Alcohol
and Substance Abuse
in Adolescence

Alcohol and Substance Abuse in Adolescence

Guest Editors
Judith S. Brook, EdD
Dan J. Lettieri, PhD
David W. Brook, MD
Editor
Barry Stimmel, MD

The Haworth Press
New York

Alcohol and Substance Abuse in Adolescence has also been published as *Advances in Alcohol & Substance Abuse,* Volume 4, Numbers 3/4, Spring/Summer 1985.

The Haworth Press, Inc., 28 East 22 Street, New York, NY 10010

Library of Congress Cataloging in Publication Data
Main entry under title:

Alcohol and substance abuse in adolescence.

Published also as v. 4, no. 3/4, spring/summer 1985 of Advances in alcohol & substance abuse.
"Selective guide to current reference sources on topics discussed in this issue": p.
1. Youth—United States—Substance use—Addresses, essays, lectures. 2. Youth—United States—Drug use—Addresses, essays, lectures. 3. Youth—United States—Alcohol use—Addresses, essays, lectures. I. Brook, Judith S. II. Lettieri, Dan J. III. Brook, David W. [DNLM: 1. Alcoholism—in adolescence. 2. Substance Abuse—in adolescence. WI AD432 v.4 no.3/4 / WM 270 A3554]
HV4999.Y68A43   1985   362.2′93′088055   84-29004
ISBN 0-86656-333-4

Alcohol and Substance Abuse in Adolescence

Advances in Alcohol & Substance Abuse
Volume 4, Numbers 3/4

CONTENTS

Alcohol
and Substance Abuse
in Adolescence

EDITORIAL

Adolescent Alcohol and Substance
Use and Abuse:
A Cause for Concern
or for Complacency

Alcohol and drug use amongst the young has always been a matter of concern. Drug use reached a peak in the late 1960s and early
1970s when alcohol consumption was superceded by the considerable use of illicit drugs, such as marijuana, hallucinogens and narcotics. At that time heroin was found to be the single leading cause
of death of young men between the ages of 15 and 35 in New York City.[1] It is encouraging that over the past decade the use of both alcohol and drugs has been decreasing.

In a 1983 survey, performed by Johnston et al., of 16,300 seniors
in schools across the country, drug use was found to have decreased
consistently over the preceding five years.[2] More important, educational programs targeted at emphasizing the risks associated with illicit drug use appeared to be finally becoming effective. Eighty-
three percent of students disapproved of regular marijuana use, as
compared to 68% in 1978, with almost two-thirds disapproving of

1

even occasional use. Almost twice the number of seniors reported the belief that marijuana users ran the risk of harming themselves compared to the proportion who held this view in 1978 (63% vs. 35%). Contrary to what might be assumed, there was no evidence that the decreased use of marijuana (5% in 1983 vs. 10% in 1978) was accompanied by a concomitant increase in alcohol consumption.

Even those adolescents considered problem drinkers appear to be overcoming this dependency. Donovan et al., following those adolescents classified as problem drinkers in 1972, found 53% of men and 70% of women to be non-problem drinkers six years later.[3]

However, as encouraging as these findings may be, one should be far from complacent with respect to adolescent drug abuse. Although the majority of problem drinkers in the Donovan study returned to normal drinking patterns, 38% of the non-problem drinking male adolescents and 15% of the non-problem drinking women became problem drinkers in adulthood. Although daily alcohol use in the Johnston survey was reported at only 5%, nonetheless, the proportion of students who had five or more drinks in a 14-day period prior to the survey was 41%.

The morbidity and mortality due to alcohol in our culture is unquestioned. As an example, one need only look at the relationship between alcohol and traffic fatalities. Although deaths due to automobile accidents decreased to 42,500 in 1983, this figure approximates the number of U.S. armed forces killed during ten years of war in Southeast Asia. Drinking is involved in 80% to 90% of vehicular accidents, with involvement of 16- to 20-year old drivers being markedly greater than that of others. Individuals under 21 years of age account for almost one in four fatalities associated with driving while intoxicated, whereas this group approximates only one in ten of the nation's drivers.[4]

The availability of illicit substances remains considerable, with 86% of seniors in the Johnston survey stating they could obtain marijuana without difficulty. Indeed, 63% of students admitted trying an illicit drug, with 40% using a drug other than marijuana in the year preceding the survey. Cocaine use was noted in 11% of students. The use of stimulants, tranquilizers and opiates was noted in 25%, 7%, and 5%, respectively. Cocaine and narcotic use, while perhaps not as prevalent a problem in certain areas of the country, within other areas is not only prevalent but also extremely damaging. In New York State, the Division of Substance Abuse Services reports one out of every twenty New York State residents, twelve years of age and older, to be currently involved in cocaine use, with over 450,000 New York State residents having used cocaine within the past six months.[5] These data indicate that adolescent alcohol and drug use remain of considerable concern.

This issue of *Advances* focuses on adolescent use of mood-altering substances in an attempt to better understand the reasons why our youth turn to drugs, the most efficacious ways to manage those so afflicted and, most importantly, how to educate youth so as to prevent their initial involvement in a process that, if not contained, can lead to severe psychological and physiological dysfunctions.

The lead paper by Lettieri summarizes the work of forty-three theorists in the drug field, classifying drug abuse theories into one's relationship to self, to others, to society and to nature.[6] In comparing theories and disciplines, the need for a "multidisciplinary, integrated theory of drug use and abuse" is emphasized, as is the complexity of existing models explaining substance abuse. The concise summaries of conceptual terms, theories and theorists will be extremely helpful to those seeking further information. The need for an integrated theory of drug use, as advocated by Lettieri, is, unfortunately, too often neglected by those in the field.

Baumrind and Moselle present a number of controversial issues regarding drug use, placing substance abuse research in a developmental-historical context.[7] Clearly this knowledge is essential to an understanding of early adolescent development. The authors provide insights into understanding the social context in which youths use drugs. If this is neglected, there is a great likelihood that the adolescent drug user will fail to be reached.

Clayton and Ritter review the major recent epidemiological studies in adolescent drug abuse.[8] These include epidemiological surveys such as the NIDA Monitoring the Future study of high school seniors, the study of military dependents conducted by Johnston et al.,[9] the Department of Defense studies of enlisted men,[10] and the youth portion of the NIDA National Survey on Drug Abuse.[11] Utilizing the data presented in these studies, they develop their own typology of multiple drug use, identifying a number of risk factors.

The paper by Hendin and Haas examines the role of marijuana in the adaptation of users.[12] Marijuana, as with other drugs, is differentially chosen for its specific psychophysiological state. The authors demonstrate how marijuana plays a characteristic, defensive role in the user's attempt to cope with inner conflicts over competition and aggression. Not surprisingly, marijuana use was strongly related to adaptive difficulties seen in long-term family and school problems. Users suffered from parental deprivation caused in part by a decrease in the family's emotional reserves. Marijuana use was found to allow expression of defiant and provocative feelings, often concerning independence issues, as well as serving as a modifier of disturbing feelings, especially anger. In addition, in the presence of depression, marijuana facilitated withdrawal from conflicts over competition and achievement.

Spotts and Shontz review the findings of an eight-year study of chronic, heavy drug users.[13] The authors report a relationship between choice of drug and differences in early stages of psychological development. Heavy drug users were more vulnerable to psychological difficulties, particularly in adolescence, than were non-users. Although drug use often began because of a failure to meet the challenge of normal individuation and a desire to achieve a certain ego state, drug use did not bring a lasting change. The importance of treatment programs, considering the differing needs of different groups of drug abusers, with treatment specifically related to the users' choice of drug, is emphasized.

Kandel reviews her findings, over the past decade, of influences on adolescent drug use.[14] Friendship is a strong determinant of adolescent illicit drug use, and illicit drug use, in turn, is a powerful determinant of friendship formation. Indeed, only sociodemographic characteristics appeared to be of greater importance in friendship formation than the use of illicit drugs. Adolescents who shared certain prior attributes tended to associate with each other and, subsequently, tended to influence each other as the result of continuing association. If major attitudinal or behavioral differences existed between adolescents, either the friendship would be terminated or one would make an attempt to alter his/her own behavior.

Although peer and parental attitudes were both important, their dominance varied with the adolescent's stage of drug use. Peer influence was found more important in initiation of marijuana use, while parental influence gained in importance for initiation into alcohol use and use of illicit drugs other than marijuana.

The paper by Brook et al., focusing on developmental mechanisms, is a continuation of the authors' studies of parental determinants of adolescent drug use.[15] The interrelationships between domains of influence are discussed, as is the use of a models approach to explore the nature of these interrelationships. The role of the father's socialization techniques, especially identification and positive and negative reinforcements, is examined, as is his role in the context of maternal and peer influences.

These papers demonstrate the complexity of adolescent drug use and abuse. For one adolescent a disturbance in early parent-child interactions or individuations, associated with a biological predisposition, may be most important, while, for another, peer influences at a later point in development in the presence of certain types of defensive character structures may be the major determinants. Other factors, such as early parental psychiatric illness, birth order, competitive achievement, maturity, current parent-adolescent relationships and prior experience with drugs, may also interact to promote drug-seeking behavior.

It is hoped that future research and intervention strategies may follow from the studies presented in this issue. These strategies not only should focus on behavior but also should incorporate information on the family, peer and larger environment and should be interdisciplinary and multifaceted, with the goal of finding a common theoretical framework.

An effective public policy must focus attention on the prevention of substance abuse through the socializing agents that most powerfully affect the development of the adolescent—the family and peer groups. The current upsurge of interest in the family, and parent-child relations in particular, reflects a growing recognition that more funds must be directed to family research and treatment programs. This intervention should occur early at a time when parental influences play a major role. Inasmuch as the influence of the peer group increases with or after the onset of adolescence, direct interventions among adolescents to prevent or minimize substance use are essential to a comprehensive policy. The efficacy of such interventions, moreover, depends on the extent to which they can utilize peer leadership, generate peer involvement, and are able to improve the interpersonal skills and intrapsychic functioning of adolescents.

Cross-sectional research, although valuable, should be integrated with longitudinal studies. This will eventually lead to the greatest understanding of the complex etiological issues involved and of the manifold effects of drug use.

The treatment of drug abusers is presently difficult, time-consuming and expensive, with little unity of opinion as to the efficacy of different methods. Successful treatment is uncertain, and relapses are common. Perhaps different techniques are successful in the hands of different practitioners with selected patients. Future research must focus on these issues and use well-formulated, well-controlled, double-blind (where appropriate) and longitudinal studies to clarify treatment issues.

In conclusion, drug use in adolescence occurs in the context of growth and development specific to that phase of life. The more that is known about adolescence as a life phase, the greater will be our understanding of what adolescents think, feel and do, including their use of drugs. Longitudinal research into normal and abnormal aspects of adolescence is essential for furthering our understanding of drug use and abuse. When combined with specific drug-oriented research, as demonstrated in the following papers, the opportunity for further meaningful progress will be enhanced.

David W. Brook, MD
Judith S. Brook, EdD
Dan J. Lettieri, PhD
Barry Stimmel, MD

REFERENCES

1. Halpern M. Deaths from narcotic addiction—A major health problem in drug abuse. In: Kemp W, ed. Current Concepts and Research. Thomas, Springfield, Illinois. 1972:61-63.

2. Johnston LD, Bachman JG, O'Malley PM. Highlights from student drug use in America 1975-1983. National Institute on Drug Abuse, Rockville, Maryland. 1984.

3. Donovan JE, Jessor R, Jessor L. Problem drinking in adolescence and young adulthood. A follow up study. J. of Studies on Alcohol. 1983; 44:109-13.

4. Grunby P. Deaths decline but drunk driving, other traffic safety hazards remain Medical news. JAMA. 1984; 251:1645-47.

5. The growing heroin and cocaine problem in New York State. New York State Division of Substance Abuse Services, New York. Outlook. 1984; 5(1):1-8.

6. Lettieri DJ. Drug abuse: A review of explanations and models of explanation. Advances in Alcohol & Substance Abuse. 1985; 4(3/4):9-40.

7. Baumrind D, Moselle KA. A developmental perspective on adolescent drug abuse. Advances in Alcohol & Substance Abuse. 1985; 4(3/4):41-67.

8. Clayton RR, Ritter C. The epidemiology of alcohol and drug abuse among adolescents. Advances in Alcohol & Substance Abuse. 1985; 4(3/4):69-97.

9. Johnston LD, O'Malley PM, Davis-Sacks MC. A world wide survey of series in the Department of Defense dependent schools: Drug use and related factors 1982. Institute for Social Research, University of Michigan, Ann Arbor, Michigan. 1983.

10. Bray RM, Guess LL, Mason RE, Hubbard RL, Smith DG, Marsden ME, Rachal JV. Highlights of the 1982 worldwide survey of alcohol and nonmedical drug use among military personnel. Research Triangle Institute, North Carolina. 1983.

11. Miller JD, Cisin IH, Gardner-Keaton H, Harrell AV, Wirtz PW, Abelson, HI, Fishburne PM. National survey on drug abuse. Main Findings 1982. National Institute on Drug Abuse, Rockville, Maryland 1983.

12. Hendin H, Haas AP. The adaptive significance of chronic marijuana use for adolescents and adults. Advances in Alcohol & Substance Abuse. 1985; 4(3/4):99-115.

13. Spotts JV, Shontz FC. A theory of adolescent substance abuse. Advances in Alcohol & Substance Abuse. 1985: 4(3/4):117-138.

14. Kandel DB. On processes of peer influences in adolescent drug use: A developmental perspective. Advances in Alcohol & Substance Abuse. 1985; 4(3/4):139-163.

15. Brook JS, Whiteman M, Gordon AS, Brook DW. Father's influence on his daughter's marijuana use viewed in a mother and peer context. Advances in Alcohol & Substance Abuse. 1985; 4(3/4):165-190.

Drug Abuse:
A Review of Explanations
and Models of Explanation

Dan J. Lettieri, PhD

ABSTRACT. This paper reviews 43 explanations of drug dependence. Summaries of each cover their drug specificity, the population studied, the disciplinary background of the theorist and the key variables utilized. In addition to a discussion of the various theoretical explanations offered in the academic literature, a brief review of the models of explanation is presented including such models as classificatory, experimental, inductive, mathematical, and reference/authority.

I. BACKGROUND

One of the early indications that research on a social problem has come of age is the quantity and quality of the explanations for it. Over the last decade interest in research on the problems of drug dependence has grown dramatically. What is particularly striking is that each of a wide array of scientific disciplines has explored the problem. Drug dependence is a complex contemporary social problem. Its complexity derives in part from the impact it has on the individual user psychologically, socially, and biologically, and in part from its effects on society, law, economics, and politics. The detailed review material which formed the basis for this paper can be found in a volume edited by Lettieri, Sayers and Pearson.[1*]

Dan J. Lettieri, is with the National Institute on Alcohol Abuse and Alcoholism, Clinical and Psychosocial Branch, Rockville, Maryland 20857. Direct Reprint Requests to: Dan J. Lettieri, NIAAA, 5600 Fishers Lane, Rm. 14-C-20, Rockville, MD 20857.
The views expressed herein do not necessarily reflect those of the Department of Health and Human Services nor of the National Institute on Alcohol Abuse and Alcoholism.

*Appendix and all tables originally published in Reference 1.

II. DEFINING THEORIES AND EXPLANATIONS

Within the scope of this paper I have chosen to use the terms theories and explanations interchangeably. It has been my express intent not to enmesh the reader in the complex issues surrounding the differentiation of these terms. Many of the authors of these explanations have labelled their positions as theories; yet clearly philosophers of science would find our usage of that term as less than optimal. The scope of this review paper is to map out the range of explanations, hunches, notions, perspectives or theories which have appeared in the substance abuse literature. Were one to impose strict definitional requirements for "theory" most of the explanations cited would be found lacking.

For practical purposes one needs a working and workable definition for theories. The question became, "What is a theory or theoretic explanation of drug abuse, and what are its components?" In general I have viewed a theory or explanation as something which addressed at least several of the following topics: (1) why people begin taking drugs, (2) why people maintain or continue their drug-taking behaviors, (3) how or why drug-taking behavior escalates to abuse, (4) why or how people stop taking drugs, and (5) what accounts for the restarting of the drug dependence behavior or cycle once stopped. Stated alternately, the five components of a theoretical explanation can be designated as (1) initiation, (2) continuation, (3) transition: use to abuse, (4) cessation, and (5) relapse. It was intended that this organizational framework could facilitate comparisons across the theories.

III. COMPARISON OF THEORIES

In order to facilitate cross-theory comparisons, a series of tables were developed (tables appear at the end of article). A listing of the theorists can be found in Appendix 1. Table 1 delineates a classification of the theories into four broad categories: (1) theories germane to one's relationship to self, (2) to others, (3) to society, and (4) to nature. Additionally, in conjunction with the primary theorists, a set of shorthand or abbreviated theory titles were developed (Table 1). A more specific classification of the theories by scientific discipline appears in Table 2. Finally, and most significantly, Table 3 entitled "Theory Boundaries" presents a concise, comparative summary of each theory, including its drug focus, the age, sex, and ethnicity of the population to which the theory applies, and a listing of key variables or concepts inherent in each theory.

Ultimately the hope of our intensive analytic effort was that we would facilitate theoretic comparisons, and perhaps, in time, someone could devise a general, multidisciplinary, integrated theory of drug use and abuse. Parenthetically we are now mapping out perspectives in the alcoholism field. Presumably the scientist's quest is for parsimony, concision and prediction. Some contend that the ultimate criterion for science is prediction. If entropy is a general trend of the universe towards death and disorder then endeavors such as these perhaps seek to bring orderliness out from the reign of chaos. For whatever reasons, it is clear that scientists continually seek explanations and models of explanation.

IV. MODELS OF EXPLANATION

Models of explanation pose a variety of unsuspecting problems. While one can operationally contend with the notion of models and theories, as we tried to do with our five theory components, the issue of explanation and/or understanding is more complex. Rather quickly one is confronted with (a) assessing the adequacy of the explanation, and (b) more to the point, how one can garner knowledge which ultimately forms the basis for an explanation.

Even a simple idea, which may have occurred to many people, achieves its greatness by the manner in which its effect on society is assessed. The ripeness of an idea is rarely the direct consequence of the thinking of the thinker himself.

The adequacy of an explanation is seldom adjudged solely on its scientific merit, but also by the ripeness of the idea within its particular social and political climate as well as its consonance with the culturally-based epistemology of the reactors. For instance, epistemology in traditional Western European thought has focused on the man-object relation. If one can measure something then one knows it. In quite a different vein, Eastern thought (particularly Confucius) has emphasized man-to-society relations. To know is to be properly interrelated with society, to achieve a transcendence. The focus is on the relationship not on the thing or object.

There have been a handful of methods which man has used to reach knowledge., and hence explanations. The methods, summarily stated are (1) recourse to reference and authority, (2) classification (Aristotle), (3) induction (Bacon), (4) deduction (Descartes), (5) the mathematical approach, (6) the experimental approach, and (7) model building. Many of these overlap and are used in combination.

The recourse to reference and authority is the most widely used method and entails citing quotations from numerous authorities. In some respects it has become a contemporary definition of scholarship. It may however be fallacious to presume that merely because so many great minds thought that way, then the matter must indeed be so. Bacon's inductive approach, while fruitful in those domains where experimental isolation of key variables is possible, has been supplanted by a new mode: measure everything in sight, correlate it, obtain a result. Such popular strategems can endanger and neglect hypotheses and fresh ideas.

V. OVERVIEW OF SELECTED THEORIES

Different disciplines or fields seem better suited to explain only certain parts of the drug behavior cycle, that is, the cycle from initiation to cessation of drug use (Figure 1). If one wishes to account for why persons continue in their use of drugs, then biomedical disciplines are probably best; in contrast, however, if one wishes to explain the initiation of drug using behavior, then social psychological explanations seem most pertinent. Sociological elements in combination with biomedical factors may be ideally suited to understanding the escalation of drug use to drug abuse, while psychological and even political and economic elements are essential to an understanding of the cessation of use. My point is that we must be cognizant of the need to incorporate variables from diverse scientific disciplines in order to fully understand the drug dependence process. No one discipline or viewpoint, alone, has successfully accounted for the multifaceted phenomenon of drug dependence.

In Table 1 there are four columns labeled Self, Others, Society, and Nature. These terms refer to the primary focus of the theory. For example, Ausubel's theory entitled "Personality Deficiency Theory" is one in which the prime focus is on man's relationship to his self; on the other hand, Becker's theory, called "Social Influence Theory" concerns itself with man's relationship to society. Perhaps one can oversimplify the categories by saying that theories

FIGURE 1

THE DRUG DEPENDENCE CYCLE

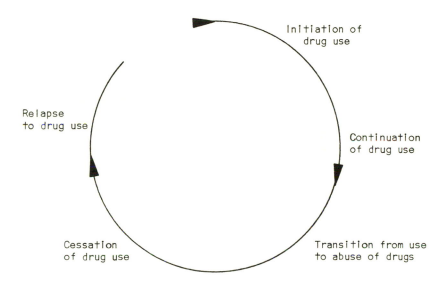

dealing with the self come primarily from the disciplines of psychiatry and psychology; theories focusing on man's relationship to others pertain to social psychology; theories relevant to man's relationship to society are essentially sociological, and theories emphasizing man's relationship to nature refer broadly to biomedical, biological, genetic, and neuroscience disciplines. In general more theories have been developed from a psychiatric, psychological and social psychological viewpoint (there are about 27 of these) than from the sociological or biomedical perspectives (there are 8 each in those two categories).

There are probably theories we have not included in this analysis; however one suspects that the prevailing psychological emphasis would be the same. The material in Table 2 may illustrate this point. For instance, under Psychiatry, there are about 12 theories in which psychiatry is seen as a primary (abbreviated as P) influence, and 8 theories that give psychiatry a secondary (abbreviated as S) influence. Viewed broadly, psychology has played a primary role in the development of 21 of the theories; and there are 34 theories in which psychology is credited with either a primary or secondary influence. Sociology has influenced 18 theories, and the combined biomedical sciences have had an influence on about 9 theories. These numbers are to be used merely for illustrative purposes. It is useful to present a brief description of some of the main themes in the theories (Table 3). A compendium of original papers for all these 43 theories is available.

Psychoanalytic Theory

The psychoanalytic position, originally stated by Freud in 1913, conceptualized addiction as a substitute for sexual pleasure and masturbation. The position was then further elaborated, and addiction was seen as a narcissistic disorder. In brief, the addict is depicted as unable to cope with adult responsibilities and consequently regresses to a more childlike state to deal with his negative feelings and poor self-esteem. The theories of Wurmser, Milkman and Frosch, and Khantzian further refine some basic psychoanalytic tenets.

For Wurmser, drugs are generally used to cope with strong negative or unhappy emotions. Specifically Wurmser argues that narcotics and hypnotics are used by those who wish to control their feelings of rage, shame, or jealousy. Stimulants are used to counteract feelings of depression and weakness. Alcohol is selected to cope with loneliness, guilt, and anxiety. And psychedelics are deployed to allay boredom and disillusionment. Most addicts have a "phobic core," that is, they fear being closed in or trapped by structures, commitments, and physical and emotional closeness. Drugs serve as a protection from these phobias and the accompanying anxiety. Wurmser also stresses the important role which early childhood physical, psychological or sexual abuse ultimately has on the use of drugs as an adult. He argues that child abuse is one of the most important determinants of later drug behavior. Drugs are a defense against the helpless feelings that have been invoked by early physical, psychological or sexual abuse.

Milkman and Frosch also stress the coping or adaptive functions of drugs to alleviate problems of depression, anxiety, and alienation. They suggest that if an alternative coping mechanism can be found then drug use will stop. While Khantzian also highlights the coping value of drugs, he places his emphasis on problems inherent in everyday interpersonal relationships, and characterizes the addict as having an impaired sense of "self-care." Khantzian argues that drugs can act as substitute for interpersonal relationships; moreover, the drug subculture affords the addict a feeling of interpersonal belonging with little personal effort.

Psychological and Personality Theories

The differences among many of the psychological and personality theories are often their differential emphasis on some psychological variable, rather than major qualitative divergencies. For Chein the emphasis is on impaired family environments which produce personality deficiencies in the young drug user. The typical potential addict is brought up in a family environment lacking affection, respect, and consistent rewards and punishments. He develops the following personality deficiencies: (a) panics and feels frustrated when faced with time consuming responsibilities or demands arising from long-term relationships with others; (b) distrusts other people; (c) perceives that relationships with others are manipulative; (d) feels useless; (e) expects to fail; (f) feels depressed; (g) has a negative self-concept; and (h) has poor sex role identification. Ultimately the addict takes drugs to make up for his feelings of emptiness as this offers an identity in a non-demanding subculture. Furthermore, by taking drugs which are a threat to society, the user is protesting and "acting out" against that society.

Ausubel adds the importance of peer influence and drug availability to the list of factors. Specifically he characterizes drug use as arising from a combination of personality factors, viz., low self-esteem, desire for immediate gratification, anxiety, depression, aggression, and environmental factors such as drug availability and peer influence.

Steffenhagen stresses the role of inferiority feelings and a pampered early childhood lifestyle. He depicts the drug user as having grown up pampered in the sense that he has become unduly accustomed to others satisfying his needs. As a consequence of depending too heavily on others for a sense of self-worth, the drug user displays an undeveloped or poor self-concept. Drugs are used to cope with his attendant feelings of inferiority, and continued drug use can serve to protect the user from life's responsibilities. Although drugs assist him to avoid interpersonal issues, he will nonetheless try to recruit others into a drug taking lifestyle as a means of increasing his peer acceptance and security.

Misra focuses on the drug user's fear of failure which results from his strong need for achievement which is demanded by a highly technological society, while Gold puts the focus on feelings of powerlessness and the resultant attempts to cognitively alter or control the external stressors. In short, for Gold, drug use occurs when an individual has difficulty in meeting societal or internal demands or expectations. The resulting conflict produces anxiety based on a feeling of powerlessness. The individual believes he cannot alter or control situations or eliminate sources of stress. To reduce the uncomfortable anxiety that has developed, the person may seek drugs.

In a more existential vein, Greaves argues that drug dependent persons do not know how to play. They are persons who have lost touch with their spontaneity, creativity, joy; moreover they often have dysfunctional sexual lives (e.g., frigidity, impotence, anger). These individuals have little interest in anything connected to the straight world—almost nothing seems to excite them. They often appear jaded and disinterested in anything around them that does not directly relate to the drug lifestyle. Having lost contact with the natural child within them, drug users have also forfeited their spontaneity, creativity and joy. They take drugs to achieve a sense of euphoria, or as a means of delimiting the pain and anxiety accompanying a humorless, unhappy lifestyle.

In a related vein Spotts and Shontz have an elaborate theory with a reliance on the role of lifestyle. They depict the amphetamine user as one who typically has had a strong, highly manipulative mother and a passive father. In turn the user tries to deny his feelings of impotence and helplessness by transforming them into hypermasculinity. Although he may, in fact, fear women, he takes great pride in displaying his sexual prowess, his high achievement needs, even some aggressive or violent behavior, and reacts against any signs of weakness or impotence. In contrast, the narcotic user's father is either tyrannical or absent, and his mother is weak. The adult narcotic addict is seen as vulnerable, isolated, lonely, unambitious, and seeking to withdraw from, rather than master life's problems. Finally Spotts and Shontz describe the barbiturate user as lacking a good relationship with either parent. He feels unloved. The user wishes to escape from these personal feelings of distress, frustration, and failure.

Social Psychological and Sociological Theories

In this set of theories the emphasis is either on the important role that the peer culture and drug cultures play on the user, or on the complex interaction of psychological factors and sociological or environmental influences. The theories of Gorsuch, Stanton, and van Dijk are perhaps the most delineated interactive theories. Van Dijk, in particular, has a very elaborate framework which depicts the etiology of drug use in terms of pharmacological effects, personal factors, social meanings and values, and environmental influences. However, van Dijk does say that in almost all instances drugs are taken for their desired pharmacological effect or their alteration of mood states. In explaining the continued use of drugs, van Dijk denotes four vicious cycles in the addiction process: namely a pharmacological cycle, a cognitive or ego cycle, a social influence cycle, and a psychic cycle. These are vicious cycles because once you get into a cycle, it is very difficult to get out. In sum, drugs are taken for their effect on mood. Personal factors contributing to drug use are: the need to relieve tension or discomfort; the lack of positive ways to deal with these feelings; mental or physical illness. Social contributors to drug use include such factors as the cultural or subcultural acceptance of the drug and the drug's symbolic meaning.

Stanton focuses on family dependence factors, while Hill prefers to highlight family independence and gratification aspects. For Stanton, not only are addicts too dependent on their families—fearing separation from this unit—but the reverse is also true. As the addict begins to succeed—whether at work or in a treatment program—he is increasing his separateness from the family. Inevitably a crisis develops within the family at which point the addict reverts to his failure behavior. The family problem then disappears. In this interdependent process, the addict's failure serves as a means of maintaining family closeness. Obversely Hill contends that the drug user's family situation has hindered him in developing independence and in the ability to delay gratification. When presented with the possibility of euphoria and instant gratification which arise from drug use, this individual is particularly susceptible to addiction.

From a different perspective the extensive work of Kandel has demonstrated that there are relatively stable stages which drug users undergo beginning with cigarettes and alcohol, then to marijuana, stimulants and depressants, psychedelics, and finally heroin. Thus Kandel's perspective is developmental in the sense that the stages are age-related, and progression to a higher ranked drug is directly related to intensity of use at the prior stage. In this regard, each prior drug stage acts as a gateway (rather than immutable progression) to the next stage.

At the other end of the sociologic continuum, Winick argues that a theory of drug use/abuse should explain the differential incidence of drug dependence, without reliance on personality characteristics which may be reflecting drug use rather than contributing to its etiology. He posits a three pronged theory in which the incidence of drug dependence will be high in those groups where there is (1) access to dependence-producing substances; (2) disengagement from proscriptions against their use; and (3) role strain and/or role deprivation.

Biomedical Theories

In this domain there are wide variations in focus, emphasis and pertinent variables. Bejerot views addiction as a biological phenomenon. He considers dependence behavior very broadly and likens drug dependence to such behaviors as gambling, overeating, pyromania and kleptomania. He suggests that dependence is a learned phenomenon, is located in the memory and not in gross physiological reactions (although memory functions do have their special physiological base), and can best be defined as an emotional fixation (sentiment) acquired through learning, which intermittently or continually expresses itself in purposeful, stereotyped behavior with the character and force of a natural drive, aiming at a specific pleasure or the avoidance of a specific discomfort. Very simply stated drugs, particularly opiates, stimulate the pleasure centers of the brain and thus give the addict great feelings of euphoria and gratification. On the other hand, Dole and Nyswander propose that opiate addiction is the result of a deficiency in the individual's metabolic system. They contend that methadone can help correct the deficiency.

Finally the theory of Jonas and Jonas conceives of addiction from a genetic and evolutionary view. They focus not on the individual but on his gene pool. In nature one finds infinite variations in population gene pools, such variation occurs to insure that at least some of the population will be able to survive even when drastic environmental changes occur. Specifically these theorists postulate that addicts carry a set of genes which were very useful and adaptive in man's distant past. These genes allowed man to be constantly alert in detecting danger from animal predators and from the environment. This trait of genetic hypersensitivity is not useful in highly technological modern society where man is presumably already overstimulated by the environment. As a consequence Jonas and Jonas suggest that persons with this gene trait take alcohol, depressants, and narcotics to reduce their hypersensitivity in a society already characterized by stimulus-overload. These theorist also suggest that the interpersonal difficulties which typify addicts are an instance of dysphoria which results from population overcrowding and social stimulus overload.

I have tried to summarily highlight a few of the contemporary theories; in no way do I imply that these are the best, but rather that they are a somewhat representative sampling of the range of contemporary ideas, conceptualizations and theoretic perspectives.

VI. THEORETICAL VARIABLES AND FACTORS

Table 3 attempts to hallmark and note the salient aspects of each of the 43 theories. In the second and third columns of this table, each theory is assessed in terms of which drug or drugs pertain to the theory. For example, Ausubel's theory is limited to opiate addiction, while Becker's theory, presumably, can be applied to account for all drugs in general, but Becker does secondarily emphasize psychedelic drugs as particularly relevant to his theory. As one reads across the columns, the age category explains whether the theory can apply to drug users of "all" ages, or is limited to certain age groups such as adolescents. In a similar fashion, descriptions are made for the "sex" and "ethnicity" or race of the drug user. Most importantly, the last column lists the major variables or concepts of each theory. This is perhaps the most difficult table to summarize because each scholarly discipline has its own unique language and argot. It is lexically complex to find terms which are sufficiently general to capture the essence of the various terms, but a preliminary attempt at classifying all the concepts into a few categories has produced the following broad domains:

1. Euphoria/Pleasure
   A) Biological Systems
        Biological drive; pleasure as a biological preference system; metabolic disease; genetic susceptibility; sensory overload; narcotic hunger; physical dependence; narcotic blockade; quality of sensory experiences; opioid receptors; endorphins; enkephalins; biological rhythms.
   B) Intrapsychic Systems
        pleasure/pain balance; abstinence syndrome; withdrawal avoidance; pain relief; euphoria; dysphoria; hypophoria; pain modulation; sense of well-being; pursuit of

altered consciousness; immediate gratification needs; sensation seeking; stimulation seeking; relief from boredom.

2. Drug Knowledge

   Knowledge about drugs; perceived drug effects; prior drug use; values; beliefs; cognitive awareness of dependence; attitudes towards drugs; controlled drug use.

3. Cognitive Factors

   A) Cognitive Variables

   social sanctions; impaired feedback; search for meaning; cognitive style; habit; self-medication; non-normative group expectations; cognitive set.

   B) Learning/Reinforcement

   learning; conditioning; dependence as a memory function; reinforcement; social learning; intermittent reinforcement

4. Tension/Anxiety Reduction

   A) Tension/Anxiety/Tension

   anxiety reduction; pain relief; discomfort relief; stress and tension reduction; stimulation avoidance; hypophoria reduction.

   B. Coping

   cognitive conflict; adaptive/defensive function; conflict/aggression reduction; coping strategies; coping abilities and mechanisms; lifestyle enhancement; behavioral styles; affective defense.

5. Interpersonal Variables

   A) Interpersonal Influence

   addict/peer/family/social influence; normative systems; social pressure; social rituals; conformity/nonconformity; social deviance; conventionality/unconventionality; drug-using culture; social control; social orientation; conduct norms; cultural modes of decorum; population density/control; social acceptance

   B) Family Factors

   disrupted family life; family systems; family homeostatic model; middle class parent culture; parental relations; parent/child over-involvement; family isolation.

   C) Interpersonal Loss and Trauma

   death/separation/loss; social constriction/entrapment; traumatic loss; role strain/deprivation.

D) Interpersonal Factors
achievement/performance competition; achievement orientation
6. Personological Features
   A) Personality Characteristics/deficiencies
      curiosity; risk-taking; claustrophobia; guilt; low self esteem; self-worth; self-concept; autonomy/independence; self-deprecation; locus of control; externalization; narcissism; rebelliousness; obedience; retreatism; escapism.
   B) Affective States
      emptiness; hopelessness; alienation; powerlessness; helplessness; hypersensitivity to stimuli; rage; apathy; emotional/affective deprivation; feelings of inferiority/superiority; fear of separation; affective regression; depression.
   C) Personality Syndromes and Characteriological Features
      inadequate personality syndrome; personality deficiency; self-destructiveness; self-care; self-preservation; self-rejecting styles; self-pathology; antisocial personality; addiction proneness; present vs future orientation; phobic core; delinquency; self-perceived behavioral pressures; tolerance of deviance; ego-state alterations; self vs ideal self; ego deficiency; arrested crisis resolution; pseudo-individuation; super-ego deficits and splits; developmental disturbance; sociopathy
7. Social/Environmental Factors
   Socioeconomic status; social class; social location; drug availability; drug distribution

CONCLUSION

As noted above not only are different disciplines better suited to explaining differential aspects of the drug dependence cycle, but different methodologies seem better suited to different disciplines and levels of analysis. The experimental method has proved effective in the physical sciences, however in the social sciences it has proved less than optimal because of difficulties in disaggregating complex social variables. Statistical techniques (e.g., causal modeling, LISREL) have been helpful and hold great promise in facilitating our disaggregation and enhanced understanding of compound social interactions. A primary weakness of the purely experimental method is that while it relies on hypotheses, we have no definite way of generating them. A hypothesis may be suggested by data, but for the hypothesis to be more than a mere summarization of the data, it is the human mind which must generate the major part of it as an idea. One encounters the same problem in those scientific disciplines where cause and effect are established on the basis of correlation rather than repeatable studies. We may imagine a causal relationship between two things simply because we can not imagine any other mechanism to account for the correlation. In other words, in many situations proof is no more than lack of imagination. Nothing is any more powerful than an idea in the mind of a single man. Fortunately the theorists in the drug dependence field have displayed great imagination and many ideas; what remains is for us to digest these ideas and condense them into a wholistic model, perhaps a predictive or mathematical model.

Underlying the mathematical approach is the intuitive feeling that complex phenomena are really made up of simpler phenomena interacting together, and that complex nature is seen suddenly to yield a simple relationship that can be expressed mathematically. The disadvantage is that the mathematical formulae often apply to rather simple, defined restricted universes, and that most universes are so complex that before that approach can succeed, we need to map out the universes. This report and prior work[1] have been attempts at making such a theoretical map. Only the combination of good ideas and hunches, boldness to fight against the tyranny of equating scientific merit with large sample size, and a willingness to occassionally take theoretical and inferential leaps can we progress in developing explanations and models of explanation. Science advances, ultimately, not by its proofs, but by its disproofs.

REFERENCES

1. Lettieri DJ, Sayers M, Pearson HW, eds. Theories on drug abuse: selected contemporary perspectives. Washington DC: US Government Printing Office, 1980. 448pp.

TABLE 1 — Theory Classification

Theorists	Abbreviated titles	Self	Others	Society	Nature
Ausubel	Personality-Deficiency Theory	•			
Becker	Social Influence Theory			•	
Bejerot	Addiction-to-Pleasure Theory				•
Chein	Disruptive Environment Theory		•		
Coleman	Incomplete Mourning Theory		•		
Dole and Nyswander	Metabolic Deficiency Perspective				•
Frederick	Learned Behavior Theory			•	
Gold	Cognitive Control Theory	•			
Goodwin	Bad-Habit Theory	•			
Gorsuch	Multiple Models Theory	•			
Greaves	Existential Theory	•			
Hendin [1]	Adaptational Theory			•	
Hill	Social Deviance Theory		•		
Hochhauser	Biological Rhythm Theory				•
Huba, Wingard, and Bentler [1]	Interactive Framework		•		
Jessor and Jessor	Problem Behavior Theory		•		
Johnson	Drug Subcultures Theory		•		
Jonas and Jonas [1]	Bioanthropological Theory				•
Kandel	Developmental Stages Theory		•		
Kaplan [1]	Self-Derogation Theory		•		
Khantzian	Ego/Self Theory	•			
Lindesmith	General Addiction Theory	•			
Loney	Hyperactive Adolescents Theory		•		
Lukoff	Sociological Theory			•	
Martin	Neuropharmacologic Theory				•
McAuliffe and Gordon [1]	Combination-of-Effects Theory		•		
Milkman and Frosch	Coping Theory	•			
Misra	Achievement-Anxiety Theory			•	
Peele	Addictive Experiences Theory		•		
Prescott	Social Neurobiological Theory				•
Robins	Natural History Perspective			•	
Schuckit	Genetic Theory				•
Simon	Opiate Receptor Perspective				•
Smart [1]	Availability and Proneness Theory	•			
Smith [1]	Perceived Effects Theory	•			
Spotts and Shontz	Life-Theme Theory	•			
Stanton	Family Theory			•	
Steffenhagen	Self-Esteem Theory			•	
van Dijk	Cyclical Process Theory			•	
Wikler	Conditioning Theory			•	
Winick	Role Theory			•	
Wurmser	Defense-Structure Theory	•			
Zinberg	Social Control Theory			•	

[1] The choosing of this classification was somewhat arbitrary; other classifications would also have been appropriate.

TABLE 2 — Disciplinary Foci of Theories

Theorists	Abbreviated titles	Psychiatry	Psychology-- general	Psychology-- learning	Social psychology	Developmental psychology	Sociology	Criminology	Anthropology	Biology	Genetics	Biomedical sciences	Neurosciences	Other
Ausubel	Personality-Deficiency Theory	P												
Becker	Social Influence Theory				S		P							
Bejerot	Addiction-to-Pleasure Theory									P				
Chein	Disruptive Environment Theory				P	S	S	S	S					
Coleman	Incomplete Mourning Theory	S		S	P	P								
Dole and Nyswander	Metabolic Deficiency Perspective			●									P	
Frederick	Learned Behavior Theory	S		P										
Gold	Cognitive Control Theory		P	S										
Goodwin	Bad-Habit Theory		P	P	S						S			
Gorsuch	Multiple Models Theory		P	S	S	S								
Greaves	Existential Theory	P	S											Clinical Psychol. (P)
Hendin	Adaptational Theory	P	S	P	S	S	S							Psychoanal- ysis (P)
Hill	Social Deviance Theory			P	P			S						
Hochhauser	Biological Rhythm Theory		S	S	S							P		
Huba, Wingard, and Bentler	Interactive Framework				P	P	P	S	S					
Jessor and Jessor	Problem Behavior Theory				P	P	S	S						
Johnson	Drug Subcultures Theory				S		P	S						
Jonas and Jonas	Bioanthropological Theory	S							P					
Kandel	Developmental Stages Theory				P	P								Epidemiol- ogy (P)
Kaplan	Self-Derogation Theory				P	S	S							
Khantzian	Ego/Self Theory	S		S	P	S	S							Psychoanal- ysis (P)
Lindesmith	General Addiction Theory			S	P		S							
Loney	Hyperactive Adolescents Theory	P												Multivariate Psychol. (P)

P--Primary
S--Secondary

24

TABLE 2 — Disciplinary Foci of Theories — continued

Theorists	Abbreviated titles	Psychiatry	Psychology--general	Psychology--learning	Social psychology	Developmental psychology	Sociology	Criminology	Anthropology	Biology	Genetics	Biomedical sciences	Neurosciences	Other
Lukoff	Sociological Perspective						P	S						
Martin	Neuropharmacologic Theory											S	P	
McAuliffe and Gordon	Combination-of-Effects Theory			S										
Milkman and Frosch	Coping Theory	S			P	P								
Misra	Achievement-Anxiety Theory		P											
Peele	Addictive Experiences Theory				P									
Prescott	Social Neurobiological Theory				S	S	S	S	S	S			P	*(P)
Robins	Natural History Perspective	P	S				P	S	S					
Schuckit	Genetic Theory	P					S	S			P	S	S	
Simon	Opiate Receptor Perspective	S						S				P	P	
Smart	Availability and Proneness Theory		P											
Smith	Perceived Effects Theory		P	S										
Spotts and Shontz	Life-Theme Theory	S	P											
Stanton	Family Theory	P	P		S	P	S		S					
Steffenhagen	Self-Esteem Theory				P	P	S							
van Dijk	Cyclical Process Theory	P			S		S							
Wikler	Conditioning Theory	P			S					S		P	S	
Winick	Role Theory	P			S		P							
Wurmser	Defense-Structure Theory	S												Psychoanalysis (P)
Zinberg	Social Control Theory	P					P							

P--Primary
S--Secondary

25

TABLE 3 — Theory Boundaries

| Theorists | Drug foci | | Population specificity | | | | Abbreviated titles | Key variables |
	Primary	Secondary	Age	Sex	Ethnicity	Other		
Ausubel	Opiates	--	All	Both	General	--	Personality-Deficiency Theory	Drug availability, euphoria, inadequate personality syndrome, anxiety reduction, coping/adjustive properties of drugs, addict/peer influence
Becker	Drugs--general	Psychedelics	All	Both	General	--	Social Influence Theory	Social set, perceived drug effects, social influence and orientation, drug knowledge, drug-using culture
Bejerot	Drugs--general	--	All	Both	General	--	Addiction-to-Pleasure Theory	Pleasure/pain balance, curiosity, peer/parent influence, biological drive, learning/conditioning, pleasure as a biological preference system, dependence as a memory function, independent will
Chein	Opiates	--	Youths, adolescents	Both	General	--	Disruptive Environment Theory	Disrupted family life, socioeconomic status, peer influence, personality deficiency, delinquency, low self-esteem, emptiness/alienation

TABLE 3 — *Theory Boundaries — continued*

Theorists	Drug foci		Population specificity				Abbreviated titles	Key variables
	Primary	Secondary	Age	Sex	Ethnicity	Other		
Coleman	Opiates	Alcohol, drugs--general	All	Both	General	--	Incomplete Mourning Theory	Search for meaning; family systems; influence; death, separation, and loss; helplessness/ hopelessness; religiosity/alienation
Dole and Nyswander	Opiates	Methadone	All	Both	General	--	Metabolic Deficiency Perspective	Narcotic blockade, metabolic disease, physical dependence, curiosity, abstinence syndrome, withdrawal avoidance
Frederick	Drugs--general	--	All	Both	General	--	Learned Behavior Theory	Learning, reinforcement, tension reduction, distructive vs. constructive factors, risk taking
Gold	Drugs--general	Opiates	All	Both	General	--	Cognitive Control Theory	Cognitive style, cognitive conflict and control, anxiety, self-deprecation, powerlessness
Goodwin	Drugs--general	Alcohol	All	Both	General	--	Bad-Habit Theory	Habit, classical conditioning, genetic susceptibility, avoidance of withdrawal symptoms, addictive cycle

TABLE 3 — Theory Boundaries — continued

Theorists	Drug foci		Population specificity				Abbreviated titles	Key variables
	Primary	Secondary	Age	Sex	Ethnicity	Other		
Gorsuch	Drugs--general	--	All	Both	General	--	Multiple Models Theory	Multiple causes, parent and peer pressure and socialization, sensation seeking, relief from boredom, conformity, pain relief
Greaves	Drugs--general	--	All	Both	General	--	Existential Theory	Impaired somatic feedback, sense of well-being, pursuit of altered consciousness, automedication, humorless lifestyle
Hendin	Drugs--general	--	All	Both	General	--	Adaptational Theory	Adaptive/defensive function, social constriction/entrapment, peer/family influence, self-destructiveness, self-esteem, achievement/performance competition

TABLE 3 — Theory Boundaries — continued

| Theorists | Drug foci | | Population specificity | | | | Abbreviated titles | Key variables |
	Primary	Secondary	Age	Sex	Ethnicity	Other		
Hill	Opiates	Alcohol	Youths, adolescents, adults	Both	Americans	--	Social Deviance Theory	Social deviance models, social control deficiencies, immediate gratification, euphoria/hypophoria, reinforcement, withdrawal avoidance, conflict/aggression reduction, drug availability, anxiety reduction
Hochhauser	Drugs—general	--	All	Both	General	--	Biological Rhythm Theory	Biological rhythms, self-medication, helplessness
Huba, Wingard, and Bentler	Drugs—general	--	All	Both	General	--	Interactive Framework	Behavioral styles: biological, intrapersonal, interpersonal, and sociocultural interactions; person-environment interactions; self-perceived behavioral pressures

TABLE 3 — Theory Boundaries — continued

Theorists	Drug foci		Population specificity				Abbreviated titles	Key variables
	Primary	Secondary	Age	Sex	Ethnicity	Other		
Jessor and Jessor	Drugs--general	--	Youths, adolescents, adults	Both	General	--	Problem Behavior Theory	Problem-behavior proneness, social influence/controls, alienation, self-esteem, locus of control, tolerance of deviance, achievement orientation, autonomy/independence, conventionality/unconventionality
Johnson	Marijuana, opiates, multiple drug use	Alcohol, drugs--general, depressants, psychedelics	Youths, adolescents	Both	General	--	Drug Subcultures Theory	Middle-class parent culture, conduct norms, values, cannabis subculture, heroin-injection subculture, drug distribution, peer culture
Jonas and Jonas	Drugs--general	Alcohol, stimulants, narcotics	All	Both	General	The individual is viewed on the basis of his/her standing (or perception of standing) within a social group	Bioanthropological Theory	Hypersensitivity to stimuli, social influence, neurophysiological influence, phylogeny, population density/control, species viability/survival, euphoria, population vs. individual gene pools

TABLE 3 — Theory Boundaries — continued

Theorists	Drug foci		Population specificity				Abbreviated titles	Key variables
	Primary	Secondary	Age	Sex	Ethnicity	Other		
Kandel	Drugs--general	Tobacco, alcohol	Youths, adolescents	Both	General	--	Developmental Stages Theory	Prior drug use, parental relations and influence, peer influence, beliefs and values, deviant behavior
Kaplan	Drugs--general	--	All	Both	General	Applies only to groups in which drug use is contra-normative	Self-Derogation Theory	Self-esteem motive, self-rejecting attitudes, non-normative group membership and expectations
Khantzian	Opiates	Drugs--general	All	Both	General	--	Ego/Self Theory	Psychopathology, ego impairment/ function, self-care/ self-preservation, aggression/rage, self pathology, narcissism, self-selection, coping strategies
Lindesmith	Opiates, opiate-type synthetics	Alcohol	All	Both	General	--	General Addiction Theory	Physical dependence, withdrawal avoidance, learning, reinforcement, cognitive awareness of dependence

TABLE 3 — *Theory Boundaries* — *continued*

Theorists	Drug foci		Population specificity				Abbreviated titles	Key variables
	Primary	Secondary	Age	Sex	Ethnicity	Other		
Loney	Drugs--general, stimulants	--	Youths, adolescents	Males	White Americans	--	Hyperactive Adolescents Theory	Aggression, rebelliousness, parental and peer influence, self-esteem, social class
Lukoff	Marijuana, opiates	Drugs--general	Youths, adolescents	Males	General	--	Sociological Perspective	Drug use as epiphenomenon, cultural and structural parameters, retreatism, social location, normative systems and socialization, peer culture/influence, family influence/ isolation
Martin	Drugs--general	Opiates	All	Both	General	--	Neuropharmacologic Theory	Opioid receptors, psychopathology, hypophoria, euphoria, depression, neurotransmitters, protracted abstinence syndrome
McAuliffe and Gordon	Opiates	Drugs--general	All	Both	General	--	Combination-of-Effects Theory	Euphoria, withdrawal avoidance, self-medication, operant reinforcement, intermittent reinforcement, lifestyle changes, insidious onset

TABLE 3 — Theory Boundaries — continued

| Theorists | Drug foci | | Population specificity | | | | Abbreviated titles | Key variables |
	Primary	Secondary	Age	Sex	Ethnicity	Other		
Milkman and Frosch	Drugs--general	Stimulants, depressants	All	Both	General	--	Coping Theory	Ego-state alteration, sensory overload, stress reduction, coping, peer influence, addictive processes
Misra	Drugs--general	--	All	Both	General	--	Achievement-Anxiety Theory	Fear of failure, apathy, achievement, anxiety, emotional inhibition, escapism
Peele	Drugs--general	Alcohol, tobacco	All	Both	General	--	Addictive Experiences Theory	Psychosocial and pharmacological interaction; perceived drug experiences; anxiety, pain, and stress relief; guilt; setting; environment; coping ability
Prescott	Alcohol, marijuana, stimulants, depressants, opiates	Tobacco, psychedelics	All	Both	General	--	Social Neuro-biological Theory	Neurophysiological needs and predispositions, social isolation, emotional/ affective deprivation, quality/ quantity of sensory experiences, stimulation seeking vs. avoidance, opiate receptors and endorphins

TABLE 3 — Theory Boundaries — continued

Theorists	Drug foci		Population specificity				Abbreviated titles	Key variables
	Primary	Secondary	Age	Sex	Ethnicity	Other		
Robins	Drugs--general	--	All	Both	General	--	Natural History Perspective	Disrupted family, nonconformity, antisocial behavior, peer influence, drug availability, antisocial personality
Schuckit	Alcohol	Drugs--general	All	Both	General	--	Genetic Theory	Genetic predisposition, socioenvironmental influences
Simon	Opiates	Drugs--general	All	Both	General	--	Opiate Receptor Perspective	Opiate receptors, opiate-induced euphoria/dysphoria, endogenous opioid peptides, endorphins/enkephalins, pain modulation/analgesia, abstinence syndrome
Smart	Drugs--general	--	All	Both	General	--	Availability and Proneness Theory	Addiction proneness, drug availability, lifestyle enhancement, escapism

TABLE 3 — Theory Boundaries — *continued*

Theorists	Drug foci		Population specificity				Abbreviated titles	Key variables
	Primary	Secondary	Age	Sex	Ethnicity	Other		
Smith	Drugs--general	--	Youths, adolescents	Both	General	--	Perceived Effects Theory	Perceived effects, self-worth/self-concept, substance availability, social influence, rebelliousness/obedience, sensation seeking, low need achievement, withdrawal aversiveness, self vs. ideal self, present vs. future orientation
Spotts and Shontz	Drugs--general	Stimulants, depressants, psychedelics, opiates	Adults	Males	General	Derived from intensive and extensive studies of individuals; may or may not apply in massed data (i.e., group averages on isolated variables measured by dimensional rather than morphogenic means)	Life-Theme Theory	Personal structure, lifestyle, ego, life themes, myths, ego deficiency, family dynamics

35

TABLE 3 — Theory Boundaries — continued

Theorists	Drug foci		Population specificity				Abbreviated titles	Key variables
	Primary	Secondary	Age	Sex	Ethnicity	Other		
Stanton	Drugs--general	Opiates	Youths, adolescents, adults	Both	General	--	Family Theory	Arrested crisis resolution, family homeostatic model, traumatic loss, fear of separation, parent/child over-involvement, pseudo-individuation, triadic interaction, family addiction cycle
Steffenhagen	Drugs--general	--	All	Both	General	--	Self-Esteem Theory	Self-esteem, drug availability, feelings of inferiority/superiority, social pressure/acceptability, coping mechanism, immediate gratification, social milieu, lifestyle
van Dijk	Drugs--general	--	All	Both	General	--	Cyclical Process Theory	Stages of use, social meaning of use, disposition, discomfort relief, psychosocial cyclical processes

TABLE 3 — Theory Boundaries — continued

| Theorists | Drug foci | | Population specificity | | | | Abbreviated titles | Key variables |
	Primary	Secondary	Age	Sex	Ethnicity	Other		
Wikler	Opiates	Drugs--general	Youths, adolescents, adults	Both	General	Applies mainly to "street addicts," for whom there is no bona fide medical indication for administration of opioids	Conditioning Theory	Euphoria/dysphoria; acute, protracted, and conditioned abstinence syndrome; social-environmental influences and stimuli; primary and secondary pharmacologic reinforcement; anxiety and hypophoria reduction; reinforcement and conditioning; exteroceptive and interoceptive stimuli; pharmacologic need/narcotic hunger
Winick	Drugs--general	--	All	Both	General	--	Role Theory	Role strain/deprivation, attitudes toward drugs, drug availability

37

TABLE 3 — Theory Boundaries — continued

Theorists	Drug foci		Population specificity				Abbreviated titles	Key variables
	Primary	Secondary	Age	Sex	Ethnicity	Other		
Wurmser	Drugs--general	--	All	Both	General	--	Defense-Structure Theory	Ego/superego deficits and splits, developmental disturbance/trauma, anxiety, affective regression/defense, sociopathy, narcissism, externalization, self-esteem, phobic core, claustrophobia
Zinberg	Drugs--general	Alcohol, heroin	All	Both	General	--	Social Control Theory	Set and setting, social sanctions and rituals, social learning, controlled drug use, cognitive conflict, cultural models of decorum

APPENDIX I — *Theorists*

David P. Ausubel, M.D., Ph.D.
Graduate School and University Center
City University of New York
and
Hochschule der Bundeswehr
Munich, West Germany

Howard S. Becker, Ph.D.
Department of Sociology
Northwestern University
Evanston, Illinois

Nils Bejerot, M.D.
Department of Social Medicine
Karolinska Institute
Stockholm, Sweden

Peter M. Bentler, Ph.D.
Department of Psychology
University of California--Los Angeles

Isidor Chein, Ph.D.
Department of Psychology
Research Center for Human Relations
New York University

Sandra B. Coleman, Ph.D.
Department of Mental Health Sciences
Hahnemann Medical College and Hospital
and
Achievement Through Counseling and
Treatment
Philadelphia, Pennsylvania

Vincent P. Dole, M.D.
Rockefeller University
New York City

Calvin J. Frederick, Ph.D.
National Institute of Mental Health
and
Department of Psychiatry
The George Washington University
Washington, D.C.

William Frosch, M.D.
Drug/Alcohol Institute
Metropolitan State College
Denver, Colorado

Steven R. Gold, Ph.D.
Department of Psychology
Western Carolina University
Cullowhee, North Carolina

Donald W. Goodwin, M.D.
Department of Psychiatry
University of Kansas Medical Center
Kansas City, Kansas

Robert A. Gordon, Ph.D.
Department of Social Relations
Johns Hopkins University
Baltimore, Maryland

Richard L. Gorsuch, Ph.D.
Graduate School of Psychology
Fuller Theological Seminary
Pasadena, California

George B. Greaves, Ph.D.
Department of Psychology
Georgia State University
Atlanta

Herbert Hendin, M.D.
Center for Psychosocial Studies
Veterans Administration
Franklin Delano Roosevelt Hospital
Montrose, New York
and
Professor of Psychiatry
New York Medical College
Valhalla

Harris E. Hill, Ph.D. (retired)
National Institute of Mental Health
Addiction Research Center
Lexington, Kentucky

Mark Hochhauser, Ph.D.
Division of School Health Education
University of Minnesota
Minneapolis

George J. Huba, Ph.D.
Department of Psychology
University of California--Los Angeles

Richard Jessor, Ph.D.
Department of Psychology and Institute
of Behavioral Science
University of Colorado
Boulder

Shirley Jessor, Ph.D.
Department of Psychology and Institute of
Behavioral Science
University of Colorado
Boulder

Bruce D. Johnson, Ph.D.
New York State Division of Substance
Abuse Services
New York City

A. David Jonas, M.D.
University of Wurzburg
German Federal Republic

Doris F. Jonas, Ph.D.
Fellow, Royal Anthropological Institute
of Great Britain
London

Denise B. Kandel, Ph.D.
School of Public Health and
Department of Psychiatry
Columbia University
New York City

APPENDIX I — *Theorists* — *continued*

Howard B. Kaplan, Ph.D.
Department of Psychiatry
Baylor College of Medicine
Houston, Texas

Edward J. Khantzian, M.D.
Department of Psychiatry
Harvard Medical School
Cambridge, Massachusetts

Alfred R. Lindesmith, Ph.D.
Department of Sociology
Indiana University
Bloomington, Indiana

Jan Loney, Ph.D.
Department of Psychiatry
The University of Iowa
Iowa City

Irving F. Lukoff, Ph.D.
Columbia University
School of Social Work
New York City

William R. Martin, M.D.
Department of Pharmacology
Albert B. Chandler Medical Center
University of Kentucky
Lexington

William E. McAuliffe, Ph.D.
Department of Behavioral Sciences
Harvard School of Public Health
Boston, Massachusetts

Harvey Milkman, Ph.D.
Drug/Alcohol Institute
Metropolitan State College
and
Department of Psychiatry
University of Colorado Medical Center
Denver

Rajendra K. Misra, D. Phil.
Northeast Community Mental Health Center
East Cleveland, Ohio

Marie Nyswander, M.D.
Rockefeller University
New York City

Stanton Peele, Ph.D.
Department of Health Education
Teachers College at Columbia University
New York City

James W. Prescott, Ph.D.
Institute of Humanistic Science
West Bethesda, Maryland

Lee N. Robins, Ph.D.
Department of Psychiatry
Washington University School of Medicine
St. Louis, Missouri

Marc A. Schuckit, M.D.
Department of Psychiatry
School of Medicine
University of California, San Diego
La Jolla

Franklin C. Shontz, Ph.D.
Department of Psychology
University of Kansas
Lawrence

Eric J. Simon, Ph.D.
New York University Medical Center
New York City

Reginald G. Smart, Ph.D.
Addiction Research Foundation
Toronto, Ontario, Canada

Gene M. Smith, Ph.D.
Erich Lindemann Mental Health Center
Harvard Medical School
Boston, Massachusetts

James V. Spotts, Ph.D.
Greater Kansas City Mental Health Foundation
Kansas City, Missouri

M. Duncan Stanton, Ph.D.
Philadelphia Child Guidance Clinic
Veterans Administration Drug Dependence
    Treatment Center
        and
University of Pennsylvania School of Medicine
Philadelphia

R.A. Steffenhagen, Ph.D.
Department of Sociology
University of Vermont
Burlington

W.K. van Dijk, M.D.
Department of Psychiatry
Psychiatric University Clinic
Academisch Ziekenhuis Groningen
Groningen, The Netherlands

Abraham Wikler, M.D.
Albert B. Chandler Medical Center
University of Kentucky
Lexington

Joseph A. Wingard, Ph.D.
Department of Psychology
University of California--Los Angeles

Charles Winick, Ph.D.
Department of Sociology
The City College of the City University
    of New York
New York City

Leon Wurmser, M.D.
Alcohol and Drug Abuse Program
School of Medicine
University of Maryland
Baltimore

Norman Zinberg, M.D.
Harvard Medical School
The Cambridge Hospital
Cambridge, Massachusetts

A Developmental Perspective on Adolescent Drug Abuse

Diana Baumrind, PhD
Kenneth A. Moselle, PhD

ABSTRACT. Adolescent drug use is placed in an historical and developmental perspective. Existing evidence concerning causes and consequences of adolescent drug use is inconclusive. In the absence of conclusive empirical evidence and cogent theories, we present a prima facie case against early adolescent drug use by defending six propositions which posit specific cognitive, conative, and affective negative consequences including impairment of attention and memory; developmental lag imposing categorical limitations on the level of maximum functioning available to the user in cognitive, moral and psychosocial domains; amotivational syndrome; consolidation of diffuse or negative identity; and social alienation and estrangement. We call for a program of research which could provide credible evidence to support or rebut these propositions, and thus address the factual claims underlying the sociomoral concerns of social policy planners.

For the past 20 years, drug use has constituted a part of the experience of being a young middle-class adolescent in the United States, and more recently has been identified as a public health problem warranting serious concern. Drug-using activity, its antecedents and its consequences are issues crucial to an understanding of early adolescent development. Therefore, when the child participants in the *Family Socialization and Developmental Competence Project*

During the preparation of this article, the authors were supported by grants from the John D. and Catherine T. MacArthur Foundation and the William T. Grant Foundation. We wish to thank Dr. Louise Richards of NIDA for her consistent support and for orienting us to the issues and literature of the field of substance abuse.

Requests for reprints of this article should be sent to Diana Baumrind, Institute of Human Development, 1203 Edward Chace Tolman Hall, University of California, Berkeley, CA 94720.

41

(FSP)* were assessed at age 14, as part of the third wave of data collection, we undertook a critical examination of the status of the drug abuse field as it pertained to the population from which we drew our subjects, namely normal middle-class young adolescents.[1,2]

In the past decade, social-behavioral studies of drug abuse have been dominated by the social-survey methods favored by epidemiologists. As a result, the natural history of the phenomenon of adolescent substance abuse over that period of time has been well-documented. However, this body of research suffers from deficiencies inherent in the use of extensive social-survey methods to assess a phenomenon which requires intensive intraindividual assessments within a longitudinal design. There is still a need for further information about why early adolescents use drugs; how the family, school and other social institutions could prevent drug use; and what strategies might intervene to prevent drug experimenters from becoming drug abusers. More attention needs to be paid to the individual and stage-related characteristics of the user, to the process of becoming a drug user, and to the drug-using experience itself. Earlier work in the field[3-5] featured just such in-depth, comprehensive analyses of the drug-using experience of small samples with variables embedded within a theoretical context. However, the data-analytic methods used by these investigators were deficient by today's standards: the sophisticated multivariate statistics and computer programs which we take for granted today were not then available. Moreover, reports were embedded in an understanding of pathological rather than normal development, or generalized from knowledge of very heavy users to the experience of moderate, regular users.[6] Today, however, the tail wags the dog: powerful data-analytic strategies frequently substitute for systematic theory and articulate hypothetical constructs, and data quality is sacrificed to obtain the large samples required by the multivariate analyses. As a result of measurement deficiencies and a theoretically undifferentiated causal model, the absence of positive findings of harmful consequences from studies which employ these impoverished measures

*The FSP is a longitudinal program of research, directed by Diana Baumrind, which has as its core objective to assess the contribution of contrasting configurations of parental socialization practices to the development in children and adolescents of instrumental competencies such as social responsibility, social agency and cognitive competence, and of dysfunctional patterns of behavior and prototypic lifestyles including drug abuse. The collection of the third wave data when the child subjects were 14 years of age was supported jointly by the National Institute on Drug Abuse under NIDA Grant #DAO 1919, by the National Science Foundation under Award #BNS 76-80747, and by the William T. Grant Foundation.

cannot be used to support the assertion that there are none, even when the studies employ a longitudinal design.

Today, the adolescent abstainer has become statistically deviant. The developmental stresses experienced in contemporary social contexts by middle-class youths may well predispose a majority of them to experiment with mood-altering and consciousness-altering substances. Adolescent substance experimentation in contemporary American society may therefore be developmentally normal as well as statistically normative behavior.[7] However, there are theoretically and empirically compelling reasons to hypothesize that various sorts of functional decrement and developmental lag result from adolescent drug use. Examination of the antecedents and consequences of adolescent drug use therefore deserves serious attention from developmentally trained behavioral scientists.

EARLY ADOLESCENCE IN CONTEMPORARY AMERICAN SOCIETY

Developmental trajectories are historically situated. In order to provide a framework for understanding the widespread use and social acceptability among adolescents, particularly on the East and West coasts, of mind-altering and consciousness-altering substances, we begin with an examination of early adolescence as a developmental period embedded within a particular social-historical context.

The Social-Historical Context

Adolescent drug use today is a conventional and not an exotic practice, and more a recreational than an ideological pursuit. In the 1960s, when LSD became widely available, consciousness-altering drug use functioned as a chemical gateway to an antinomian lifestyle and as a symbol of widespread disaffection with traditional values afflicting adult intellectuals as well as their adolescent offspring. The early 1970s marked a transition period, a coming down off the economic and emotional high, accompanied by an awareness that hard times lay ahead; the ideological supports for drug use declined. Young adolescents experiencing the anticipatory stress of entering a constricted labor market were less likely to value risk-taking for its own sake. Throughout the past decade, and continuing into the present, adolescents of the 1970s have become more conservative, achievement-oriented, and less acceptant of the ideology of "doing one's own thing." Thus, the context in which adolescent drug use occurs today is quite different, carrying little of the political or drop-out symbolism of the 1960s. As leading analysts of changing social values, including Yankelovich,[8] have shown, the youth of the 80s are painfully aware that they face in the decade ahead a hazardous economic environment; they are concerned with prestige and success as well as with self-fulfillment and will not intentionally jeopardize their ability to earn a living.

However, adolescent substance use is not a temporary aberration likely to revert to the low level of the 1950s, any more than contemporary American mores in which it is embedded are likely to revert to what traditionalists regard as a happier time. There are cogent reasons for this trend: (1) Today the gap between puberty and psychosocial maturity is wider than ever before, resulting in a prolonged status of being in-limbo, conducive to all kinds of social experimentation; (2) All social roles are in rapid transition. Generativity through work and procreation are no longer of clear positive value. Without a normatively sanctioned way to negotiate the transition to adulthood, many adolescents may choose a regressive identity based on rejection of adult roles and use illicit drugs in an attempt to remain "forever young." (3) The social role of women has been permanently altered with two possible consequences for drug use: first, to the extent that maternal presence in the home is an essential part of traditional upbringing, the countervailing force exerted by traditional upbringing will be less prominent; and second, young women are likely to engage in increasingly greater risk-taking and adult-disapproved behavior, making them as likely candidates as their male peers for drug use; and (4) Finally, as a society, the illicit status of an act has lost its value as either a moral or a practical deterrent. Thus, in probing interviews, only four of our adolescent subjects gave the fact that marijuana was against the law as a personal deterrent.[7] Abuse of substances, licit and illicit, is so widespread in our present societal context that we might well ask why some adolescents abstain, rather than why most do not.

Processes Defining Normal Adolescent Development

We employ a model of stage-sequential development as a basis for interpreting the changes that take place in childhood and adolescence. In this paradigm, development is viewed as a process characterized by alternating periods of relative disequilibrium and equilibrium, in which the global and diffuse organization of ontogenetically primitive and discrete schemes of action becomes increasingly differentiated and integrated. Novel, increasingly differentiated, and internally coherent schemes of action emerge which are better adapted to specific demand characteristics of the environment. Werner and Kaplan[9] use the term "orthogenesis" to refer to this process of developmental progress. Stage-sequential development is not a simple accretion of new behaviors, but rather a process in which schemes of actions possessing an internally coherent organization are *transformed*, in a dual sense: isolated schemes of action come to function in a more integrated fashion; and the significance of earlier systems of actions or conceptions is transformed as previously unintegrated schemes come to be incorporated into an interlocking network of implications.

A brief example illustrates some of the key features of the above-mentioned scheme: by the time children enter early adolescence, they have typically consolidated an organized body of normative conceptions derived from peer interactions which lends regularity and predictability to relations with equals. Specific conceptions may be viewed together as an intact structured whole to the extent that they reciprocally imply one another. However, the child's compliance with peer values takes on a radically *transformed* significance when such compliance acquires the implication of emancipation from parental constraint. Patterns of behavior which had previously been employed in an unreflective manner in peer interactions, in the service of play, may begin to be employed strategically in relations with parents to serve the end of emancipation. For example, the young adolescent may converse with parents using elements of argot originally derived from peer interactions, confronting the implicit right afforded parents at a younger age to determine what sort of language would be appropriate for their child to use in communication with them. The process of negotiating new role-definitions with parents may be marked by conflict and instability, followed by a period of relative stability as parents and children learn to encounter one another on a more egalitarian basis.

Adolescence is a period of development involving transitions in all the processes that make up a person. Ages 10 to 15, which are often used to bracket early adolescence, correspond to the ages of children attending middle schools and junior high schools in the United States. The concept of psychosocial adolescence implies, in addition to the accelerated physical changes of puberty, identity formation as the outcome of adolescent crisis. Identity formation, according to Erikson,[10] is the outcome of adolescent experimentation with different lifestyles, resolution of bisexual conflicts, and emancipation from childhood dependency, eventuating in crucial decisions concerning school, love and work.

Among the psychosocial and cognitive processes defining early adolescence as a period of development, we will briefly review the following: attainment of formal operations; transition from a conventional to a principled level of moral judgment; transitional status of social-conventional reasoning; increased importance of peers relative to parents as socializing agents; simultaneous increase in egocentrism and social perspective-taking, culminating in construction of ego identity; self-derogation; and finally motivation to escape altogether from the extreme disequilibrium brought about by the adolescent transition from childhood to adulthood.

By the onset of early adolescence almost all children have developed the capacity for concrete operational thought. They can therefore employ coherently and consistently basic logical operations both to comprehend observed regularities in the environment and to render their actions consistent with basic attitudes and values. However, capacity for abstract thought is limited. The rationally possible is viewed as a temporally indefinite extension of the real. It is not until the acquisition of formal operations that the child can systematically hypothecate possibilities that run counter to fact, and critique the status quo for being no more than one of a set of possible social arrangements. In societies such as ours this capacity to deal with abstract propositions and hypothetical realities is usually obtained, if at all, during the period we call early adolescence.[11] In the domain of psychosocial functioning, the adolescent's *attainment of formal operational capacities* represents both an opportunity and a danger. The adolescent is cast into a limbo between the literal, safe reality of childhood ruled by simple laws of consistency and fairness, and the complex, indeterminate reality of adulthood where what is and what could be or what ought to be may be seen as disparate. Liberated from the concrete, confining construction of reality of childhood, but not yet constrained by the social realities of adult commitment and responsibility, the social matrix in which adolescents construct their reality is still malleable and may be experienced as hypothetical and surreal. Dissatisfaction with the status quo may be countered by positing the possibility of a "better life." However, now awakened to the imperfection and hypocrisy of the adult world, and still unengaged and uncommitted, adolescents may angrily reject adult values as part of the process of emancipation.

In the early adolescent period a developmental *transition from conventional to principled morality* may take place. In order to progress from one stage to the next, a disequilibrating conflict must occur which motivates the individual to abandon the comfort of a well-integrated stage of reasoning or lifeview for a new and therefore less secure stance. The adolescent identity crisis is such a disequilibrating conflict during which adolescents question the heretofore accepted values of their parents and other adult authorities before arriving at a set of principles capable of reconciling the disparate points of view characterizing their own and their parents' generations. Adaptive risk-seeking behavior is a component of the adolescent crisis that results in identity formation, by contrast with what Erikson[10] calls a "foreclosed identity." Kohlberg and Gilligan[12] refer to the characteristic early adolescent transition from one moral stage to the next as "cultural relativism." During the adolescent transition many youths engage in socially disruptive and health-endangering behavior. However, most adolescents who experiment with drugs or other health-compromising and illicit practices do not escalate their worrisome behavior.

Important *transitions in attitudes towards social convention* also occur during adolescence. Turiel[13] identifies seven levels of social-conventional concepts through analyses of subjects' responses to a probing (Piagetian) clinical interview. The seven levels show that the process of development of social-conventional reasoning proceeds through a series of oscillations between affirmation and negation of convention and social structure. Each phase of affirmation entails a construction of concepts of convention and social structure and is followed by a phase negating the validity of the previous affirmative phase. Prior to ages 12 to 13, adherence to convention is based on concrete rules and authoritative expectations. Later, with the transition to Turiel's fourth stage, the core feature of which is a negation of conventional forms of social behavior on the grounds that they do not possess intrinsic value, young teenagers typically come to question the justification of authority and social expectation as a basis for following convention. They may then use this critique to justify flouting such convention. Acts which serve to maintain the dominant social order but which are not seen as intrinsically good or bad (e.g., dress codes) tend to be viewed as arbitrary, and therefore rules or expectations about such acts are asserted to be invalid. In the course of normal development, this negation yields to a new affirmation of convention based on systematic concepts of social organization which include role and status distinctions (level 5 in Turiel's system). In giving up a heteronomous view of parental authority as absolute and unquestionably valid, adolescents typically do not develop a negative identity which totally rejects parental values en masse. Instead, the form that adolescent negation of convention takes usually expresses simultaneous emulation and rejection of parental standards. This is generally true of drug-using adolescents as well: in emulation of their elders, adolescents use drugs to assuage immediate or anticipated discomfort, and in rejection of their elders they seize upon certain drugs of which their elders would disapprove. The use of illicit substances offers young adolescents the unique opportunity simultaneously to rebel against the rules their elders set down and to conform with the underlying attitudes which parental behavior manifests. At fourteen to sixteen, with the transition to Turiel's fifth stage, systematic concepts of social structure typically emerge and adult-supported conventions are once again affirmed, now justified by their regulative function, with the proviso that the social order is itself viewed as legitimate. However, in the absence of compelling evidence that there are harmful effects intrinsic to the use of certain drugs (most notably marijuana), adolescents are likely to subject proscriptions against the use of particular substances to the same sort of critique that is applied broadly to more clearly conventional forms of social practice. The use of consciousness-altering drugs may then consolidate the oversimplified cultural relativism characteristic of early adolescence, and thus interfere with the development in mid-adolescence of an ethic of principled conformity with legitimate social conventions.

Beginning in early adolescence *the peer group becomes increasingly significant relative to the family as a socializing context.* In the past decade dependency on peers relative to parents has increased as a result in part of withdrawal by parents from the lives of their youngsters.[14] In 1961, Coleman[15] observed that leading social cliques tended to discourage academic strivings, and this fact may not have changed substantially in the past 20 years. Superior school achievement may still reduce rather than enhance one's popularity with peers.[16] Exposure to drug-using peers, particularly a "best friend," has been shown to be a concomitant of drug use by adolescents. According to Kandel et al., [17] generalized peer influence predicts initiation to legal drugs and marijuana. The influence of a best friend leads to the initiation of other illicit drugs. However, parental rejection and alcohol use were shown to be the critical factors anteceding youthful experimentation with hard liquor. Adolescents comply with peer standards up to a point to achieve status and identity within the peer group. But status within the larger society, including educational aspirations and occupational plans, remains the province of parents.[18,19] While parents' traditionality may prevent drug use altogether, and closeness of the parent-child relationship may help shield adolescents from involvement in the more serious forms of drug use, parental influence probably stops there: once the adolescent has decided to use drugs, the harmfulness of the experience may be affected largely by the social clique which socializes the drug-using experience.

Although adolescent socialization by the peer group is developmentally appropriate in our society, adults in other societies manipulate the adolescent peer group to reinforce the dominant communal views of the society.[20,21] Bronfenbrenner[22] argues persuasively that adults, if they choose to, can produce radical changes in children's and adolescents' social and emotional development by manipulating the socialization contexts and processes that affect them. In support of his view we note that important changes in peer group attitudes towards cigarette smoking have been brought about in the last decade by effective adult manipulation of the media and educational contexts.

Early adolescence is a period of heightened consciousness of self and others, resulting in simultaneously in *increased self-centeredness and in enhanced ability to understand the perspective of another.* Greater self-consciousness becomes possible as a result of the adolescent's increasing ability to engage in recursive thought, that is, to treat as an object of contemplation his own thoughts, as well as the thoughts of others. The acquisition of mature role-taking skills occurs in early adolescence. Selman[23] believes that social perspective-taking follows an invariant stage sequence. During early adolescence youths construct an understanding of the shared perspective among individuals which exists in particular social groupings, permitting them to compare and contrast viewpoints of the self, specific others, and the generalized other. Elkind[24] emphasizes the opposite side of the coin—adolescent egocentrism. The adolescent, confronted for the first time with an awareness of his objectification in the minds of others, and overwhelmed by associated feelings of self-consciousness, uses his emerging cognitive abilities to construct a "personal fable," reaffirming his specialness and separateness. This tendency for adolescents to employ emerging structures of formal-operational thought to reconstruct their life-world in idealized terms has recently been the subject of renewed interest.[25,26]

Erikson[10] describes successive phases in the development of self-concept. The values accrued in childhood culminate in a sense of *ego identity,* of which a constituent element is the conviction that one is learning effective steps towards a meaningful, palpable future. The early adolescent constructs (or fails to construct) a unique and highly differentiated view of self and others, and coordinates impressions of the self and others. The dangers at this stage are identity diffusion in which the adolescent simply cannot take hold of life, or the consolidation of a negative identity, "i.e., an identity perversely based on all those identifications and roles which, at critical stages of development, had been presented to the individual as most undesirable or dangerous" (p. 131).[10]

Self-esteem appears to ebb at twelve or thirteen, with an increase during late adolescence.[27,28] Dramatic discontinuities in body image occur as a result of pubertal changes, so that youngsters may actually be less attractive physically at precisely the period that their awareness of self and others is developing. A decrease in self-ideal congruence occurs between ages 8 and 12,[29] together with a downward trend in self-ratings of worth. Stabilization in self-ideal congruence begins around the ninth grade[30] with recovery occurring by age 18. The low point in self-esteem in early adolescence coincides with entry into the larger and more impersonal world of middle school, which threatens the special status conferred by the family to the younger child by virtue of family membership alone. Although lowered self-esteem is normal during early adolescence, a person's self-devaluation is accompanied by real suffering, particularly since young people lack perspective to realize that their suffering is developmentally normative and temporary. Moreover, high-achieving youngsters may be especially susceptible to the loss of self-esteem brought about by change in the importance to them of peer relative to parent reference groups and the fact that peer approbation is based less on high academic achievement and more on conformity with peer standards which high-achieving youngsters may be reluctant to adopt. Kaplan[31] suggests that such youths may become deviant by adult standards as a way of coping with devalued self-esteem: the standards of drug-using peers may be less demanding of achievement and of possession of conventional good looks, and therefore may serve to reduce self-derogation which results from failing to meet the standards held by traditional adults or achievement-oriented peer reference groups.

From a developmental perspective, adolescence is the age-appropriate period to learn how to endure adaptively the suffering inherent in growth. However, many early adolescents are *motivated to escape from developmental disequilibrium* in favor of stasis and harmony. They have available a multitude of strategies for doing so with contradictory implications for drug use. Compulsive drug use may be associated with identity diffusion or development of a negative identity, whereas a risk-avoidant lifestyle could result in a foreclosed identity, in which the individual internalizes uncritically the values and behavior patterns of the parent generation. Therefore by contrast with either the principled abstainer or the experimental drug user, the risk-avoidant abstainer and the compulsive drug user may both be attempting to evade the disequilibrated state of consciousness and the assimilation-accommodation process by which development takes place.[7] While the abuse of substances is clearly not a viable strategy for resolving the crisis of early adolescence, the avoidance of drug use through foreclosure of identity cannot be viewed as an optimal solution.

COGNITIVE AND PSYCHOSOCIAL CONSEQUENCES OF ADOLESCENT DRUG USE

With this description of early adolescence as a developmental period in the contemporary United States as a background, we now argue that a prima facie case can be made against early adolescent substance use. By this we mean that there is sufficient evidence to persuade a prudent youth to abstain until more conclusive evidence can be obtained to support or refute the case we are prepared to make. It is generally agreed that, by comparison with mature adults, rapidly developing organisms are at risk from exposure to all noxious substances. Thus moderate maternal use of alcohol during pregnancy has been implicated in fetal alcohol syndrome, and there are similar concerns about even moderate use by pregnant women of caffeine and nicotine. Early adolescents are less at risk than fetuses but more at risk than mature adults.

In the sections which follow, we raise a variety of issues relevant to possible adverse consequences of drug use in young adolescents with respect to (1) Developmental Lag; (2) Amotivational Syndrome; and (3) Psychosocial Dysfunction.

Developmental Lag

In this section we will argue for the position that drug use in adolescence interferes with the process of stage-sequential development. The path of stage-sequential development may be relatively fixed by the interaction of cultural and historical factors, particular socialization encounters, and transformations in underlying cognitive-operational capacities. However, developmental progress itself is not guaranteed. It is only through commitment to courses of thought and action that depart from earlier, more stable and secure patterns that stage-transition can occur. When the underlying neurophysiological substrait is impaired, when action is curtailed and interaction with a potentially disequilibrating environment is reduced, development may be retarded.

The core developmental task at adolescence is to negotiate the transition to adult life. Young adolescents have not yet achieved the relatively secure social reality of adulthood which they can construct for themselves by negotiating successfully their school and early work experiences. Adolescents who undertake the transitional passage but do not negotiate it successfully may remain in limbo, suffering from symptoms of a diffuse identity, marked by prolonged aimlessness and lack of clarity about goals. Adolescent involvement with drugs may have a fairly comprehensive impact on stage-sequential development, due in part to the pharmacological actions of drugs commonly used, and in part to a failure to cultivate a commitment to encountering and adaptively integrating an expanded range of social interactions and conceptions.

Developmental progress occurs in order to resolve inconsistencies or fill gaps in the adolescent's highest level of understanding (with inadequacies of earlier stages having already been resolved in developmental progress to the current highest level). In other words, the acquisition of higher stages takes place at the "cutting edge" of the adolescent's understanding. Adolescents who become involved in the use of drugs may be able to effectively exercise previously acquired conceptual schemes, acquire new facts, and refine basic learning skills. Therefore their academic performance will not necessarily deteriorate, nor will they necessarily lose the ability to maintain smooth interpersonal relations with peers or adults. However, the transition to *higher* stages of social reasoning and associated patterns of social interaction, almost by definition involve a process of overtaxing what were previously the adolescents' most comprehensively effective schemes of thought and action. *Maximally* efficient functioning is required in order to resolve the disequilibration that constitutes the impetus for developmental progress. Loss of optimal cortical tone due to drug use may be reflected in the failure to consolidate a higher and more complex stage of understanding, a process which requires full "presence of mind." Developmental regression may occur if the highest level of cognitive organization is stripped away by protracted substance abuse.[32,33] Ontogenetically prior, less differentiated schemes of thought and associated forms of action previously subordinated by that highest level of functioning will then become more prominent in the drug-using behavior repertoire. With the erosion of selectivity in processing feedback from the environment, coupled with inhibition of mechanisms responsible for habituation to stimuli associated with the use of marijuana, previously acquired schemes may be employed in a perseverative manner, in situations where such schemes are no longer fully adaptive.

In the cognitive domain, adolescent involvement with drugs may impede progress from concrete to formal operations, or introduce greater instability in the exercise of incompletely consolidated formal operational schemes. In the social domain, adolescent involvement with drugs may signal entrance into a peer culture possessing a set of values and prescribed forms of social interaction that merely recapitulate earlier forms of peer interaction centering around play, without achieving an effective synthesis of conflicting claims of reason, social convention (including a work ethic in this culture), personal conscience and desire. If by "identity" we mean the adolescent's ability to conserve a sense of continuity through the act of validating simultaneously the interest of personal emancipation and the claims of mutually shared social norms, then we would hypothesize that the use of drugs would be associated with a hiatus in identity formation. By backing off from the developmentally appropriate task of synthesizing a set of principles that would serve as a basis for a critique of social convention (as opposed to a simple denial), drug-taking adolescents may behave in ways that are not congruent with conventional values and practices at the same time that their thinking continues to be bound by notions of social convention. Confronted with attempts by parents and other authority figures to instill greater compliance with conventional values and practices, but lacking a positive basis for rationalizing and justifying their own actions, the adolescent's reasoning about issues of morality and social convention may take on a defensive cast, becoming progressively more attenuated and stereotyped. The emotional turmoil so endemic to the period of early adolescence would be likely to increase the possibility of this sort of developmental lag or regression, especially when such turmoil serves as a motivating force for maintenance or increase of drug-taking.

Therefore we propose that use of consciousness-altering drugs may retard young middle-class adolescents' development in the following ways: *(1) By obscuring the differentiation between a context of work and a context of play.* Piaget[34] defines "play" categorically as the exercise of already existing schemes of action, as a predominance of *assimilation.* Adolescents who utilize the school setting primarily as a place to take drugs and socialize are in effect assimilating their educational experiences to schemes of recreation, without accommodating to the work requirements that must be satisfied for understanding and knowledge to develop. It is the rare high-school youth who has developed a sufficiently differentiated view of the social world prior to initiation into drug use to be able to distinguish between work and play contexts. The distinction would become increasingly dedifferentiated as a result of drug use, resulting in a lower level of functioning in work settings. *(2) By promoting a false consciousness of reality.* The drug ideology reinforces the drug experience as one of being "tuned in" to transcendant truths. Whereas most adults have sufficient reality-testing experience to know that there are intransigent laws of social reality, the surreal world produced by acute drug intoxication may present itself to the adolescent seductively not only as a more interesting place to live, but also as phenomenologically more real than the world view attained by engagement with the external environment. *(3) By reinforcing the sense of being special.* Whereas adolescence is the time to relinquish childhood illusions of being more special than one's peers, a drug-induced gnosis can reinforce the adolescent's conviction that such egocentric preoccupation is justified. *(4) By enabling the adolescent to avoid realistic confrontation with the demand characteristics of the environment.* College-age youths committed to a course of study may use marijuana as a tranquilizer to reduce anxiety sufficiently to enable them to study. But high-school adolescents seldom have either the commitment or the established work-skills to self-medicate in a disciplined fashion. Peer-sanctioned use of drugs enables adolescents to avoid experiencing the disequilibrating demand characteristics of an environment which would otherwise motivate them to cope, and in the process progressively to acquire more differentiated and integrated systems of action. *(5) By consolidating the cultural relativism and negative identity characteristic of early adolescents.* Consciousness-altering drugs may confer an intransigent existential validity to fabricated constructions of social reality which would otherwise be dismissed by the adolescent himself as confabulatory. The drug-using adolescent may therefore become convinced that social reality is only in the mind and so refuse to internalize consensually agreed-upon rules and mores. *(6) By masquerading as an emancipatory effort* while serving to maintain a childish pattern of family interaction in which parents feel forced by the adolescent's provocative and defiant behavior to be more controlling than they would otherwise be.

Amotivational Syndrome (AMS)

Amotivational syndrome describes a pattern of apathetic withdrawal of energy and interest from effortful activity, an uncertainty about long-range goals with resultant mental and physical lethargy, a loss of creativity, and social withdrawal from demanding social stimuli. We propose that marijuana use is implicated in AMS on the bases that: (1) the neurophysiological action of cannabinoids is to *inhibit* limbic system-cortical connections[32] which normally sustain current drive states and maintain the continuity of complex action sequences, lend an emotional tone to sensory inputs, and maintain non-specific arousal and attention states;[33,35] and (2) clinical reports testifying to (a) the unmotivated state of mind which many users intend to produce by acute intoxication, and (b) the lethargic, withdrawn condition of many chronic users who seek psychiatric help.

We do not regard marijuana use as a necessary cause of AMS since we recognize that these same symptoms occur without it, and indeed are an aspect of the normal adolescent crisis. We propose instead that prolonged marijuana use by young adolescents *intensifies* and *consolidates* AMS. The psychopharmacological effects of marijuana are to tranquilize affect, referred to in the jargon as ''cooling out'' and ''mellowing.'' Indeed many youths discover that marijuana helps them to manage their rage and frustration at being directed and contained at home and in school. The energy generated by enraging and frustrating experiences might instead be sublimated into social action, achievement, creative expression, physical fitness activities, and cognitive growth.

Drug use should be understood as largely conscious and intentional, with many of its consequences anticipated by the user. A mechanistic, linear model of cause and effect, in which marijuana is treated as an efficient cause automatically producing certain behaviors, simply is not applicable to purposive and motivated human behavior. Research investigating the relationship between drug use and AMS must be oriented towards discovering the sorts of subtle effects implied by this approach. Typically AMS is operationalized as lowered achievement level, loss of clarity concerning occupational goals, and dropping out of school. Based on these definers Kandel et al. (p. 28)[17] concludes that drug use has not been shown to lead to amotivational syndrome. She documents her conclusion with reference to three longitudinal studies, two using as subjects undergraduates at the University of California,[36,37] and one following up a cohort of 10th-grade boys.[38] Although these and other investigators do report that users are more likely to drop out of school,[38,36] have lower grades[39] and have greater difficulties in deciding on a career,[37] Kandel concludes that these problems preceded drug use and therefore cannot be attributed to the effects of marijuana. However, demonstrating that amotivational symptoms precede as well as follow marijuana initiation by no means rules out a causal relationship between marijuana use and consolidation of AMS. The process of becoming a user is *necessarily* preceded by a constellation of attitudes and symptoms continuous with those which follow drug initiation. The initiate has already decided to escape conflict and anxiety about achievement. Marijuana or other consciousness-altering drugs are used to produce the illusion of power, control and achievement in lieu of effortful activity which would otherwise be required to obtain a similar ego-enhancement.

Functional decrement resulting from AMS can only be assessed intraindividually and within a longitudinal design: initial assessments should be made prior to the adolescent crisis to estalish baseline performance and expected developmental trajectory; final outcome assessment should be made in early adulthood in order to test the hypothesis that prolonged marijuana (or other drug) use consolidates the patterns of behavior and attitudes constituting AMS.

Moreover, theoretically relevant measures must be used. Grades are not a good measure, particularly in high schools where standards are sufficiently low for bright youths to underachieve and fail to learn but still to obtain good grades by comparison with less bright youths. SAT scores would therefore provide a better index of learning than grades. If creativity suffers, as the AMS hypothesis proposes, a test of verbal fluency and flexibility requiring "good-form" responses under time pressure is indicated. Similarly, mental lethargy would be demonstrated by decrement in performance (relative to earlier test behavior) on timed intelligence or achievement tests. In addition to performance tests, the judgments of a "fair witness" rather than of the user are necessary to establish functional decrement constituting AMS. Since veridical self-perception may be interfered with by consciousness-altering drugs, perceived effects are likely to be underestimated by drug-using youths. However, by young adulthood many users (particularly those who markedly reduce their consumption or quit altogether) are able to be quite good informants much as former cultists tell a very different story after being deprogrammed. The measurement of AMS cannot be limited by convenience to grades or self-report, therefore, but must include observations of and performance on goal-oriented activities assessed over time. Whereas youthful marijuana users are generally poor informants, the same individuals as adults may be able to provide a unique retrospective view of the subjective changes which they now attribute to their adolescent drug use.

Psychosocial Dysfunction

We propose that developmental retardation produced in part by prolonged drug use results in psychosocial dysfunction including (a) escapism, (b) egocentrism, (c) external locus of control, (d) self-derogation, and (e) alienation and estrangement.

A crucial premise underlying our assertion that drug use results in psychosocial dysfunction is that young adolescents use drugs to achieve states and to facilitate functions which in the normal course of development arise from engagement in human relationships and participation in productive but stressful interactional processes. It is through extended interactions with others and practice with a variety of different role partners that increments of knowledge about the self and others are normally acquired. By opting for a chemical solution to their interpersonal problems, we contend that young people

substitute solipsistic homogenizing pseudo-encounters which de-
volve into a process Piaget[40] terms ''collective monologue'' for
complementary human engagements that preserve differences, as a
product of authentic interpersonal communication. We propose that
to the extent that adolescent drug users attain a *feeling* of closeness
and communion with others as a result of a drug-induced dissolution
of boundaries or distinctions, they will fail to acquire the skills
necessary to achieve those states without drugs. By basing personal
relationships on a private drug experience, adolescents may erode
or ''stunt'' the very relationships they seek to cultivate, thus preventing genuine intersubjective encounters. When a sense of intimacy is achieved by means of a drug, thus bypassing the usual
struggles and commitments, the end achieved will also be different.
A drug-induced sense of intimacy will lack depth, commitment and
stability, and therefore may dissolve when confronted with the reality of the other's dissimilar perspective.

The major reason given by young adolescents for using drugs is to
get high. By chronically substituting drug euphoria for negative
emotions, a habit of *escapism* is fostered. Drugs like marijuana and
the sedatives can temporarily relieve adolescent suffering, distract-
ing youths from their sources of discontent. The euphoric, tran-
quilizing, and surreal qualities of other drugs, once discovered
through experimentation to reduce pain and to alter an unsatisfac-
tory state of everyday consciousness, may become intrinsically re-
warding and thus psychologically addictive. Even though adolescents may use drugs for the same escapist reasons that adults do, the
negative effects they suffer may be more profound because adolescence is the time of life for the individual to come to terms with the
reality principle and to face the universal experiences of loneliness,
failure, frustration, and insufficiency. Drugs provide an all-too-con-
venient mechanism to enable adolescents to avoid stage-appropriate
uncomfortable disequilibrating experiences and to escape psychological and physical pain.

Use of consciousness-altering drugs may *consolidate egocentric
cognition at the expense of role-taking ability and a stable sense of
personal identity* through a dual process of (a) focusing adolescents'
attention on inner experience, and (b) enabling them to bypass the
difficult phases of relationship and interaction that occur on the way
to achievement of authentic intimacy. This claim is grounded in
Piaget's [11] treatment of the function of decentration in the stabilization of cognitive structures, and in Feffer's[41] cogent analysis of the

contribution of cognitive centrations to processes of psychopathological symptom formation.

Piaget[11] uses the term "decentration" to refer to a process of considering different points of view simultaneously. He argues that a cognitive centration on a single aspect of a situation (or a sequential centration of different aspects) will inevitably lead to distorted understandings. In the case of adolescent identity formation, an egocentric focus on personal desires and intentions, untempered by a simultaneous consideration of the contribution of external social forces to the shaping of personal motivations, may generate a paradoxical situation where adolescents essentially give themselves over unreflectively to the binding force of social norms, while believing that they are pursuing their own individualistic ends. Conversely, in the moment of identification with reference group norms, untempered by a simultaneous consideration of subjective motives and intentions, adolescents may pursue a course of social interaction in a largely egocentric, idiosyncratic manner, while believing that they have internalized a body of consensually-validated norms. In both cases, social understanding is distorted. In the case of a centration on the self, the significance of personal motivations is inflated, while an appreciation of the standpoint of others and their contribution to personal experience is minimized. It is only when the adolescent can recognize the binding force of social expectations, and comprehend simultaneously the process whereby individuals' idiosyncratic, egocentric needs and interest become institutionalized in generating that body of social expectations, that the adolescent can conserve a sense of personal identity *within* the context of social interaction. Engaged in a practice that conceals individuality while reducing thoughts, feelings, actions—and ultimately persons—to "the effects of the drug," adolescents may fail to acquire the shared perspective among individuals that arises precisely through the effort to comprehend the idiosyncracies of others viewed as active, responsible agents in their own right. At the same time, the values of the drug subculture which the adolescent has joined continue to exert a socializing force that is untempered by reflection.

With personal agency displaced into a drug, the user consolidates an *external locus of control* and evades taking responsibility for achievement-outcomes, the success of personal relationships, or the person s/he is becoming. In attempting to emancipate themselves from adult constraints through involvement with pacifying drugs and a subculture that relies upon conformity to achieve interpersonal stability, adolescents may fail to achieve the crucial recognition that sustained effort is required to alter social systems and to create new social arrangements.

We have presented a case for the view that adolescent involvement with drugs may interfere with the *process* of developing a stable identity which is normally achieved through the overcoming of egocentrism and the consolidation of mature role-taking skills. We will now make a case for the view that the *content* of adolescent identity (i.e., the adolescent's self-concept and self-esteem) may be affected adversely through involvement with drugs and complicity with the values and practices of a drug subculture.

The long-range effects of drug use may be to increase *self-derogation*. Early adolescents, as a consequence of their extreme transitional status, suffer from an ebb in self-esteem and a heightened sense of personal vulnerability. Many compensate for this vulnerability by grandiose flights of fancy. Drug-induced drop-out states in which the individual feels in control of his or her inner life may reinforce adolescents' construction of a "personal fable" including compensatory beliefs about their specialness, invulnerability, omnipotence and omniscience. The self-enhancing effects of taking drugs is at least in part a result of the euphoric mood experienced, and of cult support for restricting experiences to those which will not endanger self-esteem. A similar self-enhancing function of various patterns of psychiatric disorders, particularly paranoia, is often noted. Although the short-range effects of euphoria-producing drugs are to enhance self-esteem, the long-range effects should be the opposite. By foreclosing options for ego-enhancement via previously valued routes based upon achievement and competence, drug-using adolescents may be at a disadvantage in acquiring the skills which would provide them with a realistic sense of control over the environment. To the extent that members of mainstream reference groups continue to be important to drug-using youths, their disapprobation will negatively affect these youths' self-concept directly, as well as indirectly by foreclosing work and scholastic options which these mainstream members control.

The use of psychotropic drugs should contribute to adolescent *alienation and estrangement* in several ways: (1) The experience may interfere in general with a process of personal identity formation such that a sense of personal continuity becomes antithetical to identification with others; (2) More specifically, the experience contributes to a break in intergenerational continuity both in transmission of values and in maintenance of a viable parent-child relationship; (3) The phantasmic perception of social reality induced by the drug experience may be preserved in a generalized world view based on little actual engagement with the world; and (4) The social consequences of drug use may confirm the sense of vulnerability, powerlessness and external locus of control which are the root causes of the psychological experience of alienation.

Failure to develop a sense of personal identity that reconciles the spontaneous expression of self-interest with externally imposed constraints leaves the adolescent caught between two poles of a dialectic in which alienation is an inevitable by-product. If adolescents cannot see their own interests and needs reflected in external social norms, compliance with such norms becomes equated with estrangement from the self, with a sacrifice of the self to society. Conversely, when adolescents cannot or will not recognize the extent to which social conventions inevitably mediate their perceptions of what they view as *intrinsic* personal characteristics, their personal lives become alienated from the collective, and the possibility of genuine intersubjective encounter is greatly attenuated. Until the adolescent recognizes a reciprocal relationship between spontaneous self-interest and social conformity, estrangement from the self or from society will pervade the adolescent's experience. To the extent that involvement with drugs and a drug subculture interferes with this process of constructing a social identity, such involvement will inevitably engender alienation.

The manner in which identity is preserved at the expense of engagement with others is illustrated clearly in the *relationships of parents and drug-using adolescents.* Interactions between users and non-using parents and friends become awkward and lack mutuality, accounting for the desire of drug-takers to ''turn on'' their non-user friends. Even if parents have experimented with drugs themselves, they will be unable to share their adolescents' experience, because the experience itself is affected dramatically by the stage of development of the user and the setting in which the drug is used. Since drugs may be used to facilitate emancipation from parents, adolescents may at first welcome the break. However, parent-child relationships may then deteriorate rapidly as a result of the clash in values. By labeling the user as deviant and unworthy, and by attempting to elicit conformity through coercion, parents may help to equate conformity with alienation in the adolescent's mind. In addition, habits of work and values internalized in childhood may in fact be suppressed or subverted as a result of the dramatic alterations in mental functioning induced by psychedelic drugs and marijuana, further consolidating the generational rift. Loss of optimal cortical tone necessary to effect a process of stage-sequential development consequent to substance abuse, along with adoption of a negative identity and foreclosure of options for affirmative achievement, may prevent normal developmental progress towards acquisition of higher levels of social-conventional reasoning and the socially integrated patterns of action supported by such reasoning. Parents may then feel obliged either to reinstate age-inappropriate controls or to reject the defiant adolescent altogether.

The generalized world view produced by immersion in the drug experience and drug culture may *consolidate the surreal state of consciousness* characteristic of adolescents which reflects the reality of their "in-limbo" social status. The altered state of consciousness produced by marijuana and psychedelics may include the following elements: a sense of being "taken over" rather than of being in charge; the loss of a future time perspective and devaluation of the past; concern with experiencing rather than with doing; an ethic of personal gratification at the expense of social welfare; and a focus on freedom and non-commitment. With little or no actual engagement or struggle the drug can produce the illusion of autonomy and self-assertion while actually pacifying and immobilizing the user, and is especially insidious because it frequently presents itself to the user as cosmic enlightenment and not as a mere product of unreflective drug intoxication.

The root cause of adolescents' *alienation and estrangement* is to be found in their emerging critical capacities and the actual social conditions which adolescents are then able to critique. When basic economic processes are reified and depersonalized, rendering them too opaque to approach, youths contemplating entrance into the economy as workers may react to their sense of helplessness by estrangement and alienation.[42] The drug experience itself may further alienate the individual. The synesthetic experiences produced by drugs separate affect from the encounters which normally generate affect, sensations from the stimuli which normally give rise to them, and the perceiving ego from the physical body and surrounding environment. By artificially manipulating the body image and altering the relations between self and environment, adolescent users may fail to achieve a stable body image and may obscure the differentiations of subject and object which enable persons to monitor external stimuli and to master their environment. In sum, as a direct extension of the drug experience, and as an indirect consequence of the devaluing of that experience and of the drug-using youths themselves by members of powerful reference groups, the sense of vulnerability, powerlessness and external locus of control appropriate to adolescents' "in-limbo" status may be consolidated in enduring fatalism, alienation and estrangement.

CONCLUSION

The cumulative substantive findings in the field of adolescent substance use are too meager and tangential to resolve the major social policy issue which they should address. For example, are there major adverse personal and social consequences caused by widespread use among middle-class adolescents of marijuana and other illicit drugs? The concern of health policy planners should be especially with those adolescents for whom risk-taking behavior fails to promote personal initiative and a responsible lifestyle. We need to know why some adolescents become intensely committed to such health-compromising behavior as habitual use of harmful drugs, whereas most who experiment desist on their own. A longitudinal research design employing data-intensive assessments prior to, during, and after the adolescent transition is required to identify the actual consequences of various risk-taking behaviors thought to endanger health so that distinctions can be made between stage-appropriate, if worrisome, experimentation and a level and kind of involvement for which the secondary gains in growth enhancement do not compensate for short-range turmoil and danger.

In the absence of conclusive evidence regarding the presence or absence of concurrent effects and lasting consequences of adolescent drug use, we presented a prima facie case against early adolescent drug use by defending the following *six propositions:* (1) Developmental lag in social and work contexts will result from drug abuse. (2) Drug-using adolescents' reasoning about issues of morality and social convention becomes stereotyped and underdeveloped. (3) The use of consciousness-altering drugs further retards young adolescents' development by (a) obscuring the differentiation between a context of work and a context of play when drugs are used in work contexts; (b) promoting a drug-induced false consciousness which is misperceived as a "higher" consciousness; (c) reinforcing the childish sense of being "special" and somehow exempted from the normal claims of physical and social laws; (d) enabling adolescents to avoid guilt and anxiety which would otherwise motivate them to meet the demand characteristics of the environment; (e) generating parent-child conflict characteristic of earlier stages of development, thus impeding genuine emancipation; and (f) consolidating the cultural relativism and negative identity characteristic of early adolescence. (4) Marijuana use is implicated in amotivational syndrome through inhibition of limbic system-cortical connections which normally sustain current drive states. Indeed the lethargic, tranquilized, unmotivated state is often the sought-after effect of marijuana use. (5) Developmental retardation produced in part by prolonged drug use results in a wide variety of psychosocial dysfunctions including escapism, egocentrism, external locus of control, self-derogation and alienation. (6) The use of psychotropic drugs consolidates adolescent alienation and estrangement.

Against a backdrop of increasing competition for scarce employment opportunities, chronic drug abusers who have been unsuccessful in their efforts to develop a personally satisfying and economically viable adjustment to adult life run a greater risk of advancing to the terminal stage of substance abuse for an already alarming number of Americans—alcoholism. Alcohol abuse and addiction must be viewed as a final common pathway for a host of personal and social ills, including domestic violence, suicide, terminal medical illness, and a loss of productivity; the destructive consequences associated with the use of alcohol far surpass those associated with the use and abuse of other illicit substances.[43-45] While we would not accept an interpretation that the use of drugs such as marijuana causes alcoholism, and would certainly not entertain the hypothesis that use of illicit substances is necessary to develop a serious drinking problem, we do advance the thesis that involvement with drugs (including alcohol) will come to function as an increasingly central element in a personally and socially deteriorating developmental progression.

Societal concern with substance abuse has been expressed in moral as well as purely practical terms. But moral propositions inevitably rest upon claims of fact. It is necessary therefore to subject the various hypotheses relevant to these moral propositions to rigorous empirical tests in order to establish scientific grounds for the presumptive nexus between substance use and the subversion of those values. Thus we may ask whether, as we proposed earlier, regular marijuana use is in fact implicated in the causal nexus which produces a drop-out mentality, or lack of motivation to achieve and develop, or cognitive decrements relative to a previous level of functioning. In order to answer these questions or to test the hypotheses associated with these propositions, we must move beyond the social survey methods which have to date dominated the substance use research literature. In-depth information of the sort required to subject our prima facie case to empirical test requires intensive study, in which participants serve as their own controls.

The field of substance abuse deserves judicious and accurate scientific reporting. Youths are influenced by adult values which are expressed rationally and by scientific evidence that does not contradict their own experience. The success of the recent anti-smoking campaign testifies to the possibility of changing a negative trajectory by widespread dissemination of accurate information. In the event that the factual claims underlying the prima facie case we have made are supported by credible empirical evidence, we believe that young adolescents could similarly be persuaded to reduce their consumption of drugs shown to be harmful, or to abstain altogether.

REFERENCES

1. Baumrind D. Types of adolescent life-styles. Unpublished manuscript, University of California, Berkeley, 1971.

2. Baumrind D. Early socialization and adolescent competence. In Dragastin SE & Elder G Jr., Ed.: Adolescence in the life cycle. Washington, D.C.: Hemisphere, 1975.

3. Becker HS. Outsiders: Studies in the sociology of deviance. New York: Free Press, 1963.

4. Blum RH and Associates. Horatio Alger's children. San Francisco: Jossey-Bass, 1972.

5. Keniston K. The uncommitted: Alienated youth in America. New York: Dell, 1965.

6. Hendin H, Pollinger A, Ulman R, Carr AC. Adolescent marijuana abusers and their families. National Institute on Drug Abuse Research Monograph 40. DHHS Pub. No. (ADM) 81-1168. Washington, D.C.: Supt. of Docs., U.S. Govt. Print. Off., 1981.

7. Baumrind D. Familial antecedents of adolescent drug use: A developmental perspective. National Institute on Drug Abuse Research Monograph, in press.

8. Yankelovich D. New rules: Searching for self-fulfillment in a world turned upside down. New York: Random House, 1981.

9. Werner H, Kaplan B. Symbol formation. New York: Wiley, 1963.

10. Erikson EH, Identity and the life cycle: Selected papers. Psychological Issues, 1959; 1 (1).

11. Piaget J. The psychology of intelligence. (Piercy M, Berlyne DE, trans.) New York: Harcourt, Brace & World, 1950.

12. Kohlberg L, Gilligan C. The adolescent as a philosopher: The discovery of the self in a post-conventional world. In Kagan J, Coles R, Eds.: Twelve to sixteen: Early adolescence. New York: Norton, 1972.

13. Turiel E. Social regulations and domains of social concepts. In Damon W, Ed.: New Directions for Child Development: Social cognition, 1, 1978.

14. Bronfenbrenner U. Influences on human development. Hinsdale, Ill.: Dryden Press, 1972.

15. Coleman JS. The adolescent society. New York: Cromwell-Collier Publishing Company, 1961.

16. Gordon C. Looking ahead: Self-conceptions, race and family as determinants of adolescent orientation to achievement. Washington, D.C.: American Sociological Association, 1972.

17. Kandel DB, Kessler RC, Margulies RZ. Antecedents of adolescent initiation into stages of drug use: A developmental analysis. In Kandel DB, Ed.: Longitudinal research on drug use: Empirical findings and methodological issues. Washington, D.C.: Hemisphere, 1978.

18. Douvan E, Adelson J. The adolescent experience. New York: Wiley, 1966.

19. Brittain CV. A comparison of urban and rural adolescence with respect to peer versus parent compliance. Adolescence, 1968; 2:445-458.

20. Bronfenbrenner U. Two worlds of childhood: U.S. and U.S.S.R. New York: Russell Sage Foundation, 1970.

21. Kessen W. Ed.: Childhood in China. New Haven: Yale University Press, 1975.

22. Bronfenbrenner U. The ecology of human development: Experiments by nature and design. Cambridge: Harvard University Press, 1979.

23. Selman R. Taking another's perspective: Role-taking development in early childhood. Child Development, 1971; 42:79-91.

24. Elkind D. Egocentrism in adolescence. Child Development, 1967; 38:1025-34.

25. Edelstein W, Noam, G. Regulatory structures of the self and "postformal" stages in adulthood. Unpublished manuscript (April, 1982).

26. Labouvie-Vief G. Beyond formal operations: Uses and limits of pure logic in life-span development. Human Development, 1980; 23:141-161.

27. Bachman JG, Green S, Wirtanen I. Dropping out—problem or symptom? Youth in transition, 3. Ann Arbor, Mich.: Institute for Social Research, 1971.

28. Nickols JE, Jr. Changes in self-awareness during the high school years: A study of mental health using paper-and-pencil tests. Journal of Educational Research, 1963; 56:403-409.

29. Jorgensen EC, Howell RJ. Changes in self, ideal-self correlations from ages 3 through 18. Journal of Social Psychology, 1969; 79:63-67.

30. Yamemoto K, Thomas EC, Karns EA. School-related attitudes in middle school-age students. American Educational Research Journal, 1969; 6:191-206.

31. Kaplan HB. Deviant behavior in defense of self. New York: Academic Press, 1980.

32. Miller LL. Cannabis and the brain with special reference to the limbic system. In Nahas GG, Paton WD, Eds.: Marijuana: Biological effects. Elmford, N.Y.: Pergamon Press, 1979.

33. Luria AR. Higher cortical functions in man. (Haig B, trans., 2nd ed.) New York: Basic Books, 1980.

34. Piaget J. Play, dreams and imitation in childhood. (Gattegno C, Hodgson FM, trans.) New York: Norton, 1962. (Original work published 1951.)

35. Luria AR. The working brain. (Haig B, trans.) New York: Basic Books, 1973.

36. Mellinger GD, Somers RH, Davidson ST, Manheimer DI. The amotivational syndrome and the college student. Annals of the New York Academy of Sciences, 1976; 282:37-55.

37. Brill NW, Christie RL. Marihuana use and psychosocial adaptation. Archives of General Psychiatry, 1974; 31:713-719.

38. Johnston LD. Drugs and American youth. Ann Arbor: Institute for Social Research, 1973.

39. Kandel DB, Treiman D, Faust R, Single E. Adolescent involvement in legal and illegal drug use: A multiple classification analysis. Social Forces, 1976; 55:438-458.

40. Piaget J. The language and thought of the child. (Gabain M, trans.) New York: Meridian Books, 1955. (Original work published 1926.)

41. Feffer M. Symptom expression as a form of primitive decentering. Psychological Review, 1967; 74(1):16-28.

42. Merton R. Social theory and social structure. New York: Free Press of Glencoe, 1949.

43. California Highway Patrol. 1981 annual report of fatal and injury motor vehicle traffic accidents. California Statewide Integrated Traffic Records System, 1981.

44. National Association of State Alcohol and Drug Abuse Directors. Economic costs to society of alcohol and drug abuse and mental illness: A final report from the Research Triangle Institute. Washington, D.C., 1982.

45. National Institute on Alcohol Abuse and Alcoholism. First statistics compendium on alcohol and health. Rockville, Md., 1981.

The Epidemiology
of Alcohol and Drug Abuse
Among Adolescents

Richard R. Clayton, PhD
Christian Ritter, PhD

ABSTRACT. The primary purpose of this paper was to review systematically some of the more salient findings from a decade of research on the epidemiology of alcohol and drug abuse among adolescents. Data from most of the on-going nationwide studies regarding lifetime, past year, and past month use of various drugs were examined. While there is evidence of a downturn for some of the indicators, it is still too early to know if this is a temporary shift in rates or the beginning of meaningful trends toward lower levels of drug use. The second purpose was to challenge the alcohol and drug fields to consider more seriously the problem of multiple drug use and abuse. This was accomplished by showing that the relative percentage of youth who have used "only marijuana" has gone down as the percentage of youth who have used marijuana, other illicit drugs, and cigarettes and alcohol as well, has increased. Regression and discriminant analyses of data from the 1980 Monitoring the Future study of high school seniors reveals that variables that previously have differentiated users from nonusers are also useful in differentiating types of multiple drug users. The most important conclusion from this paper is that persons characterized as "daily" users of marijuana are better typed as multiple drug users.

The alcohol and drug abuse fields of study can be seen as strikingly similar yet quite different *or* strikingly different yet quite similar; it depends on your perspective. However, when one narrows the focus to the study of alcohol and drug abuse among adolescents, the impression of convergence overshadows the impression that the

Richard R. Clayton is with the Department of Sociology, University of Kentucky, Lexington, Kentucky 40506. Christian Ritter is with the Department of Mental Hygiene, School of Hygiene and Public Health, Johns Hopkins University, Baltimore, Maryland.
Work completed under the auspices of Grant No. DA-02646 from the National Institute on Drug Abuse.

fields are following different paths. In fact, evidence of the convergence between the areas can be seen in two specific developments.

The first is an overriding interest in measuring and describing the fact of use, the frequency and quantity of use, the characteristics of users compared to nonusers, and the consequences of use and abuse of drugs. Because of the existence of a number of cross-sectional surveys of particular populations and a smaller number of high quality longitudinal and cohort-sequential studies, it is now possible to chart trends in use. However, in spite of this apparent point of convergence, there is still some divergence. For example, the alcohol field has far more consistency across studies in how ingestion of the substance is measured. Such measurement consistency is facilitated by the fact that alcohol is regulated, it comes in a form that can be precisely measured, and there is a long history of concern about alcohol and the abuse of it. There is general agreement in the alcohol field that one must measure the frequency and quantity of intake within binge occasions, and the contexts and consequences of use and abuse. In the drug abuse field, measurement problems are much more formidable because of the lack of regulation, the variety of substances that fall under the rubric of illicit drugs, and the generally low prevalence rates for most of these drugs. From a measurement perspective then, the study of the use of illicit drugs is still in its infancy compared to the study of alcohol use.

Further evidence of convergence between the two fields can be found in the existence of several "generic" conceptual models that help organize our understanding of two important issues (e.g., the progression from use of one substance to use of other substances and the confluence of factors that "predict" not only which persons will or will not get involved in substance use, but also their level of involvement). The models that serve this function are Jessor and Jessor's[1] theory of problem behavior and Kandel's[2] theory of developmental stages in drug use. Recently, there have been elaborations of these two models in the work of Huba and Bentler[3] using maximum likelihood techniques and in Zucker's[4] psychologically based theory of alcohol use and abuse among adolescents. However, the relative position of the alcohol and drug fields is reversed when it comes to conceptual development. There is probably no other area of adolescent behavior about which more is known than drug abuse. The progress that has been made in the past decade is not limited to mere description of the changes in the incidence and prevalence, although such information is invaluable. Substantial progress has also been made in research design, measurement, and the implementation of analytical strategies that are at the cutting edge of methodology in the social sciences. Furthermore, the study of adolescent drug abuse has been characterized by an intense interest in testing causal models. Of more recent vintage, but perhaps of equal importance, there has been a concerted effort to apply knowledge gained from epidemiological and etiological research to the design and implementation of primary and secondary prevention strategies. Similar rates of progress have not occurred in the study of youthful drinking practices. As Rachal et al.[5] note: "In general, research on adolescent drinking has been characterized by little theoretical integration and virtually no systematic accumulation of knowledge, owing, in part, to the recency of the emerging focus on teenagers . . . most of the studies of teenaged drinking have contributed only descriptively to our knowledge, without systematically adding to our ability to explain adolescent drinking behavior." Rachal and his colleagues may have overstated the case somewhat, but the fact remains that the study of drug abuse among adolescents is more mature theoretically than is true for the study of alcohol abuse among adolescents.

The primary purpose of this paper is to review some of the more salient findings from a decade or so of research on the epidemiology of alcohol and drug abuse among adolescents. A secondary purpose will be to challenge both fields to begin to consider more seriously the problem of multiple drug use and abuse. At the heart of any discussion of multiple drug use is an important policy issue: whether it is best to focus attention on the pharmacological class of drugs being used most frequently, such as marijuana, or the fact that daily users of marijuana are quite likely to have used or abused a number of illicit substances other than marijuana, in addition to contemporaneous use of both cigarettes and alcohol. More will be said about this later in the paper. However, the first task will be to review the findings of epidemiological studies, focusing on each drug class separately.

EPIDEMIOLOGICAL STUDIES

It is traditional in epidemiology to examine sociodemographic differentials in the prevalence and incidence of use of specific drugs, each treated separately. This is appropriate given the pharmacological differences between drugs, varying abuse liabilities, differences in availability and usage patterns, and the greater amount of stigma attached to some drugs than others. The separate focus on specific drugs also reflects an historical fact: in the not too distant past there was a great deal more specialization in the drugs persons used. As Cohen[6] notes: "The days when substance abusers were categorically labelled—as alcoholic, cokehead, hophead, pothead, and pill-head—seem to be rapidly disappearing. Instead, we are seeing people overinvolved with a primary substance of choice, but also using a variety of others depending on availability, price, social situation, peer group usage and the latest wisdom from the so-called underground press." However, the movement toward multiple drug use does not obviate the fact that some drugs are legal and some illegal, and that it is important from policy perspectives to understand levels of use of various drugs treated separately and trends in use of these drugs over time for specific populations.

Monitoring the Future Studies

The Monitoring the Future surveys, sponsored by the National Institute on Drug Abuse (NIDA), have been conducted annually since 1975 among a nationally representative sample of high school seniors. In terms of measurement consistency from year to year, comprehensiveness of substantive content, and coverage of multiple dimensions of use of most drug classes, this series is unique. However, it should be noted that the study contains data from only those seniors present on the day the survey is administered. The 20 or so percent of each birth cohort that become school dropouts and those that are chronically absent are not adequately represented in these surveys. In addition, there are some coverage problems arising because of difficulty getting access to the classrooms and schools. While these coverage limitations may affect somewhat the levels of use of various drugs, they do not have much impact on the trend lines from year to year, according to analysis by Clayton and Voss.[7] The data in Table 1 reflect some of the changes that have occurred in prevalence since 1975 for selected drug classes.

Marijuana. It is clear that the lifetime prevalence of use of marijuana has remained essentially the same for each senior class since 1978, hovering at about 60 percent. This may indicate that lifetime prevalence has reached a rather high plateau or "ceiling." Six-out-of-ten is a rather high proportion reporting some involvement in an act that is "illegal." Recent use of marijuana, use in the past 30

TABLE 1. Drug Use Among High School Seniors: The Monitoring the Future Surveys, 1975 Through 1982

Drug Classes	Percentage Using Drugs in Survey Years							
	1975	1976	1977	1978	1979	1980	1981	1982
Marijuana								
Lifetime	47.3	52.8	56.4	59.2	60.4	60.3	59.5	59.0
Past Year	40.0	44.5	47.6	50.2	50.8	48.8	46.1	44.0
Past Month	27.1	32.2	35.4	37.1	36.5	33.7	31.6	29.0
Daily	6.0	8.2	9.1	10.7	10.3	9.1	7.0	6.3
Alcohol								
Lifetime	90.4	91.9	92.5	93.1	93.0	93.2	92.6	93.0
Past Year	84.8	85.7	87.0	87.7	88.1	87.9	87.0	87.0
Past Month	68.2	68.3	71.2	72.1	71.8	72.0	70.7	70.0
Daily	5.7	5.6	6.1	5.7	6.9	6.0	6.0	5.7
Cigarettes								
Lifetime	73.6	75.4	75.7	75.3	74.0	71.0	71.0	70.0
Past Month	36.7	38.8	38.4	36.7	34.4	30.5	29.4	30.0
Daily	26.9	28.8	28.8	27.5	25.4	21.3	20.3	21.1
Cocaine								
Lifetime	9.0	9.7	10.8	12.9	15.4	15.7	16.5	16.0
Past Year	5.6	6.0	7.2	9.0	12.0	12.3	12.4	12.0
Past Month	1.9	2.0	2.9	3.9	5.7	5.2	5.8	5.0
Stimulants								
Lifetime	22.3	22.6	23.0	22.9	24.2	26.4	32.2	36.0
Past Year	16.2	15.8	16.3	17.1	18.3	20.8	26.0	26.0
Past Month	8.5	7.7	8.8	8.7	9.9	12.1	15.8	14.0
Tranquilizers								
Lifetime	17.0	16.8	18.0	17.0	16.3	15.2	14.7	14.0
Past Year	10.6	10.3	10.8	9.9	9.6	8.7	8.0	7.0
Past Month	4.1	4.0	4.6	3.4	3.7	3.1	2.7	2.0

days, has dropped 8 percentage points since 1979, from 37 percent to 29 percent. This is a drop of one-fifth in the percentage of high school seniors reporting "recent use." The peak in "daily" use of marijuana (defined as use on 20 or more occasions in the past 30 days) has dropped from a high of 10.9 percent in 1978 to 6.3 percent in 1982. In fact, the prevalence of daily use of marijuana in 1982 was at the lowest level since 1975 when the Monitoring the Future series was initiated. There are several plausible explanations for this decline. First, and most optimistic, high school seniors are beginning to take heed of the warnings about possible health consequences associated with chronic heavy use of marijuana. It is true that a considerably larger percentage of seniors in 1982 compared to 1978 perceive "great risk" with heavy use of cannabis. A second possible explanation, though somewhat more speculative, is that these data demonstrate a "cohort" effect. Those in the Class of

1982 were born in 1964. Those in the Class of 1978 were born in 1960. It could be that those in the Class of 1978 were at considerably greater risk to begin use of marijuana than their cohorts from the Class of 1982 because of temporal proximity to the youth who fueled the drug epidemic of the 1960s and 1970s. A third possible explanation for the reduction in "daily" marijuana use is a shift in consumption patterns (i.e., an increase in multiple drug use occurring simultaneously with a reduction in the daily use of marijuana. While we will not be testing this hypothesis directly, the latter part of this paper will focus on multiple drug use and its correlates. We will suggest that there has been too great an emphasis given to pharmacological classes of drugs and too little emphasis given to multiple drug use. In particular, we will focus attention on the "daily" marijuana users, most of whom could more appropriately be called multiple drug users.

Alcohol. The lifetime as well as the past 30 day prevalence rates also indicate the existence of a "ceiling" effect for alcohol. Over 9 out of 10 high school seniors have used alcohol at some time in their lives and close to 7 out of 10 have used alcohol during the past 30 days. These figures could be higher, but only theoretically. Practically speaking, it is not likely that higher proportions could be involved. The use of alcohol in the past 30 days may be a reasonably sensitive indicator of the incredibly large number of youths "at risk" for eventually becoming problem drinkers. The proportion of youths who drink five or more drinks at a single setting is also quite high. In 1982, some 41 percent stated that on at least one occasion in the prior two-week period they had had five or more drinks in a row. It is little wonder that alcohol is implicated in over half of the automobile accidents in this country and that it is so heavily involved in the traffic fatalities occurring among youth. The data underscore the need for something to be done about consumption, restriction, on driving, or both.

Cigarettes. The lifetime prevalence figures for cigarette use show a slight decline from 76 percent in 1977 to 70 percent in 1982. Use of cigarettes in the past 30 days reveals an even more dramatic reduction, from 39 percent in 1976 to 30 percent in 1982. These data suggest that all of the publicity about the harmful effects of smoking on health may have had an impact. The focus of prevention messages on the dangers of smoking may also be associated with the downturn in the use of marijuana, particularly daily use.

Hallucinogens and PCP. The downturn shown in Table 1 for cigarettes and marijuana seems to have a counterpart in the prevalence rates for hallucinogens and PCP. In both classes, the proportion of high school seniors reporting lifetime use or use in the past 30 days is considerably lower in 1982 than was true in 1979.

Cocaine. There is some evidence that cocaine began its spread through American society in about 1972,[8] almost 7 years after marijuana began its spread in 1965. By bringing up the tail end of the epidemic, cocaine has only recently reached a peak in the young adult population and has now begun to penetrate the youth and older adult portions of the population. The lifetime prevalence rate for cocaine in the high school senior population has increased from 13 percent in 1978 to 16 percent in 1982. The rate for use in the past 30 days has remained at about 5 or 6 percent since 1979.[9]

Psychotherapeutics. Two of the psychotherapeutics (stimulants and tranquilizers) have been singled out for attention. It is clear that the lifetime prevalence rate for nonmedical use of tranquilizers has remained at about the same level over the life of the Monitoring the Future studies. However, there has been a remarkable increase in the lifetime prevalence of use of stimulants. The rate in 1978 was 23 percent; in 1982 it was 36 percent, an increase of 13 percentage points. There is some evidence that part of the increase reflects the appearance of the "look-alikes," (i.e., pills designed to resemble specific prescription drugs that are used non-medically but which contain mostly licit substances such as caffeine). It is also true that *all* of the observed increase *cannot* be accounted for by look-alikes. Part of the increase is real and may reflect, although this is speculative, the increasing pressure felt by youth as they recognize the "realities" of the job market, having seen older siblings graduate from high school and college only to find it difficult to get a job. The increase in stimulant use may also reflect some of the uncertainties generated by the economic recession of the early 1980s and late 1970s.

High School Seniors Overseas: Military Dependents

In 1982, Johnston, O'Malley, and Davis-Sacks[10] conducted a study of about 2,400 high school seniors selected randomly from 33 schools overseas that educate dependents of military personnel. Compared to their civilian counterparts, exactly the same proportion had tried illicit drugs or illicit drugs other than marijuana. Lifetime prevalence rates were nearly identical for marijuana, hallucinogens, and sedatives. Rates of use for cocaine, stimulants, the amyl and butyl nitrites, and methaqualone by the overseas seniors were lower than for seniors statewide. Use of inhalants other than the nitrities, tranquilizers, sedatives, and the opiates were somewhat higher among overseas seniors, although still quite low in terms of absolute magnitude. Daily use of marijuana was lower among the overseas seniors (4 compated to 6.3 percent) while daily drinking (8.5 compared to 5.7 percent) and daily cigarette smoking (26 versus 21 percent) were higher abroad. The similarity between the two groups of seniors regarding levels of drug use is far more striking than the differences.

Enlisted Men: Department of Defense Studies

Another group of young persons that has been studied from an epidemiological perspective is military personnel in the E1 through E5 ranks—enlisted men, most of whom are just out of high school. The study was conducted first in 1980[11] and then again in 1982.[12] The prevalence rates for the preceding 30 days decreased for all of the drug classes between 1980 and 1982. For example, 37 percent of the enlisted men reporting having used marijuana or hashish during the 30 days preceding the interview in 1980. The comparable figure in 1982 was 22 percent, a decrease of 15 percentage points. These decreases were found in all branches of service and in all theaters of assignment. The 30 day prevalence rate for all of the drug classes other than alcohol compare quite favorably in 1982 with the rates observed for the same period in the Class of 1982 Monitoring the Future sample. Alcohol is clearly an exception. In 1982, 83 percent of the E1 through E5 enlisted men had used alcohol during the preceding 30 days. A total of 13 percent reported use on 20 or more of the prior 30 days (i.e., essentially daily use). In comparison, 70 percent of the high school seniors in 1982 reported use in the past 30 days (a difference of 13 percentage points) and 6 percent used on 20 or more of those days (a difference of 7 percentage points). These are striking differences and point to a source of some difficulty vis-a-vis drug use in the military (i.e., the fact that alcohol is subsidized on military installations, at least to some extent).[13]

National Survey on Drug Abuse

Another survey sponsored by NIDA and conducted periodically is designed to represent the household population in the United States. The 1982 survey[14] is the 7th in a series that began in 1971-72 under the auspices of the National Commission on Marihuana and Drug Abuse and was picked up by NIDA in 1974. The sample is divided into three segments: youth 12 to 17 years old, young adults 18 to 25 years old, and older adults 26 years old or older. We will be focusing on the youth segment which in 1982 represented 23 million young persons.

As the data in Table 2 show, the percentage of 12 to 17 year old youth who had ever tried marijuana rose during the 1970s from 14 percent in 1972 to 31 percent in 1979.[15] In 1982, the lifetime prevalence of marijuana use among youth was slightly lower at 27 percent. This reversal in trend in lifetime use was not found, at least as clearly, in the Monitoring the Future surveys. A similar type of decline is noted for the use of marijuana during the preceding year (from 24.1 percent to 20.6 percent) and use of marijuana during the preceding month (from 16.7 to 11.5 percent). The decline in past year and past month usage rates for marijuana parallel those noted for the high school seniors. Even with this replication across studies, it is still too early to know if this change is a temporary shift in direction of the trend line, the beginning of a downturn in the use of marijuana, or merely evidence that the use of marijuana among youth in this society has reached a plateau, and what we are seeing is "noise" around the slope. Regardless of the explanation for the shift, this is the first time in a decade the rates have gone down instead of up, a welcome change from a public health perspective.

The data in Table 2 concerning alcohol consumption should be viewed with caution. In 1979 and 1982 the youth were given "private" answer sheets, which may account for the rather sharp increases in use between 1977 and 1979. However, looking at just the changes from 1979 to 1982, there is a substantial decrease across the three prevalence measures of alcohol use. Such a decrease was not found among the high school seniors. It is thus difficult to know how to interpret this decrease since it is found in only the National Survey. Changes in the sampling plan, in the distribution of youth in the birth cohorts represented by the 12 to 17 year old group, or in the availability of alcohol to these youth may explain some of the observed decrease in prevalence. Regardless, it will be important to look at how the trend line turns in the next National Survey on Drug Abuse vis-a-vis the alcohol prevalence measures. There is some convergence in the findings between the two surveys regarding use of cigarettes. The data on lifetime prevalence from the Monitoring the Future series show quite clearly a downturn in lifetime pre-

TABLE 2.   Drug Use by Youth in the National Survey on Drug Abuse
            Series: 1972, 1974, 1976, 1977, 1979, 1982

| | Percentage Using in Survey Years | | | | | |
Drug Categories	1972	1974	1976	1977	1979	1982
Marijuana						
Lifetime	14.0	23.0	22.4	28.0	30.9	26.7
Past Year	----	18.5	18.4	22.3	24.1	20.6
Past Month	7.0	12.0	12.3	16.6	16.7	11.5
Alcohol						
Lifetime	----	54.0	53.6	52.6	70.3	65.2
Past Year	----	51.0	49.3	47.5	53.6	47.3
Past Month	----	34.0	32.4	31.2	37.2	26.9
Cigarettes						
Lifetime	----	52.0	45.5	47.3	54.1	49.5
Past Year	----	----	----	----	----	24.8
Past Month	----	----	----	----	----	12.3
Cocaine						
Lifetime	1.5	3.6	3.4	4.0	5.4	6.5
Past Year	1.5	2.7	2.3	2.6	4.2	4.1
Past Month	.6	1.0	1.0	.8	1.4	1.6
Stimulants						
Lifetime	4.0	5.0	4.4	5.2	3.4	6.7
Past Year	----	3.0	2.2	3.7	2.9	5.6
Past Month	----	1.0	1.2	1.3	1.2	2.6
Tranquilizers						
Lifetime	3.0	3.0	3.3	3.8	4.1	4.9
Past Year	----	2.0	1.8	2.9	2.7	3.3
Past Month	----	1.0	1.1	.7	.6	.9
Size of n	(880)	(952)	(986)	(1272)	(2165)	(1581)

Source: Miller et al., 1983.

valence from 1976 to 1982. However, there was a slight upturn in
the past month and daily use rates for cigarettes from 1981 to 1982.
This is somewhat mirrored in the downturn from 1979 to 1982 in the
National Survey data on lifetime prevalence (from 54.1 to 49.5 percent). Unfortunately, changes were made in the questions on past
year and past month use of cigarettes in the National Survey.

Another point of convergence can be seen in the prevalence rates
for use of cocaine. Among youth 12 to 17 years old, the lifetime,
past year, and past month rates seem to be trending upward. This is
consistent with the findings from the high school seniors. What is
particularly surprising about these findings is that they occurred
when the United States was involved in a rather deep recession. Co-

caine is an expensive drug. These data may reveal a deeper penetration of cocaine into mainstream America than previously thought. Perhaps the data reveal the naivete of youth who "thought" they were getting cocaine but were really getting a substitute. Regardless of which is the correct answer, the prevalence rates for self-reported use of cocaine among adolescents are sufficiently high to generate alarm and are going in the "wrong" direction for a health conscious society.

The prevalence data on stimulants in the National Survey do not exhibit stability. If one restricts attention to changes in the rates from 1979 to 1982, it is clear that there has been an increase on each of the prevalence measures. This would be consistent with the long-term trends found for stimulants in the high school senior studies. However, Johnston and his colleagues[9] have indicated that some, but not all, of this increase in stimulant use in recent years may be attributed to the influx of "look-alikes." The increases are substantial enough to suggest that at least some is attributable to real increases in the use of stimulants. The prevalence data on tranquilizers in the National Survey reveal an increase over time while the data from high school seniors reveal a decrease. Such an inconsistency suggests the need to wait for the next additions to the trend line to see if what is being measured is a real change or is merely noise around the trend lines.

NIAAA Surveys of High School Youth: 1974 and 1978

In 1974, Rachal and his colleagues[16] conducted a study of alcohol and drug use among over 13,000 students who were part of a national sample of 7th-8th, 9th-10th, and 11th-12th graders. In 1978, Rachal and his colleagues[5] conducted another cross-sectional survey, this time among 4,918 students representative of those in the 10th through the 12th grades. The lifetime and past year prevalence rates for use of alcohol were quite similar across the two surveys and have been shown to be comparable to the alcohol use data from the Monitoring the Future studies and the National Survey on Drug Abuse Data.[5] About 87 or 88 percent of the 10th through the 12th grade students in both surveys had used alcohol at some time; 81 percent had a drink in the preceding year. The lifetime rate for 7th through 12th graders in 1974 was 80 percent; the past year rate, 73 percent. Rachal et al.[5] used frequency-quantity measures to create a typology of alcohol users ranging from abstainers to heavier drinkers. When the 10th through 12th graders in the 1974 and 1978 studies are compared, 14.9 and 14.8 percent respectively fell into the heavier drinking category (drink at least once a week and large amounts per typical drinking occasion). The percentage of abstainers increased from 19.4 percent in 1974 to 25 percent in 1978. From an epidemiological perspective, it is clear that alcohol use has stabilized among youth, albeit at a very high rate. Thus, the ceiling seems to have been reached, at least for this point in American history.

AGE AT ONSET OF MARIJUANA USE: EVIDENCE OF THE EPIDEMIC

To this point our orientation to epidemiology has been limited to incidence and prevalence rates and how they are changing in various studies. However, a key concern in any epidemiological analysis should be the age at onset of use of particular drugs. It is known that early onset of drug use, particularly alcohol and marijuana, has significant impacts on a host of role and transition related events such as marriage, divorce, parenthood, employment or periods of unemployment, involvement in deviant lifestyles, and the probability of using other substances.[17-22] Data on the age at onset of use also allow us to examine the influence of maturational, cohort, and historical effects on a phenomenon like drug use and abuse.[23]

The data shown in Table 3 were drawn from the 1979 National Survey on Drug Abuse[15] and show the spread of marijuana use through the 1944 through 1967 birth cohorts. For purposes of comparison, data on the percent who had used by age 18 and the median age at first use of marijuana are presented from the young men study.[8] This is a nationally representative sample of men born in the years 1944-54. Eighteen has been added to the birth year to get the probable high school senior year for comparison with the Monitoring the Future studies.

There are several places where historical and cohort effects on marijuana use are clear in the data found in Table 3. Reading down the column labeled "number and percentage of users," it should be noted that the percentage of 15 and 16 year olds who have ever used marijuana was already as high in 1979 as the lifetime prevalence rate for persons born in the 1944 through 1948 birth cohorts (i.e., those persons who were 31 through 35 years old in 1979). Second,

TABLE 3. Marijuana Use By Age: 1979 National Survey on Drug Abuse and the Nationwide Sample of Young Men

Age at Survey	Birth Year	High School Class	n	No. and Percent of Users	Percent Used by Age 18		Median Age at First Use	
					Nat'l Survey	Young Men	Nat'l Survey	Young Men
12	1967	1985	330	13(4)	--	--	11	--
13	1966	1984	341	44(13)	--	--	12	--
14	1965	1983	341	87(26)	--	--	13	--
15	1964	1982	380	159(41)	--	--	13	--
16	1963	1981	398	173(43)	--	--	14	--
17	1962	1980	375	206(55)	--	--	15	--
18	1961	1979	260	155(60)	60	--	15	--
19	1960	1978	251	169(67)	66	--	15	--
20	1959	1977	250	169(68)	61	--	16	--
21	1958	1976	255	174(68)	62	--	16	--
22	1957	1975	254	168(66)	52	--	16	--
23	1956	1974	247	163(66)	53	--	16	--
24	1955	1973	260	164(63)	48	--	17	--
25	1954	1972	267	167(63)	42	49	17	17
26	1953	1971	125	57(54)	34	49	18	17
27	1952	1970	134	75(51)	27	43	18	18
28	1951	1969	130	71(55)	25	33	19	18
29	1950	1968	113	58(51)	19	26	20	19
30	1949	1967	129	66(51)	18	18	19	20
31	1948	1966	115	49(42)	9	10	20	20
32	1947	1965	134	46(34)	4	8	21	21
33	1946	1964	91	33(36)	3	5	22	21
34	1945	1963	93	26(28	2	2	23	24
35	±944	1962	102	35(34)	3	3	25	26

the closest comparison with the high school senior study should be for the Class of 1979. The lifetime prevalence rate of 60 percent for the National Survey 18 year olds is identical to the 60.4 percent found among seniors in the Class of 1979.[9] In a follow-up study of a sample of youth in New York state first studied in 1971 when they were in the 10-11th grades, Kandel and Logan[20] found that 54 percent had used marijuana by age 18. This is almost identical to the 53 percent figure obtained from the 1956 birth cohort in the National Survey. Third, the historical emergence of an epidemic of marijuana use in the United States can be seen most clearly in the columns dealing with "percent used by age 18" and "median age at first use." Only 3 percent of the 1944 birth cohort had used marijuana by age 18 (i.e., 1962, prior to the beginning of the epidemic which began, according to O'Donnell et al.[8] in about 1965) compared to 18 percent of the 1949 birth cohort, which reached age 18 in 1967. This is a 600 percent increase in the percent of persons who had used marijuana by age 18, and covers only 5 birth groups. The percent who had used marijuana by age 18 in the 1955 birth cohort (48 percent) was two and two-thirds larger than the percent (18) observed for the 1949 birth cohort, only 6 birth groups older. These are remarkable increases that parallel those obtained in the national sample of young men. There *was* an epidemic of marijuana use that occurred in the mid-1960s to early 1970s. As noted earlier, it appears that the ceiling has been reached regarding lifetime prevalence and the percent having used marijuana by age 18. Whether this is a relatively permanent or just a temporary ceiling has not been determined. Further evidence of the spread of the epidemic through the population can be seen in the median age at onset columns. There is a bulking at the ages of 15 and 16 in the cohorts that would have experienced the epidemic during the years considered to be the highest ages of vulnerability to a host of behavioral acts,[24-26] including use of illicit drugs.[20] There is also evidence of a trickle-up effect as the epidemic spread through the older cohorts that were beyond the period of highest vulnerability when the epidemic began its march through the population. This is seen most clearly in the increasing median age at onset for both the National Survey sample which includes men and women, and for the young men sample.

These findings have special relevance for the etiological studies of problem behavior that are based on the notion of developmental stages or transitions.[1-2] There are "normative" trajectories for involvement in both deviant and non-deviant activities; precocity can have predictable consequences in both areas.[19-22] Involvement with substance abuse that is out-of-synch with the normative trajectory is a powerful predictor, particularly for the degree and quality of involvement in age-graded roles and the degree and type of involvement in other forms of deviance, particularly use of illicit drugs other than marijuana[18] and other consequences associated with drug abuse. The data presented in Table 3 suggest that the arch of the trajectory for involvement with marijuana has changed dramatically during the past 15 or so years, thus changing the norms governing involvement with this and other drugs as well. If the normative age at onset of drug use goes down, as it seems to have done, the normative hiatus between use of alcohol/cigarettes and marijuana or between use of marijuana and use of other drugs is also changed. Therefore, it is plausible to expect that the overall level of multiple drug use may have changed as a result of the epidemic, given that the primary ages of vulnerability "may" have remained relatively unchanged.

MULTIPLE DRUG USE

It makes a good deal of sense from epidemiological, legal, and policy perspectives to direct attention toward the incidence and prevalence of different drugs, each treated separately. After all, they vary in terms of pharmacology, biochemistry, abuse liability, usage patterns, routes of administration, and consequences. Persons have traditionally been typed according to the drug with which they are overinvolved. The terms "pothead," "addict," and "acid freak" all conjure up reasonably coherent images among those familiar with the drug scene. However, as Cohen[6] has insightfully noted, the drug scene has changed dramatically in the past several years. More often than not, the persons who are using drugs frequently, are *multiple* drug users. There are actually three sources of impetus for focusing more attention on multiple drug use and users as opposed to focusing on the drugs with which they are overinvolved. The first is conceptual (i.e., the continued reliance in the alcohol and drug fields on the "stages of development" model). The second impetus is evidence from the high school senior data concerning the relative proportion of users of illicit drugs who are using marijuana exclusively. The third impetus for directing more attention toward multiple drug use is the incredible amount of attention given to "daily" use of marijuana.

Stages of Drug Use: Considerably More Than Just Unidimensional

The several models which attempt to describe the stages of drug involvement are built, for the most part, on the unidimensionality assumption of Guttman scaling. The dominant conception of progression through stages of drug use was developed by Kandel[2] and consists of the following: (1) no use of any substance; (2) use of beer or wine; (3) use of cigarettes and/or hard liquor; (4) use of marijuana; and (5) use of other illicit drugs. In Kandel's model the focus is almost exclusively on the temporal ordering of entry into drug use. Involvement at any stage is treated dichotomously; you either have or have not used the drug at that stage. While Kandel notes that those at higher stages of development probably continue using drugs at lower stages, this information is seldom used when the staged model is employed. For example, Kandel and her colleagues[27,28] often do not include use of drugs at previous stages as predictors of drug use at subsequent stages.[18] Recently, Yamaguchi and Kandell[21,22] have suggested that nonmedical use of psychotherapeutic drugs (stimulants, sedatives, tranquilizers, analgesics) constitutes a stage between use of marijuana and use of other illicit drugs. Here again, the analytical technique is to "type" persons according to the stage they have "achieved" along the continuum of drug use, rather than to develop scores representing multiple drug use. Donovan and Jessor[24] have taken a similar tact in re-analyzing data from the 1974 and 1978 NIAAA surveys of youth. Using Guttman scaling techniques, their principal purpose was to show that problem drinking among youth may be seen as yet another stage along a dimension of involvement with licit and illicit drugs. According to Donovan and Jessor, the stages of drug involvement are: (1) nonuse of alcohol or illicit drugs; (2) nonproblem use of alcohol; (3) marijuana use; (4) problem drinking; (5) use of pills such as amphetamines, barbiturates, and hallucinogenic drugs; and (6) use of cocaine or heroin. They conclude:

> According to these data, involvement with problem drinking appears to represent a level of drug involvement that is greater than that represented by marijuana, yet not as great an involvement as that shown by adolescents who have used illicit drugs other than marijuana.[24]

Donovan and Jessor as well as Kandel have shown clearly that there is virtually an invariant pattern of onset of use of various drugs and that the drugs can be accurately arrayed along a continuum of "seriousness."[29] Involvement in the earlier stages is, for an overwhelming majority of persons, a necessary condition for involvement in the later stages. Those in the later stages are, in most cases, a subset of those who made it to a prior stage.

We have no quarrel with the ordering of the stages or the assumption about the relative invariance of the order. This is one place where there has been a substantial degree of replication across samples. The basic problem with the stages approach is: (a) there is too great an emphasis on mere use, and (b) persons at a particular stage are typed according to stage. The fact is that drugs used at prior stages are continued into later stages, and often at a higher degree of intensity and frequency. This is certainly what Donovan and Jessor found with regard to problem drinking.[24] Thus, when a person is classified as a marijuana user, he or she has probably been using beer or wine, cigarettes and/or hard liquor, perhaps for quite awhile. If they are like most people, the frequency and quantity of use of these drugs has increased since initiation. Stated differently, as one reaches each stage, the multiple nature of their drug-using career becomes more apparent. What the developmental stages model really demonstrates is considerably more important than the sequential nature of initiation into various drugs. It demonstrates that most drug users are multiple drug users, and that progression involves more than adding a new class of drugs to one's chemical repertoire. It involves a multiple interactive potential from a pharmacological and a psychological perspective. With what is now known about the half-life of various drug classes, the interactive potential for persons at the marijuana and subsequent stages, is quite substantial.

Decline in Relative Percent of "Marijuana Only" Users

Has multiple use of illicit drug increased? How much? These are important questions. It is clear from reports on the Monitoring the Future series that the percentage of high school seniors classified as having used at least one illicit drug other than marijuana has increased from 1975 to 1982, from 26 percent to 34 percent. This is not a very large increase. The overall prevalence of use of any illicit drug, including marijuana, has risen from 45 percent in 1975 to 54 percent in 1978 and 1979, and then dropped to 51 percent in 1982. The figures presented show the percentage in each of these two categories and in the marijuana only category.

Class of:	Any Use of Ilicit Drugs	Marijuana Only	Other Illicit Drugs Used
1975	45	19	26
1976	48	23	25
1977	51	25	26
1978	54	27	27
1979	54	26	28
1980	53	23	30
1981	52	18	34
1982	51	17	34

Simple visual inspection reveals that the relative percentage reporting marijuana only has dropped since 1978 when a ratio ("Marijuana only" divided into "other illicit drugs") would have been 1.0.

The ratio would have been 1.08 for 1979, 1.30 for 1980, 1.89 for 1981, and 2.0 for 1982. If it is assumed that most, if not all, of those who report having used some illicit drug other than marijuana also used marijuana in that year, then there is clear evidence for an "epidemic" of multiple illicit drug use. To check out the correlates of this potential epidemic, the ratio values (e.g., percent reporting "marijuana only in a year vis-a-vis percent reporting use of at least one other illicit drug) were examined by sex, college plans, region, and size of place of residence.

The data shown in Table 4 indicate that there is a clear trend line with regard to multiple illicit drug use for males and females such that in 1982, the percent of males reporting use of other illicit drugs was 1.6 times higher than the percent of males reporting having used only marijuana. The comparable ratio among females was 2.5 in 1982, up from a ratio of only 1.08 in 1979. An examination of the ratios relative to college plans reveals that those who did not intend to attend college have always had a higher percentage reporting having used an illicit drug other than marijuana, but that the relative percentage using only marijuana has gotten smaller in each year since 1978. A comparable but later rise in the relative percentage of college bound seniors reporting use of other illicit drugs is also seen. Comparable progressions can be seen in each column for each of the regions and each of the three categories of size of place of residence. The consistency is quite strong, regardless of the groups being compared. These data seem to indicate the emergence of an "epidemic" of multiple illicit drug use that may have followed from and even supplanted the epidemic of daily marijuana use.

"Daily" Marijuana Users: Multiple Drug Users

In recent years, there has been a great deal of publicity given to "daily" users of marijuana. In a 1980 paper, Johnston[30] said: ". . . one of the most potentially important phenomena to come onto the American drug scene in the last decade—namely the advent of large numbers of daily marijuana users in the population: the arrival of a generation which has more daily pot users than daily drinkers." One year later, Cohen[6] declared that this type of characterization based on overinvolvement with one drug, was going out of style.

Johnston's claim about the importance of the daily user of marijuana pattern led us to wonder about the *overlap* between daily use of marijuana and use of other drugs, licit as well as illicit. Data from the Class of 1980 will serve as the basis for the remainder of the

TABLE 4. Ratio of Percent Marijuana Only to Percent Using One or More Other Illicit Drugs in Each Year: Monitoring the Future, Classes of 1975 Through 1982

CLASS OF	SEX		COLLEGE PLANS		REGION OF COUNTRY				PLACE OF RESIDENCE		
	Male	Female	No	Yes	West	North East	South	North Central	Large Metro	SMSA	Non-SMSA
1975	1.13	1.73	----	----	1.40	1.00	1.53	1.71	1.20	1.37	1.44
1976	.96	1.26	1.32	.91	1.17	.90	1.21	1.18	1.04	1.18	1.10
1977	.90	1.14	1.25	.81	1.08	.97	1.00	1.17	.93	1.08	1.14
1978	.90	1.13	1.15	.82	1.21	1.00	1.00	.96	1.00	.96	1.00
1979	1.00	1.08	1.28	.89	1.43	1.03	1.00	1.04	1.10	1.12	1.09
1980	1.15	1.50	1.71	1.08	1.67	1.19	1.24	1.41	1.40	1.25	1.47
1981	1.57	2.00	2.11	1.58	2.29	1.81	1.44	2.12	1.90	1.74	1.94
1982	1.60	2.50	2.24	1.61	2.77	1.80	1.81	2.25	1.95	1.89	2.21

Note: A score under 1.0 indicates that the percentage of seniors in that category who report using only marijuana is higher than the percentage reporting use of at least one other illicit drug during that year. For example, in 1976 among males, 27 percent reported using only marijuana while 26 percent reported using some other illicit drug, perhaps, or quite likely, in addition to using marijuana. The larger the score, the greater the percentage of use of other illicit drugs relative to the percentage using only marijuana. Among males in 1982, some 20 percent are in the marijuana only mode while 32 percent are in the other illicit drugs mode.

paper, which deals with the overlap and the correlates of multiple drug use. The study of the Class of 1980 included 16,524 seniors representing 107 public and 20 private high schools. The Monitoring the Future data collection enterprise is highly routinized, having been done in exactly the same way every year. In order to keep turnover to a minimum, schools entering the sample are kept in it for 2 consecutive years. Essentially the same questions have been asked every year since 1975. There are five separate questionnaire forms with some core sociodemographic and drug use questions in each form. There is an omnibus quality to the substantive content in the five forms. For our purposes here, we will focus on Questionnaire 2 since it contains considerably more of the substantive variables that have been used in the alcohol and drug fields to "explain" drug involvement.

The first step required the development of a typology of multiple drug use. The "current" prevalence rate (use in the past 30 days) for most drugs is so low among high school seniors that the typology was developed from prevalence rates for the preceding year. The drugs chosen for inclusion in the typology were: cigarettes, alcohol, marijuana, tranquilizers, amphetamines, and cocaine. The typology was constructed using Guttman like procedures. A total of 88 percent of the Class of 1980 fell into the following "pure" scale types. The percent in each type who was classified as a "daily" user of marijuana (use on 20 or more occasions during the preceding 30 days) is listed on the right.

Typology of Multiple Drug Use	Percent and Number of Daily Marijuana Users
1. No use of any drug	0 (n=1,052)
2. Cigarettes only or alcohol only or both	0 (n=5,787)
3. Cigarettes and/or alcohol and marijuana	5.6%(n=3,426)
4. Cigarettes, alcohol, marijuana and one or two of the following: tranquilizers, amphetamines, cocaine	24.5%(n=2,972)
5. Cigarettes, alcohol, marijuana, tranquilizers, amphetamines, and cocaine	54.1%(n= 889)

If one were to combine the last two types, all of whom had used illicit drugs other than marijuana during the preceding year, 31 percent would be classified as "daily" users of marijuana. Some 86 percent of the daily marijuana users have used illicit drugs other than marijuana (e.g., tranquilizers, amphetamines, cocaine) during the past 12 months, in addition to cigarettes and alcohol. *Daily marijuana users are, for the most part, multiple drug users.* This is true not only in terms of use of licit drugs such as cigarettes and alcohol, but also with regard to the nonmedical use of tranquilizers, amphetamines, and cocaine. This is not a "new" finding. However, it points out a problem with the tendency to direct attention to specific, pharmacologically defined classes of drugs. This tendency often leads us to infer that the correlates, causes, and consequences of drug use are attributable to the class of drugs with which a person is most involved. If daily users of marijuana are more likely than those who don't use or who use only experimentally to report automobile accidents or absenteeism or symptoms of the amotivational syndrome, we are prone to attribute such to the consumption of marijuana. A more plausible inference is that these behavioral characteristics may be emergent from the ingestion of multiple substances which may be interacting pharmacologically to produce the effects/consequences.

With the typology constructed, a logical question to ask is: At what point along the multiple drug use staged continuum does the significance of multiple drug use emerge? Is it between the use and nonuse of any drugs? Is it between the use of the licit drugs and use of the illicit drugs? Or, is it between the use of the statistically normative drugs and use of the other drugs plus these?

A prerequisite for addressing this question was the development of theoretically relevant scales from the 60 substantive items in Form 2 that dealt with the behavior of the respondents or their friends, or perceptions of the respondents from the Class of 1980. These 60 items were factor analyzed using oblique rotation. Eight factors emerged with an eigenvalue above unity which accounted for 91.7 percent of the common variance. Items loading above .40 on a significant factor were formed into summated Likert type scales. The scales were analyzed using Cronbach's alpha as a measure of internal consistency. Items that did not contribute significantly to internal consistency were deleted and the scale and alpha were recomputed. Descriptions of the scales, the number and content of the items in each scale, and the resultant alpha values can be found in Appendix I.

The principal purpose of the factor analysis was to create reliable scales to use in predicting multiple drug use. Two types of analysis were then conducted. The first involves regressing the five-category, ordinal level, typology of multiple drug use on the predictor variables. This was done twice, once where 12 dummy variables were included to represent demographic variables such as sex, race, religious identification, and family structure. The second equation did not include the sociodemographic dummy variables.

Discriminant function analysis was the second technique employed. Two groups were used: the first consists of all persons who had not used anything beyond marijuana, but could have used one or more of the statistically normative drug classes (cigarettes, alcohol, marijuana) or none of these drugs. The second group consisted of those who were in the highest multiple drug use categories. Computation of the least significant difference statistic when examining mean scores on all of the predictor variables within and between all categories of the multiple drug use typology suggested this cutting point would be the most efficient for a discriminant functions analysis.

RESULTS OF THE ANALYSIS

Stepwise regression of the multiple drug use typology on the 37 independent variables in Form 2 indicated that only 21 of the variables had a statistically significant effect on the typology at the .01 level (see Column 1 of Table 5). With large samples, a large number of predictor variables, and a dependent variable constrained in terms of possible standard deviation units, statistical significance is not that difficult to attain. The data in Column 1 of Table 5 indicate that only 7 of the predictor variables produced as standardized partial beta higher than .05. These variables and their respective beta weights are: Friends smoking and drinking (.29); Friends using drugs other than marijuana (.17); Frequency of cutting school during the past four weeks (.11); Involvement in theft (.12); and Frequency of church attendance ($-.09$). The full model or equation depicted in Column 1 accounts for 43 percent of the variance in the multiple drug use typology, a very respectable total for data like these.

The second Column of beta weights are those for the model that does not include the 12 dummy variables for demographic characteristics. Only minor changes occur in the strength of the predictors

TABLE 5. Means, Beta Weights, and Discriminant Coefficients Regarding a Typology of Multiple Drug Use: Class of 1980, Monitoring the Future Study

Variables	Beta Full	Beta	Disc. Coeff.	I Mean	II Mean
Friends smoke and drink	.29	.29	.29	11.3	14.2
Freq. of cutting school	.11	.11	.23	1.5	2.3
Friends use drugs	.17	.16	.45	16.7	23.9
Involvement in theft	.12	.10	.19	4.1	5.6
Freq. of church attendance	-.09	-.07	-.16	3.1	2.6
Tickets, traffic violation	.06	.06	.11	.3	.7
Perceived phy. danger	.05	.04	.07	4.9	5.8
Perceived drug availability	.05	.06	.17	27.7	32.1
Grade Point Average	-.07	-.05	-.06	5.9	5.3
Mother's education	.04	.04	N S	----	----
Salience of religion	-.05	-.04	N S	----	----
Aggression index	.04	.04	.12	5.5	6.5
Earnings from job	.03	.03	.04	4.6	5.0
Earnings from other sources	.03	.03	N S	----	----
Size of resident city	.02	.02	N S	----	----
Freq. missed school/illness	.03	.03	.08	1.8	2.1
Healthy activities	-.03	-.05	-.11	21.3	20.0
Father's education	N S	.03	.06	3.7	3.4
Traffic accidents	N S	.03	N S	----	----
Mother's work status	N S	-.02	-.09	2.2	1.6
Black	-.04	----	----	----	----
Male	-.05	----	----	----	----
Protestant	.05	----	----	----	----
Adjusted r square	.43	.40			
Eigenvalue			.41		
Cannonical correlation			.55		

when the dummy variables are deleted. However, the second regression equation was introduced as a check and because the use of dummy variables is somewhat problematic in discriminant functions analysis.[31] The reduced equation accounted for 40 percent of the variance.

The results of the discriminant analysis for the two mnultiple drug use groups appears in Column 3 of Table 5. Stepwise selection included 15 variables which explained 30 percent of the total variance. The mean discriminant scores which summarize the location of each of the groups in the linear space defined by the discriminant function are: Group I, −.42; Group II, 1.01. The function correctly classified individual cases into their appropriate classification group 78 percent of the time.

The standardized discriminant coefficients indicate that the most efficacious predictors of membership in either the statistically normative multiple drug use group or the group that includes those who used illicit drugs in addition to marijuana and the licit drugs are: Friends who use illicit drugs other than marijuana (.45); Friends who smoke and drink (.29); Cutting school during the past four weeks (.23); Involvement in theft (.19); Perceived availability and ease of obtaining illicit drugs (.17); and Frequency of church attendance (−.16).

CONCLUSIONS

These variables (e.g., friends smoking and drinking, friends using drugs, cutting school, involvement in theft, perceived availability and ease of getting drugs, and frequency of church attendance) have a great deal of relevance from a theoretical viewpoint. The two most powerful discriminating variables for multiple drug use (use of drugs by friends and their use of alcohol and cigarettes) concern peer group behavioral norms. The salience of the peer group and the behavioral patterns exhibited by it for the initiation and continuation of drug use has been thoroughly documented.[3,8,17,27,28,32,33] Comparing adolescents in a high drinking context (France), a low drinking context (Israel), and a middle drinking context (United States), Adler and Kandel[34] found that peer effects on alcohol use in the United States were much stronger than in the other two societies. In a longitudinal follow-up of 24 to 25 year old young adults, first studied when they were in the 10th and 11th grades, Kandel[35] found that the variables that were predictive of drug use earlier, were still important in young adulthood.

> . . . in a random representative sample of young adults, marijuana involvement is associated with the same factors that had previously been reported for younger populations of junior high school, senior high school, and college students. In young adulthood, these characteristics generally reflect lower participation in conventional roles of adulthood and life histories with discontinuous rather than continuous patterns of social role participation . . . a lowered level of social achievement and psychological well-being, participation in deviant life-styles, and especially the use of other drugs (cigarettes, alcohol, other illicit drugs, and medically prescribed psychoactives) and involvement in a social network of drug-using associates. [The

latter two] are the most important factors and, when entered in multiple-regression equations, reduce the significance of most other variables.

This statement mirrors well the results found in Table 5. Use of drugs by one's friends and smoking and drinking by friends (i.e., having friends who are multiple drug users) are the strongest predictors of multiple drug use, along with involvement in deviant activities (cutting school and stealing things). The only other factor that significantly differentiates between the two multiple drug use groups is a restraining variable, frequency of church attendance, a variable that has been virtually ignored by researchers in the alcohol and drug abuse fields. Commenting on the influence of the school, home, and church in "preventing" drug abuse, Bachman, Johnston, and O'Malley[26] say:

> Those who most avoid such influence are also the most likely to be involved in all forms of substance use. . . . In other words, the kinds of young people most "at risk" tend to remain much the same, while the kinds and amounts of substances shift somewhat from year to year.

During the past 15 or so years the United States has experienced an epidemic of alcohol and drug use among its youth that is unprecedented. While there are the beginnings of favorable signs, especially with regard to the percent of youth using marijuana daily, the fact remains that the overall levels of use of all drugs are too high. In addition, there is substantial evidence of a developmental pattern of increasing levels of involvement with drugs that are licit leading to involvement with drugs that are not legal. The greater the involvement with one drug, any drug, the higher the probability that one will become a multiple drug user. The process seems to be akin to a snowball rolling down a hill. This does not mean that involvement in multiple drug use cannot be prevented. However, the best place to enter the process is at the beginning. As Yamaguchi and Kandel[21] note: ". . . prevention efforts targeted toward marijuana will be the most successful in terms of slowing down progression to higher stages of drug involvement. Such efforts may lead to a real decrease of involvement not only in marijuana but in illicit drugs other than marijuana. For all drugs, prevention efforts will be more effective if they are targeted at reducing the risk of initiating the use of drugs rather than on decreasing use among users since former and not only current use of drugs at a lower stage increase the risk of progression to a higher stage.''

The data presented in the latter part of this paper suggest that we must take seriously the problem of multiple drug use among youth. The risk factors that are of primary importance are already known. Precocious involvement in cigarette and alcohol use, early involvement in marijuana use, early problem drinking; all of these along with a movement away from the influence of restraining institutions and toward the influence of peer groups whose values are in defiance of the institutions, have an impact on the incidence and prevalence of multiple drug use. It is time for the alcohol and drug abuse fields to recognize the significant impact of multiple drug use on society, and to begin to develop prevention and treatment interventions that counter all drug use, not just the use of specific drugs.

REFERENCES

1. Jessor R, Jessor, S. Problem behavior and psychosocial development—A longitudinal study of youth. New York: Academic Press, 1977.

2. Kandel, DB. Stages in adolescent involvement in drug use. Science 1975; 190:912-14.

3. Huba, GJ, Bentler, PM. A developmental theory of drug use: Derivation and assessment of a causal modeling approach. Life-Span Dev. & Beh. 1982: 4:147-203.

4. Zucker, RA. Developmental aspects of drinking through the young adult years. In: Blane, HT, Chafetz, ME., eds. Youth, alcohol, and social policy. New York: Plenum, 1979.

5. Rachal, JV, Maisto, SA, Guess, LL, Hubbard, RL. Alcohol use among youth. In: Alcohol consumption and related problems. Alcohol and Health Monograph 1. Rockville, MD: National Institute on Alcohol Abuse and Alcoholism, 1982, 55-95.

6. Cohen, S. The effects of combined alcohol/drug abuse on human behavior. In: Gardner, S., ed. Drug and alcohol abuse: Implications for treatment. Rockville, MD: National Institute on Drug Abuse, 1981, 5-20.

7. Clayton, RR, Voss, HL. Technical review on drug abuse and dropouts. Rockville, MD: National Institute on Drug Abuse, 1982, 1-44.

8. O'Donnell, JA, Voss, HL, Clayton, RR, Slatin, GT, Room, RGW. Young men and drugs—A nationwide survey. Rockville, MD: National Institute on Drug Abuse, 1976.

9. Johnston, LD, Bachman, JG, O'Malley, PM. Highlights from student drug use in America 1975-1982. Rockville, MD: National Institute on Drug Abuse, 1982.

10. Johnston, LD, O'Malley, PM, Davis-Sacks, ML. A worldwide survey of seniors in the department of defense dependent schools: Drug use and related factors, 1982. Ann Arbor, MI: Institute for Social Research, University of Michigan, 1983.

11. Burt, MR, Biegel, MM. Worldwide survey of nonmedical drug use and alcohol use among military personnel: 1980. Bethesda, MD: Burt Associates, 1980.

12. Bray, RM, Guess, LL, Mason, RE, Hubbard, RL, Smith, D.G, Marsden, ME, Rachal, JV. Highlights of the 1982 worldwide survey of alcohol and nonmedical drug use among military personnel. Research Triangle, NC: Research Triangle Institute, 1983.

13. Mosher, JF, Mottl, JR. The role of nonalcohol agencies in federal regulation of drinking behavior and consequences. In: Moore, MH, Gerstein, DR, eds. Alcohol and public policy: Beyond the shadow of prohibition. Washington, DC: National Academy Press, 1981.

14. Miller, JD, Cisin, IH, Gardner-Keaton, H, Harrell, AV, Wirtz, PW, Abelson, HI, Fishburne, PM. National survey on drug abuse: Main findings 1982. Rockville, MD: National Institute on Drug Abuse, 1983.

15. Fishburne, PM, Abelson, HI, Cisin, I. National survey on drug abuse: Main findings: 1979. Rockville, MD: National Institute on Drug Abuse, 1979.

16. Rachal, JV, Williams, JR, Brehm, ML, Cavanaugh, E., Moore, RP, Eckerman, WC. A national study of adolescent drinking behavior, attitudes and correlates. Research Triangle, NC: Research Triangle Institute, 1975.

17. O'Donnell, JA, Clayton, RR. Determinants of early marijuana use. In: Beschner, G, Friedman, A, eds. Youth drug abuse: Problems, issues, and treatment. Lexington, MASS: Lexington Books, 1979, 63-110.

18. O'Donnell, JA, Clayton, RR. The stepping-stone hypothesis—marijuana, heroin, and causality. Chemical Dependencies 1982; 4:229-41.

19. Clayton, RR, Voss, HL. Shacking up: Cohabitation in the 1970s. J Marr & Family 1977; 39:272-84.

20. Kandel, DB, Logan, JA. Patterns of drug use from adolescence to young adulthood—I. Periods of risk for initiation, continued use and discontinuation. Am J Public Health 1984, in press.

21. Yamaguchi, K, Kandell, DB. Patterns of drug use from adolescence to young adulthood—II. Sequences of progression. Am J Public Health, 1984, in press.

22. Yamaguchi, K, Kandel, DB. Patterns of drug use from adolescence to young adulthood—III. Predictors of progression. Am J. Public Health, 1984, in press.

23. O'Malley, PM, Bachman, JG, Johnston, LD. Differentiation of period, age, and cohort effects on substance use among American youth 1975-1980. Ann Arbor, MI: Institute for Social Research Working Paper, 1982.

24. Donovan, JE, Jessor, R. Problem drinking and the dimension of involvement with drugs: A Guttman scalogram analysis of adolescent drug use. Am J Public Health, 1983; 73: in press.

25. Jessor, R, Chase, JA, Donovan, JE. Psychosocial correlates of marijuana use and problem drinking in a national sample of adolescents. Am J Public Health 1980; 70:604-13.

26. Bachman, JG, Johnston, LD, O'Malley, PM. Smoking, drinking, and drug use among American high school students: Correlates and trends, 1975-79. Am J Public Health 1981; 71:59-69.

27. Kandel, DB, Treiman, D, Faust, R, Single, E. Adolescent involvement in legal and illegal drug use: A multiple classification analysis. Social Forces 1976; 55:438-58.

28. Kandel, DB, Marguilies, RZ, Davies, M. Analytical strategies for studying transitions into developmental stages. Soc of Educa 1978; 51:162-76.

29. Clayton, RR, Voss, HL. Young men and drugs in Manhattan: A causal analysis. Rockville, MD: National Institute on Drug Abuse, 1981.

30. Johnston, LD. The daily marijuana user. Paper presented at meeting of the National Alcohol and Drug Coalition, Washington, DC, 18 September 1980.

31. Klecka, WR. Discriminant analysis. Beverly Hills, CA: Sage, 1980.

32. Jessor, R. Marihuana: A review of recent psychosocial research. In: DuPont, RL, Goldstein, A, O'Donnell, JA, eds. Handbook on drug abuse. Rockville, MD: National Institute on Drug Abuse, 1979, 337-55.

33. Brook, JS, Whiteman, M, Gordon, AS. Qualitative and quantitative aspects of adolescent drug use: Interplay of personality, family, and peer correlates. Psy Reports 1982; 51:1151-63.

34. Kandel, DB, Adler, I. Socialization into marijuana use among French adolescents: A cross-cultural comparison with the United States. JHSB 1982; 23:295-309.

35. Kandel, DB. Marijuana users in young adulthood. Arch Gen Psychiatry. 1983; 41:200-09.

Appendix I

Friends Use Drugs

Twelve items in which the respondents are asked to estimate how many of their friends use (1) cigarettes, (2) marijuana or hashish, (3) LSD, (4) other psychedelics, (5) amphetamines, (6) quaaludes, (7) barbiturates, (8) tranquilizers, (9) cocaine, (10) heroin, (11) other narcotics, and (12) inhalants. The response alternatives are none, a few, some, most, all and the scores range from 1 to 5. The scale has a potential range from 12 through 60. The alpha coefficient for this scale was .94.

Perceived Drug Availability

The question stem for the 9 items in this scale was: How difficult do you think it would be for you to get each of the following types of drugs, if you wanted some? The drugs were: marijuana (pot, grass), LSD, some other psychedelic (mescaline, peyote, psilocybin, PCP, etc.), amphetamines (uppers, pep pills, bennies, speed), barbiturates (downers, goofballs, reds, yellows, etc.), tranquilizers, cocaine, heroin (smack, horse), some other narcotic (methadone, opium, codeine, paregoric, etc.). Each item was scored as follows: probably impossible = 1, very difficult = 2, fairly difficult = 3, fairly easy = 4, very easy = 5. The range of scores was from 9 through 45 with an alpha coefficient of .93.

Perceived Physical Danger

This scale contains four items asking: During the past 12 months, how often the following events have occurred: (1) has someone injured you with a weapon (like a knife, gun, or club)?, (2) has someone threatened you with a weapon, but not actually injured you?, (3) has someone injured you on purpose without using a weapon?, (4) has an unarmed person threatened you with injury, but not actually injured you? Each item was scored as not at all = 1, once = 2, twice = 3, 3 or 4 times = 4, and 5 or more times = 5. The scale had a potential range of 5-20. The alpha coefficient was .72.

Healthy Activities

The five items in this scale concerned the frequency with which the respondent engaged in healthy activities. How often do you eat breakfast, eat at least some green vegetables, eat at least some fruit, exercise vigorously, get at least 7 hours of sleep? The response alternatives were never = 1, seldom = 2, sometimes = 3, most days = 4, nearly everyday = 5, and every day = 6. The potential range was 5-30 and the alpha coefficient was .73.

Friends Smoking and Drinking

How many of your friends would you estimate engage in the following activities? (1) smoke cigarettes, (2) smoke marijuana or hashish, (3) drink alcoholic beverages, (4) get drunk at least twice a week. Each item was scored none = 1, a few = 2, some =3, most = 4, all = 5. The scale had a potential range of 4-16 and an alpha of .81.

Aggression Index

During the last 12 months, how often have you engaged in the following: (1) hit an instructor or supervisor, (2) gotten into a serious fight in school or at work, (3) taken part in a fight where a group of friends were against another group, (4) hurt someone badly enough to need bandages or a doctor, (5) used a knife or gun or some other thing (like a club) to get something from a person. Each item was scored not at all = 1, once = 2, twice = 3, 3 or 4 times = 4, 5 or more times = 5. With a range of 5 through 25, the alpha coefficient for the aggression index was .71.

Involvement in Theft

During the last 12 months, how often have you engaged in the following: (1) taken something not belonging to you worth under $50; (2) taken something not belonging to you worth over $50; (3) taken something from a store without paying for it? Each item was scored as follows: not al all = 1, once = 2, twice = 3, 3 or 4 times = 4, 5 or more times = 5. The potential range on the scale was 3-15 and the alpha coefficient of reliability was .73.

The Adaptive Significance
of Chronic Marijuana Use
for Adolescents and Adults

Herbert Hendin, MD
Ann Pollinger Haas, PhD

Over the last decade and a half, research by ourselves and others[1-5] has linked the appeal of drugs such as heroin, LSD, and amphetamines among young people to the specific psychophysiological states which each produces. This work has suggested that these drugs have particular adaptive or defensive functions which help to explain their differential use by particular types of individuals within the overall drug-using population. In spite of the fact that marijuana has consistently been the most widely used of all illicit drugs, relatively little attention has been given to identifying the functions which this substance plays in the adaptation of those who use it.

In an attempt to fill this gap, we have undertaken a series of studies which have sought to obtain psychological understanding of the adaptive significance of marijuana for chronic users as distinct from the broader population of casual marijuana-smoking individuals. Our initial investigation of this topic, part of a larger study of drug abuse among college students, used a series of intensive unstructured interviews, rather than the much more widely employed self-report questionnaire or single-interview approach, in order to understand both the drug-taking and related behaviors in the context of the individual's total psychosocial adaptation. In the case of college youngsters who smoked marijuana heavily and exclusively, we found that their drug behavior was not responsible in any direct of simplified way for poor school performance, as some have maintained. Neither could it be considered a reaction to academic

Herbert Hendin and Ann Pollinger Haas are with the Center for Psychosocial Studies and Dept. of Psychiatry, New York Medical College.

The research described in this article was supported by Grants no. DA-01489 and no. DA-02730 from the National Institute on Drug Abuse.

difficulties, nor an incidental concomitant of a change to a non-achievement-oriented lifestyle, as others have claimed. Rather, marijuana was seen as playing a characteristic, definable defensive role in these students' attempts to deal with conflict over competition and aggression which had become intolerable. A common pattern found among the 15 heavy marijuana-smoking students who were intensively studied was the equation of success with destructiveness and failure with humiliation. Finding it impossible to accept either alternative, these students used marijuana in the service of withdrawing from the conflict. In addition, marijuana abuse in each of these students appeared to be related to adaptive difficulties which derived in major part from troubled family relationships. Parents, in particular, were consistently and intimately tied up with these young persons' sense of being caught up in an impossible position regarding achievement and competition.[6-8]

ADOLESCENT MARIJUANA ABUSERS AND THEIR FAMILIES

This apparent connection of the drug behavior to longstanding difficulties within the family led us to a subsequent study focusing on white middle and working-class adolescents who were long-term heavy marijuana smokers and who were still living at home.[9-11] Using the Representative Case Method,[12-14] 17 youngsters were selected from among approximately 300 marijuana-abusing adolescents who were identified through Family Court, schools, social agencies, mental health clinics, and private referrals within the New York metropolitan area. In no sense were these individuals chosen because they represented the "average" adolescent marijuana user; rather, each was specifically selected to epitomize particular patterns seen among the larger group.

The subjects of the research included not only the marijuana-abusing youngsters, but also their parents, and in most cases, a non-marijuana-abusing sibling who served as a control. The primary data-collection method involved a prolonged series of intensive interviews with all participants in each family.

A major goal of the study was to understand the family dynamics in the context of which a marijuana-abusing youngster as well as a close age-order sibling who did not abuse drugs had emerged. Several different patterns were observed across the families who were studied, even though in virtually every case we found that the marijuana abuser had received the worst rather than the best of what the parents had to offer. In some cases this occurred because the youngster was born after the family's emotional reserves had been drained by prior children. In such families, difficulties among the family members as well as the individual problems intensified with each succeeding child. In other families, the marijuana-abusing youngster had long been seen as mirroring the parents' limitations, anxieties, and insecurities, while his or her sibling was regarded as having the parents' best characteristics. Each child tended to be treated accordingly.

In some families the parents' exaggerated and rigid expectations of a favorite child, and their subsequent disappointment in that child, resulted in a shift in their affections to another of the siblings. Among other families parental difficulties caused problems for a particular child when he or she was quite young and even though the parents had resolved these difficulties the child's troubles persisted.

As elaborated below, marijuana was found through this study to have a variety of functions for adolescents: as a defiant or provocative act directed against parents, in particular, and by extension, to other authority figures; as a self-destructive act; as a modifier of disturbing emotions such as anger; as a reenforcer of fantasies of effortless, grandiose success; and as a help in withdrawing from conflicts concerning competition and achievement.

Defiance and Provocation

With some of the adolescents, like one young man who grew marijuana plants in his basement, and who fought constantly with his parents over his right to smoke as much marijuana as he pleased, their provocativeness was apparent. Marijuana for such adolescents represented an assertion of their independence and their desire to be free from parental control. The ambivalent nature of this desire however, is suggested by the fact that such provocative use of marijuana elicits parental reaction and intervention in ways that more covert use does not.

Some of the heaviest of the marijuana users managed to keep their usage from their parent's awareness for years despite coming home stoned nearly every day. Although the parents' need not to know is involved here as well, these youngsters used this need to their advantage, while others were determined to force their marijuana abuse on their parents' consciousness. Those who were more secretive about their marijuana use were usually provocative or defiant in other ways, however, from refusing to do household chores to staying out at night without informing their parents.

The defiance which almost all of the adolescent marijuana abusers demonstrated in behavior toward their parents was also evident in their relationships with other authorities, in particular, their teachers, principals, and school counselors. Since most of the youngsters were cutting class to smoke and since their marijuana abuse was often related to an attempt to escape from the pressures of school, at times school authorities appeared to be more aware of such abuse and more in conflict with youngsters over it than were their parents. In almost every case, however, the marijuana-abusing adolescent's school behavior was a reflection of long-standing patterns of provocative interaction with adults that had developed in the family.

Self-Destructiveness

It is important to recognize that not all behavior that is self-destructive in its consequences is self-destructively motivated. With drug abuse, the consequences may be the price that one is willing to risk for the effect of the drug. Yet among these adolescent marijuana abusers, as with drug abusers in general, self-destructiveness—reflected in such behavior as car accidents, unwanted pregnancies and suicide attempts—was often an integral part of the motivation for their drug behavior.

Although most of the adolescents initially talked of their marijuana use as a conflict-free source of pleasure, in time almost all expressed greater ambivalence. One young man of 17, who claimed to be joyfully high on marijuana whenever he could, eventually admitted that he felt he was wasting his life by being constantly stoned, and spoke of marijuana as taking away his ambition and drive, and thwarting his ability to express himself. One young woman, who initially presented her marijuana as harmless, later admitted that while others probably took drugs for pleasure, she often approached this behavior with a "let something bad happen to me" attitude.

The intensive interviews with these youngsters provided psychodynamic evidence of both the self-destructive nature of their marijuana abuse and the sources of that self-destructiveness. The case of one 17-year-old, upper-middle class suburban boy made this particularly clear. From infancy this youngster had suffered from a lack of nurturance from his emotionally detached career-oriented mother. His birth had been unplanned and occurred during the final months of a two-year maternity leave which his mother had taken in order to have the boy's older brother. Although both boys had received relatively little from their mother during childhood and adolescence, a sense of deprivation was particularly marked in the younger boy as a result of his mother's absence from his earliest days. By the age of 14, he was using massive quantities of marijuana in an attempt to obliterate the pain and frustration of this relationship. During the course of the interviews with him, he dreamed that his mother was offering him a cup of "tea" (slang for marijuana) which was poisoned. He perceived his mother as having poisoned his life by failing to meet his needs while seeming to be offering to so, and marijuana appeared to be serving a similar function.

Anger

If marijuana was often seen as a defiant or self-destructive act, it functioned more importantly in attempts to modify unpleasant, disturbing feelings and emotions, and in particular, to diminish the experience of anger. For some youngsters, the anger they experienced toward their families was often felt to be uncontrollable and was part of a deeper and more disturbing feeling that they hated their parents. Some dreamed or fantasized killing or otherwise eliminating all their family members. Some became extremely frightened by the extent of the violence they engaged in when angry. Marijuana helped these youngsters subdue their rage and control their violent impulses. Many reported avoiding fights with their families through using marijuana to ease their tension and anger at home.

One angry 15-year-old young woman from an upper-middle class family living in a fashionable urban neighborhood has been smoking marijuana since she was 11 and heavily for the past year. Her family saw her as a devil because of her provocativeness in staying out late, not doing her schoolwork, and being nasty to them. Her older sister was seen as an angel, and both girls seemed to try to act out their roles.

The marijuana-abusing youngster was described by her parents as defiant, disobedient, and "fresh." Her father was particularly upset by her lying and her mother by her poor schoolwork. Her older sister was seen by the family as more intelligent, more attractive, more popular, and better adjusted. Whatever was confident and secure in the parents' relationship was focused on the older sister, while the younger one was the focus of all their anxiety and discomfort.

The difference in parental attitudes toward the two girls started virtually at birth. The older child was described as a wonderful, beautiful baby, born during a happy period soon after the parents' marriage. When the younger daughter was born, the husband was often away, traveling on his job or entertaining clients, and his wife would wait up for him to return or to call. She said her younger daughter was a poor sleeper but this may reflect some resonance with her own tension during this period.

A story the family frequently told that occurred when the subject was a year old was felt by her to reflect where she stood with them. The family was taking a trip and went off in a cab when they remembered that they had left her behind. That the incident occurred was remarkable enough, but that the parents persisted in retelling it as a funny story showed an even more remarkable insensitivity to the pain and rage their telling it aroused in her. Her current misbehavior made it impossible for her parents to forget her. She was unrelenting in her anger toward her parents, expressed affectionate feelings toward them rarely, and was bitterly unforgiving of their deficiencies.

That she had incorporated her parents' picture of her was suggested by the fact that on two occasions after fights with her family she dreamed that the devil was inside her and cutting her off from her friends. Marijuana seemed to relieve her anger and tension and made it possible for her to be more comfortable with her friends as well as her family.

Psychodynamic evidence of the link between these youngsters' overwhelming anger toward their families and their self-destructiveness was invariably present. This was vividly seen in the case of a 14-year-old young man from an Irish Catholic working-class family. Throughout his childhood this youngster had reflected his father's academic failure and his mother's anxieties in social situations. Beginning in elementary school he had been in almost constant academic and disciplinary trouble and was finally placed by the court in a residential treatment center at the request of his parents. When seen several months later, he was preoccupied with thoughts of suicide. He had recurrent fantasies of escaping from the center, going home and shooting all the members of his family, and then dying in a gun battle with police. In a similar vein, he dreamed his whole family was killed by the Russians in a nuclear attack, during which he decided to fight rather than take shelter since he was going to die anyway.

Similar psychodynamics were evident in another case of a young-ster from a Catholic working-class background. His father and mother, who worked respectively as a school bus driver and wait-ress, had come to live vicariously through their eldest son. The boy's father was particularly intent on using his son's considerable athletic abilities to achieve a degree of recognition and success that had eluded him in his own life. The sense of being used and not valued for himself filled this young man with an overwhelming rage toward his family. Fearing his potential for violence toward them, he frequently talked of blowing himself away with a shotgun in-stead. He linked this with getting "blown away" by smoking mari-juana, an image which suggests how marijuana can be the link be-tween containment of anger and self-destructiveness.

Grandiosity

Many of the marijuana-abusing adolescents related feeling de-pressed to their sense that they amounted to nothing within the con-text of their own families. In the case of many of the young men, feelings of grandiosity appeared to help alleviate such feelings and encouraged their sense that magical transformation without effort was possible. The use of marijuana to transform their mood was consistent with this aspect of their personalities.

One young man from a middle-class suburban family was given the nickname "burnt-out Bobby" by his classmates because of his heavy use of marijuana. His difficulties at school went back to his early childhood and together with his sloppy appearance, messy room, and failure to carry out his responsibilities at home, led to dif-ficulties with both parents and to his father treating him with con-tempt.

He talked frequently, however, of his special luck, believing that unusual things happened to him. If he needed something he felt he would find it or without his asking, someone would give it to him. These grandiose feelings were reflected in a dream in which he was an outfielder playing professional baseball, was given a special glove that made every ball come into it, and became an immediate star.

He had this dream the night following an interview in which, after raising the question of what he was getting from the interview ses-sions, he talked about his recurrent thoughts of finding "a bottle with a genie in it." His attitude that he should get his high school diploma without having to study, his desire to be paid for a job without having to work, and his dream of being a star in a sport that he did not actually play, all reflected the attitude he brought to the interviews that in some magical way, without effort on his part, they should transform him. Marijuana helped sustain these illusions in such youngsters.

None of the young women marijuana abusers showed the type of grandiose fantasy found to be common among the young men, although they likewise tended to be highly unrealistic in their expectations of themselves and others. Particularly common among these young women was a feeling of invulnerability to any consequences of their behavior. They would talk of going on to college when they were at the time flunking out of high school. They would describe impossible relationships with boyfriends who consistently abused them as somehow destined to end up well. Chances taken in their sexual relationships, they felt, would not end in pregnancy and they would escape any harmful consequences of reckless marijuana abuse.

A comparable attitude of invulnerability was often reflected in the risks and chances the young men took with cars and motorbikes. Among both the young men and young women there was clearly a psychological link between invulnerability and depression, between grandiosity and damaged self-esteem, between the dual ideas that ''nothing can happen to me'' and that ''if it does, what's the difference?''

Escaping Competitive Conflicts

Although college youngsters used marijuana to deal with difficulties with achievement and competition that were the outgrowth of problems with their families, the youngsters who turned to heavy marijuana use in high school had usually abandoned traditional aspirations for success through effort and achievement. They were so overwhelmed by the pain and frustration of their early relationships with their families in which they lost out in a more basic competition for affection, that they were unable to sustain effort or achieve in competition with others.

One young man, who was one of the brightest subjects we saw, had been an outstanding student up until early adolescence when he stopped doing schoolwork and attending classes, and dropped out of high school in his junior year. He had been a favored child, handsome, bright, and friendly in contrast to a younger brother who had been seen by his mother as not nearly so bright, sociable, or attractive. His mother was aware of the friction with her favored son since his childhood because of her need for him to fulfill her expectations. At the age of four he made his own bed, but she reacted critically because he had not made it as she wished it to be made. By the age of 12 he was no longer excited by his triumphs nor bothered by his failures. His mother reacted to his abandoning his goals for achievement with frustration, fury and rejection and he countered with provocative behavior of which his marijuana smoking was but a part. By 17 he moved away from home, drove a cab sporadically to support himself, and continued to long for acceptance from his mother which was not forthcoming. His younger brother did much better in school and in life largely because he had been spared his mother's expectations and disappointment.

In all of its functions, marijuana served to detach these adolescents from the problems of the real world—from their anger and unhappiness with their parents, and from the need to work and compete to achieve success. In so doing, it permitted some to appear casual or light-hearted while inside they felt miserable. For all of them, marijuana helped sustain, in illusory ways, the desire for power, achievement and control.

Although this study provided considerable insight into the adaptive significance of marijuana for these young people, the adaptation of adolescents is often highly fluid and this applies to their drug use as well. Follow-up interviews with these youngsters which have continued approximately every six months over the last four years, have revealed changes in many. Among those who moved away from their families, some positive outcomes have been observed in the direction of diminished drug use and more stable social adaptations. Others, however, have become further entrenched in a drifting, aimless existence, including in some cases heavy use of cocaine or alcohol. For still others, marijuana patterns begun during adolescence appear to have become an established part of their daily routines, despite the changes which have occurred in their life circumstances.

CHRONIC MARIJUANA USE AMONG ADULTS

Our earlier work has raised many questions about the role of marijuana in the lives of adults who, while generally no longer enmeshed in the struggles with parents and siblings which characterized the adolescents we studied, are often coping with the pressures of jobs, relationships, marriage, and perhaps even children of their own. To answer some of these we undertook to explore the use of marijuana among adults who had smoked daily and heavily over a period of many years.[15] All subjects selected indicated current use of at least six days per week, and use both during daytime and evening hours. As a group, they smoked an average of more than three marijuana cigarettes every day.

Based on the responses obtained from 150 such adults on a collaboratively developed Marijuana Questionnaire,[16] 15 individuals were selected for intensive study, again through the use of the Representative Case Method. In order to illuminate patterns of heavy chronic marijuana usage which had not previously been explored, our leanings in selecting these individuals were in the direction of those who were older, married or in a stable relationship, committed to a particular occupation, and who overall appeared to be relatively settled in their lives. The eight men selected included a successful Harvard-educated lawyer, a divorced salesman raising three young children, a bright young accountant, and a free-lance screenwriter and film director. Represented among the seven women were a recognized writer from a socially prominent family, a suburban housewife, and a former prostitute who was currently employed in a middle management position in a large corporation.

Using a similar protocol to that which we developed for the adolescent study, these adults were seen, in most cases, over a two-year period. The results of this study provide a valuable perspective on the adaptive significance and consequences of chronic marijuana usage against which our findings regarding adolescents may be compared and contrasted.

Defiance and Provocation

Among the adults whom we studied, the defiance and provocation of parents that was reflected to such an extent in the adolescents' use of marijuana had in most cases evolved into a more general break with parental and conventional societal values. This was evident in the emancipation felt by one woman who in her late twenties had broken away from life as a doctor's wife in favor of what she saw as the unrestricted freedom of a California lifestyle which included heavy use of marijuana. It was even more directly evident in those like the as-yet unsuccessful screenwriter-director who identified himself with revolutionary groups and minority causes, and referred to himself as a "nigger of the world." For most of the adult chronic marijuana users their efforts to obtain a constant supply of the drug, to sell marijuana if only to pay for their own supply, and to use the drug while avoiding difficulties with the law, was associated with a view of themselves, often with some satisfaction, as behaving in ways that did not have societal sanction.

Self-Destructiveness

If their perceived differences with the lives of others around them were expressed in less personal terms than was true of the adolescent marijuana abusers, the adults also showed a different pattern with regard to the self-destructive aspect of heavy marijuana usage. Although some of the adults we studied had used drugs like heroin, LSD, or cocaine in earlier more self-destructive periods of their lives, none of them were found to currently use marijuana in the adolescents' overtly self-destructive way that alienated parents, led to school or work failures or to encounters with police.

Anger

The use of marijuana by our adolescent subjects to diminish an overwhelming or otherwise uncontrollable anger was likewise reflected differently in our adult subjects. Some like the successful corporate lawyer, who had been raised to perform and achieve and who regarded himself as a "cut-throat bastard" at work, saw marijuana as necessary to reduce their competitive aggression sufficiently to enable them to relax when they were away from work. Others like the salesman, whose passivity and submissiveness had consistently cost him advancement in his career, smoked throughout the day to avoid having to deal with their fears around competitiveness and aggression.

If the adults did not use marijuana to deal with acute overwhelming anger as did our adolescent subjects, most used it to ease the chronic anger and frustration produced by unhappy relationships. In facilitating their detachment from the unpleasant reality of a current situation, marijuana enabled many of these men and women to exist for years in troubled relationships without feeling any urgency to do anything about them. One woman in her mid-thirties, for example, who told herself she was not bothered by her husband's distance or lack of consideration, spent virtually every evening smoking marijuana while reading science fiction in the bathtub. For others, marijuana diminished the reality of the other person to an extent that they were able, by being high during sexual relationships, to achieve satisfaction with marital partners whom they otherwise found distasteful. Still others were aware of their use of marijuana to repress dreams in which they expressed violence and rage toward a spouse or child.

Grandiosity

Regarding the function of marijuana in sustaining grandiose fantasies of success and achievement, certain variations were observed between the adolescent and adult marijuana users. In a small number of the adults the adolescent's difficulty of reconciling fantasies and possibilities was clearly reflected, as for example, in the case of the aspiring director whose belief in the greatness of his talent made it virtually impossible for him to work in any way that would be remunerative. Although he realized the strain this put on his wife and child, he regarded it as the price they needed to pay until his work was recognized.

Among most of the male adult subjects the transformation in mood produced by the use of marijuana was associated with grandiosity in subtler ways. For example, the lawyer had a sense of himself while smoking that he was a "philosopher-king" who had profound insights into other people. Such a perception contrasted sharply with his remarkable need to avoid any insights into himself. Another man whose life had been a series of painful frustrations pictured himself as a St. Bernard dog who could survive and overcome all hardships while he used marijuana to avoid facing the fact that he had paid a price for not attempting to deal with them.

The illusion of invulnerability which was a common feature among the female adolescents who used marijuana heavily was also seen among many of the adult women. The adolescents believed that there would not be harmful consequences to their destructive behavior or from relationships that were destructive to them. Many of the adult women marijuana users had continued such behavior and relationships together with an illusion of invulnerability well into their thirties.

Escaping Competitive Conflicts

Regarding the use of marijuana to escape from conflict regarding achievement and success, interesting similarities as well as differences emerged between the adolescent and adult marijuana users.

None of the high school students and few of the college students we saw who were heavily into marijuana were able to combine such usage with academic or work success. Most were deeply involved in conflicts with their families that had so negatively permeated their attitudes toward ambition and achievement as to make them intolerable or impossible goals.

By contrast, heavy marijuana usage was found to be compatible with significant career success in at least some of the adult cases. The established lawyer and woman writer were good examples. Both came from ambitious and successful families, and both had incorporated parental goals for achievement even though they diverged from parental values in other respects. It is significant that these individuals and the others like them conscientiously avoided smoking marijuana during the working day. Such men and women were consistently found to make a careful split between their working persona and their social selves and regarded marijuana as an integral part of their ability to relax and to "play."

Others of the adults we studied were reasonably successful in what they did but were operating well below their abilities. For these individuals marijuana enabled them to avoid the challenge of their own capabilities. For still others, heavy use of marijuana throughout the day fostered their resigned acceptance of a lack of occupational success and allowed them to withdraw from the competitive aggression of the working world in a way which paralleled the withdrawal behavior seen in adolescents reacting to the pressures of school.

It may be significant that those individuals who were successful in their work had started their heavy marijuana usage in adult life—in the lawyer's case, for example, after he was in practice, and in the case of the accomplished writer, after she had been teaching, had divorced and was living independently. By contrast, the unsuccessful salesman who smoked during the day, passively resigned himself to not moving ahead in his work, and used marijuana both to reenforce his behavior and as a consolation, had started to smoke heavily at 17. At the age of 35 this man bore a strong resemblance to the adolescent marijuana abusers.

Closeness and Intimacy

In addition to providing both confirming and contrasting perspectives on the functions heavy marijuana use was found to perform for adolescents, the adult marijuana users also evidenced certain dynamics which, while not so clearly evidenced among the adolescents, appeared to be closely tied up with chronic use of the drug. One of the most important of these involved difficulties with closeness and intimacy. Even though all of the high school and college-age heavy marijuana users we studied had problems with intimacy, because such problems are so common among adolescents generally and because their use of marijuana did not seem to play a significant role in their avoidance of closeness (in the way that heroin use clearly did), we did not consider the keeping of emotional distance a primary function of marijuana in this age group.

Problems in close relationships were present in virtually all of the adult users and here, marijuana clearly played a major role in creating an illusion of intimacy while restricting closeness and commitment. The suburban housewife, who linked commitment to entrapment, suffocation and death, provided a particularly good example of this. Although currently in a second marriage with a man for whom she felt affection and respect, she insisted on retaining "fantasy tickets" to other involvements which gave her a sense of safety and independence while making sure her commitment to her husband remained less than total. Such fears of closeness and deep connection were echoed as well in others of the adult chronic marijuana users.

The need to restrict closeness was paradoxically linked in many of these individuals to the perception that marijuana enhanced their sexual pleasure. As in the housewife's case, the enhancement often involved sexual fantasies or behavior in which someone was included other than or in addition to the person with whom they were most involved. One man, for example, was aroused by fantasies stimulated by marijuana in which he was having sex with one woman and was being watched by another. Interestingly, when this man became involved with a woman in which limited commitment was part of the relationship, his need for marijuana-stimulated fantasies which restricted closeness became less necessary.

Introspection

Marijuana is often thought to be a drug that encourages contemplation, and the chronic adult users, far more than the adolescents, saw it that way. Most felt it increased their understanding of themselves and others, making them more philosophical and insightful about what was going on around them.

Yet, we were impressed that with each of the representative cases marijuana permitted the individual to lead an unexamined life strikingly free of introspection. Marijuana enabled many to avoid looking at the pain and frustration of their early lives and to avoid seeing the effects of their early experiences on their personality and character. The use of marijuana to avoid self-awareness in adult life was strikingly exemplified by the lawyer who went through two long-term marriages with no sense of his own contribution to their failure; by the screenwriter who lived in a world of grandiose fantasy in which the limitations and realities of his life could be almost totally ignored; by the writer's belief in astrology as a guide to relationships and her reluctance to look at the impact of her own needs and character on her attachments; and by the housewife's ability to escape from commitment through her "fantasy tickets."

How is the marijuana users' view of their heightened awareness to be reconciled with the absence of introspection that seems to go with chronic use of the drug? The interviews indicated that becoming detached from the feeling and reality of current situations gave these individuals the impression of transcending the situation and augmenting their perspectives. The woman who told herself that her husband's selfishness and lack of consideration were not important to her insisted, "That's just the way he is and I refuse to let it bother me." But she needed marijuana, science fiction, and a warm bath to maintain the illusion that she was not troubled by his behavior.

On the basis of those with whom we worked, it appeared to be less insight than the transcendence of painful vision that characterizes heavy marijuana smokers. Detachment enabled these men and women to see their problems as less important; the ability to minimize was consistently confused with insight.

Magical Transformation

Finally, for these adults as well as for the adolescents, marijuana was not simply a drug of passivity, withdrawal, and denial. For almost all of them, as for most of the adolescents, marijuana was associated with a sense of magical transformation—the transformation from a housewife fearing commitment to husband and children to the holder of fantasy tickets to sexual adventure, from driven lawyer to "philosopher-king," from unsuccessful screenwriter unable to support his family to talented director for whom his family's needs must be sacrificed. One young mother and former dancer, after her first interview, dreamed of herself as dead and in the company of Mr. Rourke from the TV program "Fantasy Island." She described him as a "God-like individual" who was going to lead her into a new life. Her associations made clear that the dream was stimulated by her hope that some such change would take place through the interviews.

Perhaps most magical of all was the substitution of a sensory illusion of life for boredom and fear of lifelessness that afflicted these men and women. Such magical transformation became for many a substitute for the effort of real change. Belief in astrology was common among even some of the best educated of our subjects. The belief in a fate dictated by the stars was consistent with the use of marijuana to change one's fate in fantasy rather than in reality. Regardless of the degree of success or accomplishment they had achieved, each of these individuals used marijuana to avoid seeing, understanding, or dealing with their personal situation.

SUMMARY

To the degree that the adults were aware of their difficulties, they saw marijuana as an escape from them, or as providing relief or enhancing their ability to cope with them. Neither they nor we saw marijuana as the cause of their problems. Rather, it served for most to help maintain them in a troubled adaptation, reenforcing their tendency not to look at, understand, or attempt to master their difficulties. It served to detach them from their problems, and helped them to regard even serious difficulties as unimportant. Marijuana provided a buffer zone of sensation that functioned as a barrier against self-awareness and closeness to others.

Marijuana enabled the adolescents to avoid choices and challenges associated with growing up. The adults we studied appeared to have been obliged by time to make choices for which they were not prepared, and with which they were not satisfied. To the extent that their futures had caught up with them, they used marijuana in an attempt to diminish awareness of their limitations and convince themselves their problems were insignificant. If the adolescents used marijuana to detach themselves from troubled relationships with their families and to avoid planning for the future, what we have learned from the adult marijuana users provides a perspective on what these young persons' lives are likely to become.

REFERENCES

1. Wieder H, Kaplan E. Drug use in adolescents: psychodynamic meaning and pharmacogenic effect. Psychoanal Study Child. 1969; 24:339-431.

2. Milkman H, Frosch W. On the preferential abuse of heroin and amphetamine. J Nerv Ment Dis. 1973; 156:242-248.

3. Hendin H. Students on heroin. J Nerv Ment Dis. 1974; 156:240-245.

4. Hendin H. Amphetamine abuse among college students. J Nerv Ment Dis. 1974; 158:256-257.

5. Hendin H. Beyond alienation: the end of the psychedelic road. Am J Drug Alcohol Abuse. 1974; 1:11-23.

6. Hendin H. Marijuana abuse among college students. J Nerv Ment Dis. 1973; 156:259-270.

7. Hendin H. The age of sensation. New York: Norton and Co., 1975.

8. Hendin H. Psychosocial theory of drug abuse: a psychodynamic approach. In: Lettieri DJ, Sayers M, Pearson HW, eds. Theories on drug abuse: selected contemporary perspectives. National Institute on Drug Abuse Research Monograph 30. DHHS pub no (ADM) 80-976. Washington DC: Supt of Docs, US Government Printing Office, 1981.

9. Hendin H, Pollinger A, Ulman R, Carr A. Adolescent marijuana abusers and their families. National Institute on Drug Abuse Research Monograph 40. DHHS pub no (ADM) 81-1168. Washington DC: Supt of Docs, US Government Printing Office, 1981.

10. Hendin H, Pollinger A, Ulman R, Carr A. The functions of marijuana abuse for adolescents. Am J Drug Alcohol Abuse. 1981-82; 8:441-456.

11. Hendin H, Pollinger A, Ulman R, Carr A. American adolescent marijuana abusers and their families. Inter J Sociol Family. 1982; 12:202-215.

12. Shontz FC. Research methods in personality. New York: Appleton-Century-Crofts, 1965.

13. Spotts J, Shontz FC. The life styles of nine american cocaine users: trips to the land of Cockaigne. National Institute on Drug Abuse Research Issues 16. DHEW pub no(ADM) 76-392. Washington DC: Supt of Docs, US Government Printing Office, 1976.

14. Spotts J, Shontz FC. Cocaine users: a representative case approach. New York: Free Press, 1980.

15. Hendin H, Haas A, Singer P, Ellner M, Ulman R. Chronic marijuana use among adults. National Institute on Drug Abuse Research Monograph. Washington DC: Supt of DOCS, US government Printing Office, in press.

16. Huba G, Bentler P, Newcomb M. Assessing marijuana consequences: selected questionnaire items. National Institute on Drug Abuse Research Issues 28. DHHS pub no (ADM) 81-1150. Washington DC: Supt of Docs, US Government Printing Office, 1981.

A Theory of Adolescent Substance Abuse

James V. Spotts, PhD
Franklin C. Shontz, PhD

ABSTRACT. This report applies a theory of psychological individuation to inferences drawn from an 8-year series of clinical studies of men who practice heavy, chronic use of different drugs. Each man was studied intensively over a period of 4-5 months, using interviews and a comprehensive battery of dimensional and morphogenic assessment procedures. Users of barbiturates and sedative hypnotics were found to be least mature, followed by users of opiates, users of amphetamine, users of cocaine, and nonusers of drugs, who were found to be most mature. A theory is described which conceives adolescent substance abuse as rooted in dysfunctional relationships with parental figures which block or delay the normal individuation process. Comparable sets of representative case studies of heavy, chronic users of alcohol and marihuana are recommended to facilitate the development of treatment programs that take into account the special needs of persons who practice heavy, chronic use of different substances.

I. INTRODUCTION

The problems associated with substance abuse have a long history in America. However, adolescent substance abuse did not become a matter of major social concern until the mid-1960s. At that time, an explosion in substance abuse began among adolescents and young adults which continues to the present day. Current projections indi-

James V. Spotts is Assistant Director, Greater Kansas City Mental Health Foundation. Franklin C. Shontz is Professor of Psychology, University of Kansas.

This program of research has been supported by contracts and grants from the Psychosocial Division of the National Institute on Drug Abuse. The authors wish to thank Dr. Daniel J. Lettieri for his encouragement and helpful suggestions.

117

cate that adolescent substance abuse will continue to be a problem through the remainder of this century.[1]

The belief that substance abuse reflects personal maladjustment is implied in many published studies. This belief takes several forms and includes the ideas that: (1) substance abuse is related to the psychological needs of the user; (2) the personalities of chronic users of one substance (such as heroin) differ from those of chronic users of another (such as amphetamine); and (3) heavy, chronic substance abuse stems from personality disturbance or psychopathology.

Although published studies which bear upon drug use-personality relationships number in the thousands, research findings tend to be fragmentary, confusing and contradictory and often are of little practical value to practitioners who want to increase their understanding in order to improve their effectiveness with individual substance abusers.

The quality of research in this area varies greatly. Many studies contain serious design flaws which limit their usefulness.[2] Some investigations which study only drug users who are incarcerated or in treatment may present an inaccurate picture of substance abusers for such persons are likely to show more personality disturbance than substance abusers who are free. Furthermore, published research is often based on findings obtained with a single instrument. Although some studies do suggest that there are differences in the personality characteristics of persons who abuse different drugs[3-6] systematic, comparative research in this area is all but nonexistent.

In 1974 we conducted a series of NIDA sponsored studies of persons who practiced heavy, chronic use of cocaine.[7] A review of the literature on drug abuse/personality relationships undertaken at that time revealed the confusing and contradictory status of research in the field. In light of this review we carried out an interlocking series of intensive, multidimensional, studies of individuals who practice heavy, chronic use of different drugs. This research program has continued for 8 years, with funding from NIDA. During this time, we have studied carefully selected individuals who are heavy, chronic users of cocaine, amphetamine, opiates, barbiturates/sedative hypnotics, and nonusers of drugs. To our knowledge, these investigations constitute the first systematic comparative studies of heavy, chronic drug users in the field of substance abuse. This report provides an overview of this program of research and summarizes theoretical inferences drawn from it.

II. METHOD

Our research employs the *Representative Case Method,*[7-10] a powerful and cost efficient way to conduct *clinical* studies of individuals. It calls for the intensive, holistic study of persons, who are not sampled from a population but are deliberately sought out because they epitomize a condition of theoretical or practical interest, or present an extraordinarily clear opportunity to critically examine hypotheses about an important human state or problem.

In this type of research, generalization proceeds from individuals who are studied as whole persons to other individuals who are studied as whole persons, not from individuals to group means. Findings from this type of research take into account the complexity and uniquenesses of personal psychological structures. Although its purpose is not primarily to describe populations or test specific hypotheses, this type of research generates findings that are particularly useful to therapists, counselors, and other practitioners who deal with persons one at a time.[11-15]

When careful attention is paid to the sequential selection of persons, the Representative Case Method permits individuals to be combined into groups that may be described by summary statistics and permits quantitative comparisons among groups.[2] If the persons studied are heterogeneous on factors such as age, socioeconomic status, and education, but are matched across groups on these variables, generalizability across levels of these variables is enhanced.

This type of clinical research has a long and respected history. It begins by carefully identifying persons who most clearly epitomize a particular condition (e.g., a disease, like AIDS) and then comprehensively and systematically examines these individuals in order to explicate the dynamic constellation of factors which produce or contribute to the condition.

A. Participants

Paid intermediaries and the participants themselves were used as finders to identify in the community of drug users in the Kansas City area more than 1,000 candidates for the research. On the basis of screening interviews with the finders, and personal interviews with the candidates who passed screening; 45 men were selected for intensive study. Thirty-six were committed to the heavy, chronic use of one of four drugs or classes of drugs under investigation and a comparable group of nine were committed to the nonuse of hard drugs. None of the participants were hospitalized or incarcerated. All were living independent (though not necessarily legal) lives in their communities. None of the drug users was an experimental, occasional, or social-recreational user. The criteria for selection were that all drug users had experimented with use of a variety of substances; had developed an intense commitment to their drug(s) of choice; and had used them on a regular basis for long periods of time. Consequently, each could speak as an expert about the drug of choice, its effects, and the factors associated with its use. Detailed descriptions of the personal and drug use characteristics of these men are presented in other reports.[2,11-15]

All groups were comparable in *age, sex, IQ,* and *socioeconomic background.*[2,12,15] In addition, participants were matched across groups in terms of *life style.* Participants were drawn from all sectors of society and included persons engaged in heterogeneous legal and illegal occupations. Each group contained: a musician or entertainer; a blue collar worker; a thief, burglar or strong-arm robber; an intense, achievement oriented individual; a manager of some type of performers (musicians, actors, etc.); a scion of an exceptionally wealthy family; an entrepreneur; a social misfit; and a two worlder who maintained full-time legal employment to mask another illegal occupation. Diversity in life style guaranteed that a sufficiently wide variety of life styles were examined (in each study series) to justify statements about substance abuse in several different contexts. A more detailed discussion of the participant selection procedures is presented in Spotts and Shontz.[7:44-48]

All drug users were also comparable in *level of educational achievement.* However, it proved impossible to obtain nonusers who were comparable to users in other respects and in educational achievement as well; nonusers had more education than any drug user group or combination of drug user groups.[2] The nonusers selected had been reared under conditions where they were as much "at risk" for drug use/abuse as the other paticipants but were persons with an intense commitment not to use hard drugs.

Each participant was studied for 12-15 days over a period of 4-5 months with extensive life history and drug use interviews and a comprehensive battery of dimensional and morphogenic assessment procedures;[2,7] data collection took approximately 1.5 years for each cohort of nine men (Table 1). A detailed account of the administra-

Table 1

Description of the Basic Battery of Assessment Procedures
Employed in the Studies of Heavy, Chronic Drug Users and Nonusers

---

1. Life History Interview (20-30 hrs. per participant)

2. Drug Experience Interviews (15-30 hrs. per participant)

3. Drug Effects Interviews: Drug of Commitment (20-30 hrs. per participant)

4. Wechsler Adult Intelligence Scale (WAIS)

5. Revised Beta Examination

6. Minnesota Multiphasic Personality Inventory (MMPI) with scoring for the 11 Supplementary Scales (Ego Strength, Maladjustment, Anxiety, Repression, Dependency, Dominance, Social Responsibility, Prejudice, Social Status, Control, McAndrews Addiction Scale); and 10 Content Scales (Depression, Poor Morale, Psycholicism, Phobias, Organic Symptoms, Authority Conflict, Manifest Hostility, Family Problems, Hypomania, Social Maladjustment).

7. Cattell 16 Personality Factor Scale, Forms C and D with scoring for Supplementary Scales (Extroversion, Anxiety, Tough, Poise, Motivational, Distortion

8. Eysenck Personality Inventory

9. Zuckerman Sensation Seeking Scales (Form IV)

10. Pearson Novelty Experiencing Scales

11. Garlington and Shimota Change Seeker Index

12. Drug Preference Ratings (administered 3 times)

13. Semantic Differential Ratings of 10 concepts (Drugs in General, Amphetamine, Cocaine, Heroin, Speedball, Barbiturates, LSD, Marihuana, Beer, and Hard Liquor) with 26 nine-point scales

14. Q-Sort descriptions of Usual Self, Typical Self, Ideal Self, Worst Self, Predrug Self, Drug Self, Post-Drug Self, Typical Drug User, and Typical Nonuser, administered 3 times to each participant under both Standard and Individualized conditions

15. Kelly Rep Test

---

tion of the various assessment procedures used in this research is presented in Spotts and Shontz.[7]

It may appear that the number of persons studied in these investigations is insufficient to support generalization. However, due credit must be given for the care taken in participant selection, the comprehensiveness of the studies of each individual selected, and the careful matching procedures employed. The difference between generalizability and significance must also be borne in mind. Variations in group size does alter the size of critical ratios required for statistical significance, but small group size, per se, is no deterrent to generalization. Generalizability is *not* determined by the number of persons studied but by the relevance, quality, and quantity of data and the investigator's skill in integrating and interpreting findings in a logical and meaningful fashion.

III. RESULTS

Though more exploratory than analytical in nature, this series of carefully designed clinical investigations permitted us to draw a clear and consistent set of inferences. We found that heavy, chronic users of cocaine, amphetamine, opiates, barbiturate/sedative-hypnotics, and nonusers differ systematically with respect to: (1) early family backgrounds and family dynamics; (2) patterns of adult adjustment; (3) attained levels of psychological maturity; (4) temporal orientations; (5) types of deficiencies in individuation exhibited as adults; (6) performance on a variety of widely used psychological tests (Table 1); and (7) gravitation to the heavy, chronic use of drugs which produce strikingly different effects.

A. Theory

Integration of these findings into a broader conceptual framework requires use of theory. The following section describes a theory that accomplishes this purpose. This theory[12] is not a set of hypotheses that have been "tested by" our data but a conceptual schema that we have applied to facilitate understanding them. No suggestion is made that other theories could not be used with equal success.

B. Psychological Development and Individuation

This theory draws heavily from the ideas of Jung,[16-20] Neumann;[21,22] Edinger;[23] Whitmont;[24,25] and Campbell.[26] The theory is outlined in Figure 1. Table 2 presents the definitions of the major theoretical concepts employed in the theory. Briefly, this theory postulates that psychological growth procedes through stages.[12,15] Each stage includes a number of maturational tasks that must be accomplished if normal individuation is to occur. According to the theory, each person must undergo a series of psychological *crises* or *transformations,* in each of which earlier patterns are radically altered or cut away to permit emergence of new attitudes, behav-

Figure 1. Stages of Psychological Individuation[a]

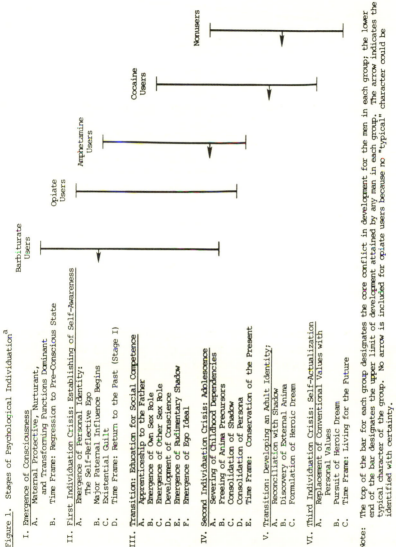

Barbiturate Users   Opiate Users   Amphetamine Users   Cocaine Users   Nonusers

I. Emergence of Consciousness
   A. Maternal Protective, Nurturant, and Transforming Functions Dominant
   B. Time Frame: Regression to Pre-Conscious State

II. First Individuation Crisis: Establishing of Self-Awareness
   A. Emergence of Personal Identity:
      The Self-Reflective Ego
   B. Major Paternal Influence Begins
   C. Existential Guilt
   D. Time Frame: Return to the Past (Stage I)

III. Transition: Education for Social Competence
   A. Apprenticeship to the Father
   B. Emergence of Own Sex Role
   C. Emergence of Other Sex Role
   D. Development of Conscience
   E. Emergence of Rudimentary Shadow
   F. Emergence of Ego Ideal

IV. Second Individuation Crisis: Adolescence
   A. Severing of Childhood Dependencies
   B. Freeing of Anima Precursors
   C. Consolidation of Shadow
   D. Consolidation of Persona
   E. Time Frame: Conservation of the Present

V. Transition: Developing an Adult Identity:
   A. Reconciliation with Shadow
   B. Discovery of External Anima
   C. Formulation of Heroic Dream

VI. Third Individuation Crisis: Self-Actualization
   A. Replacement of Conventional Values with Personal Values
   B. Pursuit of Heroic Dream
   C. Time Frame: Living for the Future

Note: The top of the bar for each group designates the core conflict in development for the men in each group; the lower end of the bar designates the upper limit of development attained by any man in each group. The arrow indicates the typical character of the group. No arrow is included for opiate users because no "typical" character could be identified with certainty.

[a] Abridged and adapted from Spotts and Shontz (12).

Table reprinted with permission D.B. Kandel. © 1978 by The University of Chicago, American Journal of Sociology, 84: 427-36. All rights reserved.

123

Table 2

Definitions of Major Theoretical Concepts Employed
in the Theory of Psychological Individuation

ANIMA - In men, the unconscious image of femininity which is first
        encountered in the mother, then repressed, and typically
        re-encountered in a lover at the time of emergence of the Heroic
        Dream. The "external anima" becomes an essential source of
        psychological support during the pursuit of that dream. (18)

EGO - The psychological region of contact between person and
      environment, typically experienced as a focussed awareness of
      stimuli and personal responses.

EGO IDEAL - A figure or image drawn from experience which epitomizes
        what the person would like to become.

EXISTENTIAL GUILT - A reaction of self-blame to imagined injuries done
        to parental images when separation from them takes place.

HEROIC DREAM - A fantasied life goal that requires for its attainment
        the overcoming of obstacles and conquest of enemies or challengers

INDIVIDUATION - The process of growth and differentiation which has as
        its goal the development of the distinctive, individual
        personality.

PERSONA - The social facade or "mask" developed by the individual to
        facilitate interaction with others on a conventional but
        superficial basis.

SHADOW - The primitive aspects of the personality, the dark-side
        components of the personality which the individual fears, hates or
        despises, and has not integrated into consciousness. The Shadow is
        usually kept outside conscious awareness by repression and is concealed
        from others by the persona.

iors, and thought patterns that are more appropriate for contemporaneous circumstances. Parental figures play a crucial role in determining how smoothly individuation procedes, for they can ease or facilitate the child's passage through a particular crises or can impede, delay, or even block the individuation process.

The theory postulates four major crises in life. The first crisis (Stage II) occurs in childhood and is associated with emergence of self-awareness and the autonomous, self-reflective Ego. The second crisis (Stage IV) occurs in adolescence and is described in detail later in this report. The third and fourth crises occurs in the adult years and are described elsewhere.[12] The third crisis is included in Figure 1 only to demonstrate the continuity of the individuation process. These crises can have such serious consequences that in an earlier article[12] we employed the metaphor of the *Dragon Fight* to denote that there are points in life where the individual must fight for his individuality if he is to achieve or retain it.

No crisis is resolved with a single act; each requires a span of time, even years to reach completion. During Transition Periods

(Stages III and V of Figure 1) the person works towards completion of the developmental tasks at the stage already achieved, attempts to complete tasks left over from earlier crises and gathers strength for the next one.[12]

Unlike physical development, which typically unfolds of its own accord, psychological individuation is *not* automatic. It is achieved through conflict, struggle, and strife; is paid for with guilt, pain, and anxiety; and always entails the possibility of failure.[15] Under ideal conditions, psychological individuation proceeds at a pace roughly commensurate with physical maturation. However, given the vagaries of early life experiences psychological individuation often lags behind biological or chronological age indicators.

Although derived from the study of men, this theory assumes that both men and women traverse the same stages. However, it does not assume that both sexes experience or manage the crises in the same ways.

The theory postulates (1) that the predisposition to heavy, chronic drug use originates early in life; (2) that heavy chronic use of a particular substance results from failure or partial success in meeting a particular challenge of normal individuation; and (3) that persons who practice heavy, chronic use of particular substances do so because the drug of commitment produces a distinctive *ego state*[11-15] which either allows temporary escape from problems generated by failures in individuation or creates the illusory experience that they have been overcome by pharmacological means. In either case, the drug experience is counterfeit because it produces no enduring changes in personal structure.

IV. DESCRIPTIONS OF PERSONS WITHIN THE GROUPS STUDIED

Based on everything we learned about each individual, the theory described above was applied to the life of each man we studied. Although a range of psychological maturation was evident for each group (Figure 1), the five groups differed in level of achieved individuation. Nonusers demonstrated the highest level of maturity followed by cocaine users, amphetamine users, opiate users, and barbiturate/sedative-hypnotic users in that order.[12] We inferred that the men in each group were wrestling with similar constellations of developmental difficulties.

Space limitations do not permit a detailed presentation of the results obtained in this program of research. However, the discussions that follow present brief capsule descriptions of the personal characteristics of these groups derived from the various assessment procedures employed in this research. For more detailed information, the interested reader is referred to the findings summarized in other published reports.[2,7,11-15,27,28] Additional findings will be presented in forthcoming publications.

A. Barbiturate/Sedative Hypnotic Users

The barbiturate/sedative-hypnotic users we studied had been reared in economically successful but emotionally depriving families. Most described their fathers as disinterested or violent and abusive persons and their mothers as weak, timorous, and ineffectual women who were unable to provide their sons the love and security they needed. These men blamed themselves for their absence of love and affection and, though angry with their status, saw themselves as undesirable and unlovable. We speculated that serious psychic injury occurred in these men's lives as early as Stage II-A, and centered upon pervasive feelings of abandonment-rejection.

Clinically, heavy, chronic users of barbiturates/sedative hypnotics resembled the borderline personality described by Kernberg,[29,30] Materson,[31] and others. Although extroverted and sexually active, their social relationships were unstable and their vocational histories were spotty and reflected underachievement. These men resented authority and had serious difficulties with persons occupying such positions; they were pessimistic persons who lived in an unhappy present and saw themselves as having no future. They lived with high levels of tension and anxiety, were chronically depressed and plagued by doubts, and feelings of worthlessness.[14] In interviews, they reported an alarming incidence of self-destructive acts, i.e., serious accidents, fights, barroom brawls, auto wrecks, and drug overdoses. When stressed (which was frequently) they turned to barbiturates and sedative-hypnotics to obliterate self-awareness and escape to a consciousless state of Oblivion.[14]

B. Opiate Users

Heavy, chronic opiate users were isolated men who lived narrow, constricted lives; cynical and distrustful people who seemed unable to tolerate intimate relationships. In life history interviews they either reported that their fathers were absent during their developmental years, or described them as violent and overwhelming tyrants. They described their mothers as overprotective or as persons who fostered dependency through seduction or the exercise of raw power. Life history data suggest that most of these men had not successfully managed the transformations at Stage II, which allows the person to establish a secure, separate identity. The outcome was failure or only partial success in the First Individuation Crisis.

As adults, opiate users avoided intense emotionality, did not feel at home in the world, showed little interest in the tasks of adulthood, and seemed unable to cope consistently with work, marriage, family or other adult activities. Heavy, chronic users of opiates evidenced little interest in adult sexuality. They engaged in criminal activities in the pursuit of drugs but otherwise avoided conflict. They preferred to withdraw from the problems of life than attempt to conquer them. These men seemed to become easily exhausted in their efforts to cope with the problems of adult life. They reported they used opiates to withdraw to a primitive, (paradisical) state of peace, contentment and serenity to find the respite they feel they need to contend with a world that is too complicated, stressful, and demanding.[12]

C. Amphetamine Users

The heavy, chronic users of amphetamine and its congeners described their fathers as weak and ineffectual persons who had been psychologically emasculated by their stronger wives. They described their mothers as complex, seductive, and manipulative women who superficially seemed to encourage independence but practiced complex acts of guilt and deceit to keep their men under their control.

As adults, heavy, chronic users of amphetamine tended to be driven, sometimes violent and impulsive, but achievement-oriented men who reacted strongly against threats of weakness or impotence. Although amphetamine users were extroverted and sexually active, their interpersonal relationships were superficial. Though fascinated by women, amphetamine users feared them and felt compelled to conquer, exploit, and even punish them. These men reported they used amphetamine to maintain a high energy level, ward off depression, reinforce strivings for dominance and sexual potency, and to aid them in their efforts to cope with a hostile world. Amphetamine users were tied to the present. They had no heroic dream;[32] could not settle down, maintain regular employment, marry, raise a family or commit themselves to the tasks of adulthood, for they were still enmeshed in the tasks of adolescence (Stage IV).

D. Cocaine Users

Heavy, chronic users of cocaine seemed to have achieved self-awareness and control and to have established a stable Ego and self-identity. Most had apparently had managed passage through the Second Individuation Crisis (Stage IV) but seemed severely scarred by the experience. Cocaine users described their fathers as supportive and concerned, but as plodders, men to be respected but surpassed. They described their mothers as stronger, more energetic and resourceful than their fathers but also as cold, stern, and dictatorial.

As adults, cocaine users were proud, ambitious, and intensely competitive men; stubborn and willful individuals who were ready to fight or outwit others to achieve their goals. However, they were also isolated loners who attempted to repress or deny normal human frailties and avoided dependency of any kind. Though sexually active, cocaine users dominated women and showed little interest in developing mutual relationships with them. They reported that cocaine expands experience, produces euphoria, lifts them out of depression, provides a brief but ecstatic feeling of unity and completeness, and reinforces their beliefs that they needed no one *except* cocaine.[13] Most cocaine users had an heroic dream of conquest that dominated their lives. Some accomplished a great deal, but none were able to keep or enjoy success for their dreams of glory were either abandoned with bitterness and despair or led to the downfall, disgrace or death of their perpetrators.[7,13]

E. Nonusers

Nonusers had achieved self-awareness and control, stable Egos and secure self-identities. The majority described their fathers as strong and steady persons, hard workers, and good providers though not necessarily ambitious people. The fathers were remote persons who were feared, respected, and perhaps even hated, but were never friends or confidants of their sons.[12] The mothers of nonusers were described as warm, close, and protective but also as strong and fearless fighters, and effective disciplinarians in the home. These men reported that their mothers actively encouraged them to become independent, trained them, provided them incentives for growing up, fostered and even provoked strivings for autonomy, and pointed them firmly towards conquest of the external world.

As adults, the typical nonuser was an aggressive and self-confident individual who had harnessed his talents and energies for achievement. Unlike the drug user groups, most nonuser were identified with the larger society and saw a place for themselves in it. The typical nonuser had a clear sense of purpose and had formulated an heroic dream which made vocational activity central in his life. Nonusers were cheerful, pragmatic men who faced reality in a tough, straightforward manner. They were sexually active, but like cocaine users, most avoided intimacy with women. They staunchly refused to use drugs because they feared their use would reduce their control over their own destinies.[12]

V. THE THEORY OF ADOLESCENT SUBSTANCE ABUSE

A. The Theory of the Adolescent Individuation Crisis

In the theory proposed in this report, the Second Individuation Crisis is the crucible of adolescence and for some youth, substance abuse seems to offer a way to avoid or circumvent this crisis. The psychological image of the mother is central during this period, for it epitomizes the dependencies of infancy and childhood. According to the theory, the image of the father remains somewhat in the background. He stands as the somewhat remote figure who represents the far off world of adulthood or as the carrier of conventional values. Once the Second Crisis has been passed, the father image may assume a more intimate role as teacher and personal ideal.

Before birth, the infant is protected and sustained in the maternal womb. Following birth, and for a number of years afterward, the growing child receives its sustenance, security, and guidance in the family, within a second womb as it were.[26] During infancy and childhood, parental figures serve as extensions of the child's Ego and shape its development. With the onset of adolescence, however, the person must extricate himself from infantile dependencies and become emancipated from the parents of childhood.[33] However, before a person can become an adult, he must stop being a child[34] and this requires a qualitative change or transformation.

The Second Individuation Crisis (Stage IV, Figure 1) may cover a painful and protracted span of years which involves a major reorganization of mental life.[35-38] The person's self-concept is affected as are relationships with other people. A new set of attitudes, values, and behaviors are created and a world view evolves which more closely approximates those of adulthood.

During this period, the individual not only must shed the dependencies of childhood, but must also: define and consolidate a personal identity; control heightened sexual drives; develop a *persona,* or social presence which facilitates relationships with others; decide upon a final sexual identity; develop a capacity for intimacy; establish ways to maintain meaningful relationships with peers; come to terms with the more primitive aspects of experience, the *shadow;*[18] develop a sense of competence and personal worth; establish a value system that can guide relationships with others; and formulate at least some ideas about what he/she wants to do with his life.[12,33,37,39-42]

Two other factors complicate resolution of the Second Individuation crisis. First, while biological milestones denote entrance into adolescence (attainment of puberty;[43]), no comparable indicators tell the youth when adulthood has been achieved. Second, during adolescence there is a massive upsurgence of ego-alien (numinous) experiences which are often given spiritual significance by youth. This surge of spirituality subsides in early adulthood but reappears in the Fourth Individuation Crisis. It is partly responsible for the emotionality, idealism, introversion, moodiness, and self-analysis observed in adolescents. It also may fuel some aspects of adolescent substance abuse and may be one reason for the high incidence of religious conversions during this period.

Stierlin[44] has observed that the adolescent's conflicts with parental figures in the adolescent individuation crisis ideally should be a "loving fight" in which the protagonists mutually affirm the other's rights to existence and differentiation. Offer and Offer[45] have demonstrated that this can occur. However, few people are reared under ideal circumstances, and our theory postulates that the Second Individuation Crisis is the *most dangerous* period in life for, if improperly managed, it can become a brutal and protracted struggle in which traumata, psychosis, and death are ever present possibilities.[12]

Most adolescents are able to manage this crisis and move on to adulthood, but some fail, and others are only able to partly manage the passage. Some settle for a passive existence;[12] others stubbornly refuse to give up childhood.[46-47] Others are overwhelmed and become the psychiatric casualties seen in adolescent neurosis, depression, and psychosis.[48-52] The fears, anxieties, frustrations, and failures of this period also find expression in juvenile alcoholism, drug abuse and antisocial behavior.[41,53-62] Finally, death always lurks in the wings. It is no accident that adolescence is associated with a high incidence of traffic fatalities and accidental deaths (which are often poly-motivated), suicides, suicide attempts, and drug overdoses.[63-74]

B. Adolescent Substance Abuse

Based on retrospective reports of adolescent experiences, provided by the persons we studied, our theory postulates that adolescent substance abuse represents one of several directions an individual may take in efforts to avoid, manage, or contain failures, delays or blockages in individuation. In this theory, the adolescent substance abuser is a person who is having difficulty "putting away childish things," letting go of past behaviors, and accepting the new ones of the future. Some adolescents turn to heavy use of alcohol or other drugs to avoid the painful tasks of the Second Individuation crisis; others use drugs in attempts to arrest the forward flow of life and maintain a static adolescent state; still others abuse substances to help them tolerate the pain and suffering that can accompany the normal maturational process. In this theory, adolescent substance abuse is anchored in the individuation process (particularly the Second Individuation Crisis) and is rooted in the failures, conflicts, and dysfunctional relationships with parental figures which make it impossible for individuation to proceed in a normal manner.

According to this theory, if death does not intervene most individuals eventually manage passage through the Second Individuation Crisis and move on into adulthood. As these tasks (and those left over from earlier periods) are completed the need for pharmacological props and supports declines. This process of "maturing out" has been described even in the lives of chronic opiate users though it occurs considerably later for these individuals.[75-76]

This theory is consistent with the findings of large scale research and represents one of those rare instances where there is direct convergence of the findings of large scale research and studies of individuals. Numerous epidemiological studies have suggested that substance abuse emerges in early adolescence, reaches its peak at ages 18-25, then subsides in the early to mid-30s.[55,60,77-82] Our studies elaborate upon these findings by showing how they apply in the lives of individuals.

C. Stages of Drug Involvement

Reports from the men we studied suggest that initial contact with drugs during adolescence is mainly a matter of social exposure. As adolescents, these men were often in situations where drugs were used; fully 72 percent of them said they were introduced to use of drugs by friends. Rarely were drug dealers involved and, as might be expected, alcohol and marihuana were usually the first drugs (besides caffeine, tobacco, and medicines) tried. Alcohol was the first drug used (before age 18) by 69 percent of the drug users and 89 percent of the nonusers. Excluding alcohol, marihuana was the first illegal drug tried by 64 percent of the drug users and 77 percent of the nonusers.[2]

Most men reported that, after initial exposure, they experimented with a variety of substances. They discovered that different substances produce predictably different psychological experiences, and gravitated to the chronic use of the substance(s) that best filled the deficiencies in their personal structures.[11,13,14] Our findings indicate that for the vulnerable individual, once such a substance is found and a source of supply has been established, social support is no longer required. The person-drug relationship becomes self-sustaining.

VI. AREAS FOR NEEDED FUTURE RESEARCH

There is a need for comparable clinical studies of persons who abuse other drugs, particularly *alcohol* and *marihuana,* two of the most widely used and abused drugs in America today.

Alcohol is typically the first drug tried by adolescents. It therefore has a high temporal priority to become the individual's drug of choice. It is readily available, relatively inexpensive, and is often "legal" at relatively early ages. It is an exceptionally "flexible" drug. Though most individuals use it for sedative purposes it can facilitate social interaction or produce withdrawal and isolation; muffle aggression or serve as a trigger for outbursts of violence; produce euphoria or depression; suppress sexuality or lower sexual inhibitions; produce loss of consciousness or act as a precipitant for a wide variety of destructive acts.[83]

Descriptions of the personality characteristics of some alcohol abusers provided by experts in the field[84-91] suggest these individuals are similar, in many respects, to the barbiturate/sedative hypnotic users we studied. However, the men we studied did not exhibit the high level of dependency some have reported with alcoholics.[92-94] Barbiturate abusers often abuse alcohol and alcoholics are frequent abusers of barbiturates, sedative hypnotics, and tranquilizers.[95-97] Carefully constructed representative case studies of "pure" alcohol abusers could go far in showing how alcohol abusers are similar to and different from individuals who abuse other substances.

Gersick, Grady, Sexton, and Lyons,[98] Kandel,[99] and Jessor[100] have reviewed much of the published research on the personal characteristics of marihuana users. Though this literature is extensive, intensive studies of the personal characteristics of persons who practice heavy, chronic use of marihuana are limited. In one such study, however, Hendin and his associates[101] found severe personality disturbance characteristic of both chronic adolescent marihuana users and their families. Intensive studies of heavy, chronic marihuana users could contribute significantly to our understanding of the relationship between marihuana abuse and personal maladjustment.

If persons who abuse alcohol and marihuana are selected to be comparable in all other respects to persons already studied in our research, and if the same data collection techniques are used, the findings of all series will comprise an integrated whole. The result will be a body of clinically relevant knowledge that is more comprehensive in scope and penetrating in depth than any currently in existence.

VII. CONCLUSIONS

The inferences described in this report are the products of one of the first comprehensive efforts to conduct systematic comparative studies of individuals who practice heavy, chronic use of different drugs. The findings of these investigations indicate that the personalities of individuals who practice heavy, chronic use of cocaine, amphetamine, opiate, and barbiturate/sedative hypnotics differ strikingly from each other and from those of persons committed to the nonuse of drugs. Our data suggest that the men we studied were practicing heavy, chronic use of different substances in efforts to manage distinguishably different constellations of problems in individuation. A theory of psychological individuation has been presented which encompasses the diverse patterns of adjustment displayed by the differing groups. This theory anchors adolescent substance abuse in the individuation process and links it to dysfunctional relationships with parental figures which resulted in failures or only partial success in managing normal crises of psychological individuation. The systematic, multidimensional studies described in this report are unique. They comprise a series of *benchmark studies*,[2] against which data from future studies of substance abusers, incarcerated or nonincarcerated, in treatment or out of treatment, may be compared. Completion of comparable studies of men committed to the heavy use of alcohol and marihuana, would make available, for the first time, standards against which men in future studies of almost all the major substances of abuse could be compared and would facilitate development of treatment programs which take into account the special needs of particular substance abuser groups.

REFERENCES

1. Richards LG, ed. Demographic trends and drug abuse, 1980-1995. (NIDA Research Monograph No. 35, DHHS Pub. No. (ADM) 81-1069.) Washington, D.C.: U.S. Government Printing Office, 1981.

2. Spotts JV, Shontz FC. Psychopathology and chronic drug use: A methodological paradigm. Int J Addict. 1983a; 18:633-680.

3. Hekimian LJ, Gershon S. Characteristics of drug abusers admitted to a psychiatric hospital. JAMA. 1968; 205:125-130.

4. Hill HE, Haertzen CA, Davis H. An MMPI factor analytic study of alcoholics, narcotic addicts and criminals. Quart J. Study Alcoh. 1962; 23:562-582.

5. Penk WE, Fudge JW, Robinowitz R. Personality characteristics of compulsive heroin, amphetamine, and barbiturate users. J Consul Clin Psychol. 1979; 47:383-385.

6. Rardin DR, Lawson TR, Kruzich DJ. Opiates, amphetamine, and alcohol: A comparative study of American soldiers. Brit J Addict. 1974; 9:891-898.

7. Spotts JV, Shontz FC. Cocaine users: A representative case approach. New York: Free Press, 1980a.

8. Shontz FC. Research methods in personality. New York: Appleton-Century-Crofts, 1965.

9. Shontz FC. Single organism designs. In: Bentler PM, Lettieri DJ, eds. Data analysis strategies and designs for substance abuse. (Research Issues No. 13.) Rockville, MD.: National Institute on Drug Abuse, 1976:25-44.

10. Shontz FC. Single organism research and the Representative Case Method. In: Lettieri DJ, ed. Drugs and suicide: When other coping strategies fail. Beverly Hills, CA.: Sage Publications, 1978:225-246.

11. Spotts JV, Shontz FC. A life theme theory of chronic drug abuse. In: Lettieri DJ, Sayers M, Peterson HW, eds. Theories of drug abuse: Selected contemporary perspectives. (NIDA Research Monograph No. 30, DHHS Pub. No. (ADM) 80-967.) Washington, D.C.: U.S. Government Printing Office, 1980b.

12. Spotts JV, Shontz FC. Ego development, dragon fights, and chronic drug abusers. Int J Addict. 1982; 17:945-976.

13. Spotts JV, Shontz FC. The phenomenological structures of drug induced ego states: I. Cocaine: Phenomenology and implications. Int J Addict. 1984a; 19:2.

14. Spotts JV, Shontz FC. The phenomenological structure of drug induced ego states:

II. Barbiturates and sedative-hypnotics: Phenomenology and implications. Int J Addict. 1984b; 19:3.

15. Spotts JV, Shontz FC. A new perspective on intervention in heavy, chronic drug use. Int J Addict. (In press.)

16. Jung CG. Modern man in search of a soul. New York: Harcourt, Brace and World, Inc., 1933.

17. Jung CG. Psychology and alchemy. The collected works of Carl G. Jung (Vol. XII). (Hull RFC, trans.) New York: Bollingen-Pantheon, 1953:25.

18. Jung CG. Aion. In: deLaszlo VS, ed. Psyche and symbol: A selection from the writings of C. G. Jung. Garden City, N.Y.: Doubleday & Co., Inc., 1958. (Originally published, 1951.)

19. Jung CG. Analytical psychology. Its theory and practice. The Travistock Lectures. New York: Vintage Books, 1968.

20. Jung CG. On the relation of analytical psychology to poetry. In: Campbell J, ed. The portable Jung. (Hull, RFC, trans.) New York: The Viking Press, 1971:302-322. (Originally published, 1922.)

21. Neumann E. The origins and history of consciousness. (Hull RFC, trans.) Princeton, N.J.: Princeton University Press, 1954. (Originally published, 1949.)

22. Neumann E. The great mother: An analysis of the archetype. (Manheim R, trans.) Bollingen Series XLVII (2nd ed.) Princeton, N.J.: Princeton University Press, 1972. (Originally published, 1955.)

23. Edinger EF. Ego and archetype: Individuation and the religious foundation of the psyche. Baltimore, MD.: Penguin Books, 1973.

24. Whitmont EC. The symbolic guest. Princeton, N.J.: Princeton University Press, 1978.

25. Whitmont EC. Return of the goddess. New York: Crossroad Publishing Company, 1982.

26. Campbell J. The hero with a thousand faces. Bollingen Series XVII. Princeton, N.J.: Princeton University Press, 1949.

27. Spotts JV, Shontz, FC. Correlates of sensation seeking in heavy, chronic drug users. Percept. & Motor Skills. (In press.)

28. Spotts, JV, Shontz, FC. Drugs and personality: Extraversion-introversion. J. Clin. Psychol. (In press.)

29. Kernberg O. The treatment of patients with borderline personality organization. Int J Psychoanal. 1968; 49:600-619.

30. Kernberg O. Borderline conditions and pathological narcissism. New York: Science House, 1975:163-177.

31. Masterson JF. Psychotherapy of the borderline adult: A developmental approach. New York: Brunner/Mazel, 1975.

32. Levinson DJ, Darrow CN, Klein EB, Levinson MH, McKee B. The seasons of a man's life. New York: Ballantine Books, 1978.

33. Blos P. The adolescent passage: Developmental issues. New York: International Universities Press, 1979.

34. Beiser HR. Ages 11 to 14. In: Greenspan SI, Pollock GH, eds. The course of life: Psychoanalytic contributions toward understanding personality development, Vol. II: Latency, adolescence and youth. (DHHS Pub. No. (ADM) 80-999.) Washington, D.C.: U.S. Government Printing Office, 1980:293-308.

35. Adatto CP. On the metamorphosis from adolescence into adulthood. J Am Psychoanal Assoc. 1966; 14:485-509.

36. Erikson EH. The problem of ego identity. J Am Psychoanal Assoc. 1956; 4:56-121.

37. Erikson EH. Identity and the life cycle: Psychological issues (Vol. 1). New York: International Universities Press, 1959.

38. Geleerd E. Some aspects of ego vicissitudes in adolescence. J Am Psychoanal Assoc. 1961; 9:394-405.

39. Group for the Advancement of Psychiatry. Normal adolescence (Vol. VI), Report No. 68. New York: Group for the Advancement of Psychiatry, 1968.

40. Harley M. Some reflections on identity problems in prepuberty. In: McDevitt JB, Settlage CF, eds. Separation-individuation. New York: International Universities Press, 1971:385-403.

41. Noshpitz JD. Disturbances in early adolescent development. In: Greenspan SI, Pollock GH, eds. The course of life: Psychoanalytic contributions toward understanding personality, Vol. II: Latency, adolescence and youth. (DHHS Pub. No. (ADM) 80-999.) Washington, D.C.: U.S. Government Printing Office, 1980:309-356.

42. Szurek SA. The need of adolescents for emotional health. In: Howells JG, ed. Modern perspectives in adolescent psychiatry. New York: Brunner/Mazel, 1971:100-125.

43. Khatchadourian H. The biology of adolescence. San Francisco, CA.: WH Freeman, 1977.

44. Stierlin H. Separating parents and adolescents. New York: Quadrangle, 1974.

45. Offer P, Offer J. Three developmental routes through normal adolescence. In: Feinstein SC, Giovacchini PG, eds. Adolescent psychiatry. New York: Jason Aronson, 1975:121-141.

46. Bruch H. The golden cage: The enigma of anorexia nervosa. Cambridge, MA.: Harvard University Press, 1978.

47. Sours J. The anorexia nervosa syndrome: Phenomenologic and psychodynamic components. Psy Quart. 1969; 1:167-187.

48. Feinstein SC, Miller D. Psychoses of adolescence. In: Noshpitz J, ed. Basic handbook of child psychiatry. New York: Basic Books, 1979.

49. Holzman P, Grinker RR Sr. Schizophrenia in adolescence. In: Feinstein SC, Gioracchini PI, ed. Adolescent psychiatry. New York: Jason Aronson, 1977.

50. Hudgens RW. Psychiatric disorders in adolescence. Baltimore, MD.: Williams and Wilkins Co., 1974.

51. Lorand S. Adolescent depression. Int J Psychoanal. 1967; 48:53.

52. Schoolar JC, ed. Current issues in adolescent psychiatry. New York: Brunner/Mazel, 1973.

53. Cahalan D, Room R. Problem drinking among American men (Monograph 7). New Brunswick, N.J.: Rutgers Center of Alcohol Studies, 1974.

54. Friedman CJ, Freedman AS. Drug abuse and delinquency. Part I: Drug use in three groups of lower class adolescent boys. Drug abuse in America. Problems in perspective, (Vol. 1). Patterns and consequences of drug use. National Commission on Marihuana and Drug Abuse. Washington, D.C.: U.S. Government Printing Office, 1973:398-436.

55. Huba GJ, Wingard JA, Bentler PM. Adolescent drug use and intentions to use drugs in the future: A concurrent analysis. J Drug Ed. 1979; 0:145-150.

56. Jessor R, Collins MI, Jessor SL. On becoming a drinker: Social-psychological aspects of an adolescent transition. In: Seixas FA, ed. Nature and nurture in alcoholism. Annals of the New York Academy of Sciences, Vol. 197. New York: Scholastic reprints, 1972.

57. Jessor R, Jessor S. Problem behavior and psychosocial development: A longitudinal study of youth. New York: Academic Press, 1977.

58. Johnston L, O'Malley P, Eveland L. Drugs and delinquency: Search for causal connections. In: Kendel DB, ed. Longitudinal research on drug use: Empirical findings and methodological issues. Washington, D.C.: Hemisphere-Wiley, 1978:132-156.

59. Kandel D. Interpersonal influences on adolescent illegal drug use. In: Josephson E, Carroll E, eds. Drug use: Epidemiological and sociological approaches. Washington, D.C.: Hemisphere-Wiley, 1974:207-240.

60. Kaplan HB, Pokorny AD. Alcohol use and self-enhancement among adolescents: A conditional relationships. In: Seixas FA, ed. Currents of alcoholism (Vol. IV): Psychiatric, psychological, social, and epidemiological studies. New York: Grune and Stratton, 1978:51-75.

61. Kaplan HB. Deviant behavior in defense of self. New York: Academic Press, 1980.

62. Margulies R, Kessler RC, & Kandel D. A longitudinal study of the onset of drinking among high school students. Quart J Study Alcoh. 1977; 38:897-912.

63. Baechler J. Suicides. New York: Basic Books, 1979.

64. Cusky WR. Self-destruction: Suicide and drugs. In: Lettieri DJ, ed. Suicide and drugs: When other strategies fail. Beverly Hills, CA.: Sage Publications, 1978:193-224.

65. Glaser K. Attempted suicide in children and adolescents: Psychodynamic observations. Am J Psychother. 1965; 19:220-227.

66. Jacobs J. Adolescent suicides. New York: John Wiley Interscience, 1971.

67. Jacobziner H. Attempted suicides in adolescence. JAMA. 1965; 191:7-12.

68. Lettieri DJ, ed. Drugs and suicide: When other coping strategies fail. Beverly Hills, CA.: Sage Publications, 1978.

69. Margolin NL, Teicher JD. Thirteen adolescent suicide attempts. J Am Acad Child Psy. 1968;7:296.

70. Mason P. Suicides in adolescents. Psychoanal Rev. 1954; 41:48-54.

71. Saxon S, Aldrich SY, Kuncel EE. Suicide and drug abuse. In: Lettieri DJ, ed. Drugs and suicide: When other strategies fail. Beverly Hills, CA.: Sage Publications, 1978:167-192.

72. Sellers EM, Marshman JA, Kaplan HL, Giles HG, Kapur BM, Busto U, MacLeod SM, Stapleton C, Sealey F. Acute and chronic drug abuse emergencies in metropolitan Toronto. Int J Addict. 1981; 16:283-303.

73. Teicher JDA. A solution to the chronic problem of living: Adolescent attempted suicide. In: Schoolar JC, ed. Current issues in adolescent psychiatry. New York: Brunner/Mazel, 1973:129-147.

74. Toolan JM. Suicide and suicide attempts in children and adolescents. Am J Psy. 1962; 118:719-724.

75. Beckett HD, Lodge KJ. Aspects of social relationships in heroin addicts admitted for treatment. Bull Narc. 1971; 23:29-36.

76. Winick C. Maturing out of narcotic addiction. Bull Narc. 1962; 14:1-7.

77. Abelson HI, Fishburne PM, Cisin I. National survey on drug abuse; 1977: Vol. 1, Main findings. (National Institute on Drug Abuse DHEW Pub. No. (ADM) 78-618.) Washington, D.C.: U.S. Government Printing Office, 1977.

78. Clayton RR, Voss HL. Young men and drugs in Manhattan: A causal analysis. (National Institute on Drug Abuse, Research Monograph #39, DHHS Pub. No. (ADM) 81-1167.) Washington, D.C.: U.S. Government Printing Office, 1981.

79. O'Donnell JA, Voss HL, Clayton RR, Room R. Young men and drugs: A nationwide survey. (National Institute on Drug Abuse, Monograph #5, DHEW Pub. No. (ADM) 76-311.) Washington, D.C.: U.S.: Government Printing Office, 1976.

80. Fishburne PM, Cisin I. National survey of drug abuse: Main Findings, 1979. (National Institute on Drug Abuse DHHS Pub. No. (ADM) 80-976.) Washington, D.C.: U.S. Government Printing Office, 1980.

81. Johnston L, Bachman J, O'Malley P. 1979 Highlights. Drugs and the nation's high school students, Five year national trends. (National Institute on Drug Abuse DHEW Pub. No. (ADM) 79-930.) Washington, D.C.: U.S. Government Printing Office, 1979.

82. Kandel D, ed. Longitudinal research on drug use. Washington, D.C.: Hemisphere Publishing Corporation, 1978.

83. Krystal H. Character disorders: Characterological specificity and the alcoholic. In: Pattison EM, Kaufman E. eds. Encyclopedic handbook of alcoholism. New York: Gardner Press, 1982:607-617.

84. Goodwin DW, Crane JB, Crane CB. Felons who drink. Quart J Stud Alcoh. 1971; 32:136-148.

85. Khantzian ES. The alcoholic patient: An overview and perspective. Am J Psychother. 1980; 34:4-19.

86. Knight RP. The psychodynamics of chronic alcoholism. J Nerv Ment Dis. 1937; 86: 538-548.

87. Owens PL, Butcher NJ. Personality factors in problem drinking: A review of the

evidence on some suggested directions. In: Pickens R, Heston L, eds. Psychiatric factors in drug abuse. New York: Grune & Stratton, 1979.

88. Menninger CA. Man against himself. New York: Harcourt Brace Jovanovich, 1938.

89. Winokur G, Reich T, Rimmer J, Pitts FN. Alcoholism, II: Diagnoses and familial psychiatric illness in 259 alcoholics probands. Arch Gen Psych. 1970; 23:104-111.

90. Goodwin DW. Alcoholism and suicide: Associated factors. In: Pattison EM, Kaufman E, eds. Encyclopedic handbook on alcoholism. New York: Gardner Press, 1982: 655-662.

91. Krystal H, Rashkin H. Drug dependence: Aspects of ego functions. Detroit, MI,: Wayne State University Press, 1970.

92. Balint M. The basic fault. London: Tavistock, 1968.

93. Khantzian EJ. On the nature of the dependency and denial of problems of alcoholics. J Ger Psych. 1979; 2:191-202.

94. Kaufman E, Pattison EM. The family and alcoholism. In: Pattison EM, Kaufman E, eds. Encyclopedic handbook of alcoholism. New York: Gardner Press, 1982:663-672.

95. Ashley MJ, le Riche W, Ollin JS. Mixed drug-abusing and pure alcoholics: A socio-medical comparison. Brit J Addict. 1978; 73:19-34.

96. Devenyi P, Wilson M. Abuse of barbiturates in an alcoholic population. Can Med Assoc. 1971; 104:219-221.

97. Freed X. Drug use by alcoholics: A review. Int J Addict. 1973; 8:451-473.

98. Gerseck KE, Grady K, Sexton E, Lyons M. Personality and sociodemographic factors in adolescent drug use. In: Lettieri DJ, Luford JP, eds. Drug abuse and the American adolescent. (NIDA Research Monograph #38, A RAUS Review Report, DHHS Pub. No. (ADM) 81-1166.) Washington, D.C.: U.S. Government Printing Office, 1981: 39-56.

99. Kandel DB. Drug use by youth. An overview. In: Lettieri DJ, Ludford JP, eds. Drug abuse and the American adolescent. (NIDA Research Monograph #38, A RAUS Review Report, DHHS Pub. No. (ADM) 81-1166.) Washington, D.C.: U.S. Government Printing Office, 1981:1-24.

100. Jessor R. Marihuana: A review of recent psychosocial research. In: DuPont R, Goldstein A, Brown B, eds. Handbook on drug abuse. Washington, D.C.: U.S. Government Printing Office, 1979:337-355.

101. Hendin H, Pollinger A, Ulman R, Carr AC. Adolescent marihuana abusers and their families. (NIDA Research Monograph #40, DHHS Pub. No. (ADM) 81-1168.) Washington, D.C.: U.S. Government Printing Office, 1981.

On Processes of Peer Influences in Adolescent Drug Use: A Developmental Perspective

Denise B. Kandel

ABSTRACT. Data from longitudinal studies of adolescents carried out over the last ten years are reviewed to provide an integrated and dynamic perspective on the nature of friendships and processes of peer influence in adolescent drug involvement, within a general developmental perspective. Four interrelated questions are examined: (1) What individual attributes are especially important in the formation of friendships among adolescents? (2) Which of two processes, selection or socialization, account for the similarity in values and behaviors observed in ongoing friendship dyads, and how important is similarity in friendship formation and dissolution? (3) What is the nature of friends' influence as compared to parents', and in which domains of adolescent's life do these influences exert themselves? (4) What mechanisms, role modeling or social learning, underlie processes of interpersonal influences?

Relational dyadic and triadic samples of adolescents matched to a parent and/or a best friend and observed at one point in time as well as over time provide important and relatively rare sources of data on processes of interpersonal influence. Sociodemographic characteristics are the strongest determinants of friendship formation, with participation in illicit drugs following next in importance. Both selection (assortative pairing) and socialization contribute to observed similarity in friendship pairs. Adolescents coordinate their choice of friends and their values and behaviors, in particular the use of marijuana, so as to maximize congruency in the friendship dyad. If there

Denise B. Kandel is with the Department of Psychiatry and School of Public Health, Columbia University, and the New York State Psychiatric Institute.

This is a revised version of a paper presented at the Conference on Integrative Perspectives on Youth Development: Person and Ecology, May 1983, Berlin, West Germany, and to be included in R. Siberseisen and K. Eyferth (eds.), *Integrative Perspectives on Youth Development: Person and Ecology.* Springer Verlag, 1984. Preparation of this manuscript was partially supported by research grants DA0064 and DA01097 and Research Scientist Award DA00081 from the National Institute on Drug Abuse. The assistance of Mark Davies and Victoria Raveis is gratefully acknowledged.

139

is a state of unbalance such that the friend's attitude or behavior is inconsistent with the adolescent's, the adolescent will either break off the friendship and seek another friend or will keep the friend and modify his or her own behavior. Both parents and peers can have strong influences on adolescents, depending upon the arena of influence. Parents are especially important for future life plans, while peers are most important for involvement in illicit drug use. However, for drug use itself, there are different patterns of influence depending upon the stage of drug involvement. Peers are especially important for initiation into marijuana use, while parental factors gain in importance in the transition from marijuana use to the use of other illicit drugs. Interpersonal influences of peers on ongoing marijuana and alcohol use result from modeling and imitation more than from social reinforcement and the transmission of values.

Peers have been identified as one of the most important factors in the use of legal and illegal drugs by adolescents.[1-12] In this paper, I review selected findings from the work that I have carried out over the last decade in order to provide an overview of what has been learned about the nature and role of peer influences in adolescent drug involvement within a developmental context. An integrated and dynamic perspective on the nature and processes of peer influences and on the role of friendships in adolescence emerges.

Adolescence is traditionally considered to be the period in the life span when peer influences are most intense. Because adolescents are still members of parental family units and occupy the social roles of children toward whom parents have since their births exerted important socialization functions, a basic issue in adolescent socialization is the extent to which adolescent development proceeds in response to peer or to parental influences.[13-15] A pervasive notion is that there is a "generation gap," with adolescents assumed to function completely independently and in opposition to the world of adults. Social commentators have stressed the emergence of strong adolescent subcultures and the increased separation between parents and their adolescent children.[16-18] The emergence of these distinct subcultures has been attributed to structural changes in social organization: the fact that adolescents spend most of their lives segregated in schools with peers of their own age; the lengthening of schooling; and the reduced responsibilities for participation in the labor force. Insulation from parents and other adults is assumed to result in the elimination of parental ability to influence their adolescent children.

This thesis is too simple-minded, as will be documented shortly.

Adolescent drug use represents one area of adolescent life subject to strong peer influence, however, and a behavior uniquely suited to the study of the role of peer influences and friendships in adolescence.

Four interrelated questions are addressed:

1. What characteristics are shared by adolescents who make friends with each other and how important is drug use in adolescent friendships?
2. What processes underlie friendship formation and dissolution in adolescence and how important are assortative pairing and socialization in accounting for similarity observed at one point in time?
3. What is the nature of friends' influence as compared to parents', and in which domains of adolescent's life do these influences exert themselves?
4. What mechanisms, role modeling or social learning, underlie processes of interpersonal influences?

ON THE NATURE OF FRIENDSHIP STUDIES

The studies we have carried out differ in important respects from most other studies of peer influences. We have examined real-life adolescent friendships over time, with independent data obtained from each friend, and we have examined these friendships within the context of parental relationships. By contrast, most existing adolescent studies rely for the most part on the subjects' reports of the characteristics of their friends.[19] The influence process is inferred from the effect of the perceptions of friends' characteristics on the adolescents' own behaviors or attitudes (e.g.,[20]), or from the youths' responses to hypothetical situations involving potential conflicts between parents and peers.[13,21-23] Longitudinal studies of real-life friendships in which independent data are obtained from one or more friends are rare. Exceptions include Newcomb's classic study carried out 1961[24] and the more recent research of Hallinan,[25-26] Epstein,[27-28] Coleman,[29-31] the further analyses of the Coleman data by Cohen,[32] as well as the work of Duck[33-34] and Curry and Kenny.[35]

Because in our studies we obtained independent assessments of each interacting member in adolescent-best friend dyads and adolescent-best friend-patient triads, we could investigate such issues as actual similarity in friendship pairs, intergenerational transmission of values, or interpersonal influence without having to rely exclusively on the respondents' reports of the other persons' attributes. This strategy has very strong methodological advantages. Indeed, we have shown that the perceptions of another's characteristics, which are generally indexed as sources of interpersonal influences, are partially determined by the perceiver's own attributes that these perceptions are assumed to explain[36] or by the perceiver's social roles.[37] In addition, because we followed a sample of friendship pairs over time we could analyze the processes of friendship formation and dissolution, as I will describe in greater detail shortly.

METHODS

A large scale longitudinal survey was carried out on a representative sample of the adolescent population attending public secondary schools in New York State in 1971-72, drawn from 18 public high schools throughout the state. Students were given self-administered structured questionnaires in their classrooms twice in the course of a school year, in Fall 1971 and Spring 1972, at a 5-to-6-month interval. In five schools, adolescents were asked to nominate their best friend in school and everyone in the school was surveyed. In addition, a questionnaire was mailed to every parent of every student in the 18 schools, alternately mothers and fathers, in order to obtain independent data from one parent for each adolescent. Sixty-six percent of the parents returned their questionnaires. (For further details, see[10,38-39].)

The following samples are available for analysis: 4,033 adolescent-parent dyads; 1,879 adolescent-best school friend dyads; and 1,112 adolescent-best-school-friend-parent triads. In addition, 959 friendship dyads could be traced over the 5-to-6-month interval.

Most friendships were of long duration: 73% of the adolescents had known their friend three or more years, only 11% one year or less. Forty-one percent of the choices were reciprocated. The restriction of the best friend nomination to a best friend in school still allows us to generalize to best friends in general, since in 79% of cases the best-school-friend is also the best friend overall, in and out of school. Furthermore, the very limited relevant data available in the literature suggest that data on a single best friend provide acceptable estimates of the influence of a group of close friends. Thus, the zero-order correlation between adolescents' and best friends' educational aspirations is .45 when based on five friends[40] compared with .37 for one friend.[41] The similarity in these correlations suggests that social networks are characterized by a substantial amount of homophily.

SIMILARITY IN FRIENDSHIP PAIRS

Characteristics shared in common by friends may indirectly throw light on the determinants of interpersonal attraction and interpersonal influence. As noted above, most of our knowledge about friendships and interpersonal attraction beyond childhood derives from laboratory studies. These have suggested that similarity in values and attitudes provides the most important basis for interpersonal attraction. However, these results may be determined by the research paradigm that underlies these inquiries. By requiring subjects to attend to characteristics selected by the experimenter, laboratory studies may artificially distort the relevance of certain factors in interpersonal attraction.[42]

Indeed, data from our research on real life adolescent friendship pairs indicate that the most frequent attributes shared in common by friends are not values and attitudes but sociodemographic characteristics such as age and sex,[15,43-44] as has also been found in adult friendships.[45-46] Behaviors, especially the use of illicit drugs, are next in importance. Similarity is lowest on attitudes and psychological factors. Thus, similarity (as measured by weighted Kappas) ranged from .837 for grade in school or .638 for age, to .459 for using marijuana or .338 for smoking cigarettes, to .309 for educational aspirations, but only .234 for attitudes toward the legalization of marijuana or .135 for depressive mood.

The important role of illicit drugs in adolescent friendships is illustrated further by data on the proportion of focal adolescents who report having ever used marijuana as a function of the degree of self-reported life-time marijuana experience of the nominated best-school-friend. When the best friend reports never to have used marijuana, only 15% of focal adolescents report to have used marijuana; when the best friend has used marijuana once or twice, 50% of the choosers have also used marijuana. This proportion increases to 79% when the best friend reports having used marijuana 60 or more times.

The important role of the peer group in the use of illicit drugs is also observed at a further stage in the life span. We reinterviewed a subsample of these adolescents nine years later at the average age of 24.7 years. Perceived extent of marijuana use in one's social networks, involving friends among those single and the spouse/or partner as well as friends among those married or living with a partner, is the strongest predictor of current marijuana involvement in young adulthood.[47]

PROCESS OF FRIENDSHIP FORMATION

Similarity among individuals at one point in time could result from one or two processes: selection (or assortative pairing) and socialization. Under selection, similarity between friends, such as drug use, preexists the friendship and is a causative factor in the association. Under socialization, similarity develops over time as the result of association and its resulting interpersonal influence. An unusual set of relational longitudinal data on stable and unstable friendship pairs and their associated members-to-be, newly chosen members and relinquished members allowed us to address this issue.[39]

A sample of 959 friendship pairs drawn from the same schools in the fall and spring of the same academic year was identified. In a number of these pairs (N = 290), the person named as best friend changed over time. For a number of these changing unstable pairs, information was available not only about the two members of the dyad at each point in time, but also about a third person: information at Time 1 about the friend-to-be (N = 266 pairs), and information at Time 2 about the former friend (N = 233 pairs). The relatively short time interval between the measurement points allowed close monitoring between potential changes in individual attributes and changes in friendship patterns. These data made it possible to assess similarity among adolescents before they become friends, while they are friends, and after they cease being friends. Inferences could be made about the role of similarity in the formation and dissolution of friendships.

We found that both processes, selection and socialization, are important. Adolescents who share certain characteristics are more likely to become friends; and those who associate with each other become more similar over time. To place similarity in illicit drug use within a broader developmental context, we investigated similarity on four attributes that can change over time: marijuana use, educational aspirations, participation in minor delinquency and political attitudes. (Participation in minor delinquency was ascertained from a seven item index that asked adolescents how often in the last 3 months they had participated in such activities as "taking things of some value worth $2 to $50 that did not belong to you" or "had cheated on a class test.") Overall levels of similarity in friendship dyads decrease from the first to the last of these four attributes (Table 1). Levels of similarity vary systematically with the stage of friendship: whether it is in the process of formation, in a stable phase, or has recently dissolved. Similarity in existing friendships measured at Time 1 shows differences in levels according to the subsequent fate of the friendship, a fate that was not yet known at the time of the initial assessment. These patterns are most striking for marijuana use. When the pairs are classified according to their subsequent history, those that would dissolve between the fall and the spring of the school year are characterized by lower similarity *prior to the dissolution* (see row 1) than those that remained stable (row 4). Newly formed pairs are more similar than pairs of friends-to-be (row 3 versus row 2). Among the stable pairs, similarity further increases over time, as can be noted by comparing row 5 with row 4. The highest similarity is observed among stable reciprocated pairs (row 7); stable unreciprocated pairs have much lower similarity. Interestingly enough, at Time 1, *similarity is higher among friends-to-be* (row 2) *than among existing friendships that are going to dissolve over the next several months* (row 1). *As regards marijuana use, similarity is lowest in the unstable friendships, both prior to the dissolution* (row 1) *and especially afterwards* (row 6). Similar patterns are obtained among the other three characteristics: educational aspirations, political attitudes and participation in minor forms of delinquency, although the differences are most striking with respect to marijuana and least striking with respect to educational aspirations. Similarity is lowest prior to the dissolution of the friendship and after its dissolution; it is highest during the active phase of the friendship itself.

Thus, the sharing of certain attributes contributes to interpersonal attraction and is strengthened further as the result of association. Statistical analyses[39] indicate that selection and socialization contribute about equally to levels of intra-friendship similarity observed at one point in time.

Table 1

Homophily[a] on Behaviors and Attitudes Among Friendship Dyads at Various Stages of

Formation and Dissolution

Type of Friendship Dyad[b]		Time When Homophily Assessed[c]	Frequency Current Marijuana	Educational Aspirations	Political Orientation	Minor Delinquency
1. Unstable: changed friend at T2	A_1F_1	Time 1	.239	.327	.145	.158
2. Friends-to-be at T2	A_1N_1	Time 1	.327	.348	.107	.248
3. New friends	A_2F_2	Time 2	.405	.406	.106	.296
4. Stable pairs	A_1F_1	Time 1	.451	.349	.201	.255
5. Stable pairs	A_2F_2	Time 2	.505	.382	.248	.286
6. Former friends (friends at T1)	A_2O_2	Time 2	.220	.380	.185	.167
7. Stable pairs: reciprocated	A_1F_1	Time 1	.580	.369	.263	.307
8. Stable pairs: unreciprocated	A_1F_1	Time 1	.302	.327	.127	.203

[a]As measured by Kendall's T_B.

[b]A = Adolescent chooser; F = Friend chosen; N = Friend-to-be; O = Former friend.

[c]Time 1 = Fall; Time 2 = Spring.

Reprinted with permission from Kandel DB. Am J Sociol 1978; 84:427-36.

ON THE RELATIVE INFLUENCE OF PARENTS AND PEERS

What is the overall role of peer influence in an adolescent's life, especially as regards the use of illicit drugs? How strong is that influence relative to the influence of other potential sources of socialization, especially parents?

Both parents and peers are influential, but each have their realms of influence. The proper question to ask is not: To what extent are adolescents under the general influence of their friends as compared to their parents?, but: What are the areas of influence for friends and what are the areas of influence for parents? Indeed, in certain areas, peers are most influential; in other areas, parents are the influential force. For issues and concerns of immediate relevancy to the adolescent's life, peers play a crucial role. For issues relevant to basic values, such as religiosity, and to the adolescent's future, such as educational aspirations, parents are much more important than peers. These processes are illustrated strikingly in two different realms, marijuana use and educational aspirations.

Two alternative explanations of adolescent's involvement in illicit drugs have been posited. According to one interpretation, adolescent involvement in illicit drugs results exclusively from peer influences: participation in a drug subculture and association with other drug using peers. According to another interpretation, even a behavior such as marijuana use which is typical of the youth culture and deviant according to adult standards, could represent continuity between the generations and constitute a juvenile manifestation of behaviors engaged in by adults. Adolescent drug users may come from families in which the parents use various drugs, either socially accepted drugs, such as alcohol, or medically prescribed psychoactive drugs, such as tranquilizers or stimulants.

In order to test these two alternative hypotheses, the drug behavior of focal adolescents was examined as a function simultaneously of the parent's self-reported use of alcohol (distilled spirits) or medically prescribed psychoactive drugs and of the best school friend's use of marijuana.[8-12]

For adolescent's marijuana use, while parental drinking and best friends' marijuana experience both have an independent effect, the effect of peers is far larger than the effect of parents. This is best seen in those triads in which the adolescent is exposed to conflicting role models because parent's and friend's behaviors diverge, one using drugs and the other not. When faced with such conflict, adolescents are much more responsive to peers than to parents. In this particular sample, 58% of adolescents used marijuana when their best friends also used marijuana although their parents did not drink distilled spirits regularly. By contrast, only 22% of adolescents used marijuana when their parents drank regularly but their best friends had not used marijuana. Parental influence can, however, synergize with and potentiate peer influence. The highest rates of adolescent marijuana use (70% in this sample) occurred when both parent and peer reinforced each other's influence on the adolescent; the lowest rate (12%) when neither used drugs. Given particular patterns of peers' use of drugs, parental behavior becomes important in moderating peer influences. Children of non-drug using parents are somewhat *less* likely to be using drugs than their peers, whereas children of drug using parents are *more* likely to do so.

The same trends appear when parental behavior is indexed by parental use of medically prescribed drugs or when the adolescent's behavior is the drinking of hard liquor. When adolescent's drinking of hard liquor is examined as a function both of drinking by parents and by the best school friend, results similar to those with respect to marijuana are observed, although the differences among the groups are not as striking. When their best friend has not used alcohol at least three times in their lives, the proportion of adolescents having drunk alcohol at least three times is 31% when their parents are not regular users of alcohol and 39% when their parents are regular users. These proportions increase to 52% and 61% respectively, when friends have drunk alcohol at least three times in their lives. The preeminent influence of peers as compared to that of parents is still very evident.

Estimates of influence based on a causal path model indicate that the total modeling effect of peer marijuana use on adolescent marijuana use is ten times as high as the effect of parental alcohol use among girls (.52 versus .05) and almost seven times higher among boys (.47 versus .07) (Table 2).

Completely opposite patterns of influence appear in connection with the formation of educational aspirations in these same triads of respondents. Levels of educational aspirations were examined as a function of the parent's aspirations for their children and the best friend's aspirations for themselves.[36] The effect of parents on adolescent's aspirations is much stronger than the effect of the best friend, a conclusion also reached in an earlier study.[48] When their best friends have no college aspirations for themselves, 15% of

Table 2

Parental and Peer Influences on Adolescent Marijuana Use

Among Boys and Girls

(Standardized Coefficients are presented.[a])

	Boys	Girls
Parental alcohol use[b]	.07	-.05
Parental marijuana use attitude[b]	-.22*	-.35
Best friend marijuana use	.47*	.52*
Best friend marijuana attitude[b]	-.06	-.16
R^2	69%	61%
N$\geq$	446	606

[a]Coefficients for measurement model and error variances and covariances are not presented.

[b]Multiple indicator latent variable.

*Greater than twice its standard error.

focal adolescents plan to attend college if their parents have no college aspirations for them as compared to 68% if the parents have such aspirations; parallel proportions when the best friend has college aspirations are 32% and 89%. The contrast with drug behavior is striking.

Coefficients estimated in a causal model indicate that the effect of parents is several times as strong as the effect of the best friend: seven times as strong in the case of boys and one and a half times as strong in the case of girls (Table 3).

ROLE OF PEERS AND PARENTS AT DIFFERENT STAGES OF DRUG INVOLVEMENT

It is clear that parental influences are especially important for the future life plans of adolescents, while peers are more important for involvement in illicit drug use. However, with respect to drug use itself, there are different patterns of influence depending upon the

Table 3

Psychosocial Model of Interpersonal Influences on Adolescents' Educational Aspirations.

Parental Influence Measured by the Parent's Self-Report of Aspirations for their Child,

Among Boys and Girls. (Standardized Coefficients are presented.[a])

| | BOYS (N=312) | | | | GIRLS (N=449) | | | |
	GPA	Parental Aspirations	Best Friend Aspirations	Adolescent Aspirations	GPA	Parental Aspirations	Best Friend Aspirations	Adolescent Aspirations
SES[b]	.19*	.37*	.13*	.07	.19*	.34*	.11*	.06
Grade point average	–	.33*	.25*	.36*	–	.29*	.20*	.29*
Parental aspirations for adolescent	–	–	–	.35*	–	–	–	.31*
Best friend aspirations for self	–	–	–	.05	–	–	–	.20
R²				41%				37%

[a]Coefficients for measurement model and error variances and covariances are not presented.

[b]Multiple indicator latent variable.

*Greater than twice its standard error.

specific drug and the stage of drug involvement. Relative to other predictors, peers are especially important for initiation into marijuana use, while parental factors gain greatly in importance in the transition from marijuana use to the use of other illicit drugs. This trend is clearly demonstrated in longitudinal analyses that examined the determinants of initiation to each of the three major stages of drug involvement, i.e., alcohol, marijuana, and other illicit drugs over a six month period, among adolescents at risk for transition into each of these stages at the beginning of the time interval.[10] Four domains of variables were included among the predictors: parental influences, peer influences, beliefs-values and behaviors. The effect of each cluster, within and across stages of drug use, was indexed by the total variance accounted for by each summary cluster considered alone as well as by the increments to the total explained variance contributed by each successive cluster to the variance already accounted for by the preceding clusters. To facilitate comparisons across stages, the increment in variance explained by each cluster was calculated as a percentage of the total variance for each stage.

Parental factors explain a much greater portion of the total explained variance in initiation to the use of other illicit drugs than initiation to the other two stages, 40% compared to 23% for initiation into hard liquor and 14% for marijuana. By contrast, peer influences explain a greater proportion of the variance of initiation into marijuana (48%) than for initiation into hard liquor (34%) or other illicit drugs (33%) (see also[10]).

DURATION OF INTERPERSONAL INFLUENCE

There is some inferential evidence that parental influence may have a longer lasting impact than the influence of friends made at a particular point in time. Suggestive differences appear in the predictive power of parental and peer influences in explaining initiation to marijuana use in longitudinal investigations that make these predictions over differing time intervals. When the interval and time lag is short, such as the five-to-six months interval in our study, peer influence on marijuana use is much stronger than parental influence[10-11] By contrast, over a longer three year interval with controls on personality and family domains of variables, peer factors were found by Brook, Lukoff and Whiteman[1] not to have any effects. Similarly, Lucas, Grupp and Schmitt[49] found that perceived marijuana use by college students' reference group in the freshman year weakly predicted marijuana initiation two years but not four years later. Because peer attachments may change relatively rapidly over the course of adolescence, the results suggest an important hypothesis about the nature of peer influence to be tested in future work. Namely, that peer influences are immediate and relatively transitory in comparison to parental influences.

DIFFERENTIATION OF ADOLESCENT SUBCULTURES

Not only must peer versus parental influences be conceptualized in terms of specific issues, but peer influences and peer groups themselves must be differentiated according to their prevailing orientation. Not all peer groups promote an anti-adult ideology. There exist striking differences in the behaviors and values of adolescents in different adolescent subgroups.[50] Two contrasting subgroups were identified among the adolescents in our sample who interacted greatly with their peers. An index of degree of peer interaction was constructed based on five items that measured the frequency of getting together with friends outside of school, dating, attending parties, hanging around with groups of kids and driving around with friends. Adolescents scoring in the upper third of the distribution were defined as high in peer involvement. These high interacting youths were classified according to the extent of perceived marijuana use among their friends. Adolescents answering that "most" or "all" of their friends had used marijuana (10.3% of the sample) were considered to move in circles with high levels of exposure to marijuana use and were contrasted to those reporting that "none" of their friends were users (6.7% of the sample). Both groups of adolescents were actively involved with their peers, as reflected, for example, in the fact that 59% and 65% respectively reported seeing their best friend daily out of school. These two groups are characterized by very different values, orientations and behaviors. Compared to members of non-marijuana using groups, those who belong to marijuana using groups are more likely to be using marijuana (89% versus 5%) and other illicit drugs (76% versus 9%), to be less close to their parents (40% score high on an index of closeness to their mother versus 64%) but closer to their friends (56% versus 32% score high on an index of peer orientation), to perform less well in school (41% versus 51% had an overall grade average of at least B), to be less religious (19% versus

40% attended services once or twice a month), to be more depressed (45% versus 26% scored high on an index of depression), and to hold more liberal political attitudes (62% versus 29% defined themselves as liberal).

That different peer groups and cliques are different in their behaviors and attitudes appears an obvious and trite finding. Yet, discussions of peer influences in adolescence disregard for the most part variations and differentiations among peer groups and assume that all peer groups are consistently antagonistic toward adults. As documented by the data, the crucial factor in an adolescent's feelings toward adults is not involvement in peer groups per se but involvement in certain groups, for example a group in which its members use marijuana. A high degree of interaction with peers can coexist without necessary rejection of parents.

PROCESSES OF INTERPERSONAL INFLUENCE

To the extent that adolescents influence each other, how does this influence come about? Social learning-theory[51-53] suggests that interpersonal influence can arise from two processes: (1) imitation, when one person models the behavior or values of another; and (2) social reinforcement, when one person adopts another's values which in turn affects his or her behavior. These two processes parallel functions of significant others as role models and as definers.[54]

Distinctions can also be introduced regarding the manner in which interpersonal influence is exerted. Influence can be (1) *direct,* when the example set by the significant other (role modeling) and the definition of norms (social reinforcement) have direct and immediate consequences for the individual. However, influence can also be (2) *indirect,* when one individual influences the development of another person's values, attitudes or behaviors other than the specific behavior of interest, including the formation of interpersonal ties, which in turn determine the behavior of interest; and (3) *contingent,* when one source of influence modifies a person's susceptibility to the influence of another. Indirect and contingent effects can take place with respect to each basic learning process, whether modeling or defining. The direct effects of interpersonal influences are those most often discussed in the socialization literature.

A test of these two hypotheses was carried out with respect to alcohol and marijuana use.[55] We examined the effects of the significant others' self-reported drug use and drug-use attitudes on the focal adolescent's own use of that same drug. The test for peers could be carried out with more precision than for parents, since the drug behaviors and drug related attitudes were the same as those of the focal respondent, either alcohol or marijuana. Modeling of parental drug behavior was indexed by the consumption of distilled spirits since very few parents had used marijuana. The uses of alcohol and of marijuana were examined at two different phases of involvement: initiation in a longitudinal sample, and on-going use in a cross-sectional sample.

The basic socialization processes are found to vary depending upon the source of influence, the specific drug, and the phases of behavior engaged in by the adolescent. While modeling of peers appears both for alcohol and for marijuana, although it is more important for marijuana, modeling of parents appears only for alcohol. However, parents play a stronger role as role models in the initiation phase of involvement in alcohol as compared to later phases, while the reverse is true for peers both for alcohol and for marijuana. With respect to peer influences, modeling is consistently stronger than defining for frequency of alcohol and marijuana use; defining is more important than modeling for initiation to marijuana. The ratio of the total effects of imitation to social reinforcement for adolescent frequency of alcohol use is 14 for parents (.14 versus .01) and 5 for best friends (.29 versus −.06); for frequency of marijuana use the ratio is .18 (.04 versus .22) for parents and 1.82 (.51 versus .28) for best friends (see Table 4). Not only does modeling of peers and parents by adolescents have differential importance at different phases of drug behavior, modeling also exerts itself differently at the different phases. At initiation of a drug, to the extent that modeling effects occur, they are direct. On the ongoing drug behavior, as indexed by frequency of use, parental behaviors have mainly indirect effects either through their influence on the choice of friends made by their children or through the children's explicit awareness of the parental behaviors. By contrast, direct imitation of peers occurs over and beyond the indirect effects of friends' behaviors, especially for marijuana. The indirect effects are channeled through the perceptions of friends' behaviors and through the influence of these perceptions on the adolescent's attitudes.

Tests for the presence of contingent effects, in which interaction terms of parental closeness with parental self-reported behaviors and adolescent perception of parental behaviors were entered in the equations, were consistently negative.

Table 4

Modeling versus Defining: Decomposition of Parental and Peer Effects

on Adolescent Drug Behaviors[a]

Effects on:	Total Effect	Direct Effect
Frequency of Alcohol Use:		
Parental effects		
Attitude	-.01	.03
Alcohol use	.14*	-.01
Best Friend's effects		
Attitude	-.06	.02
Alcohol use	.29*	.10*
Initiation into Alcohol Use:		
Parental effects		
Attitude	-.13*	-.10
Alcohol use	.15*	.12*
Best Friend's effects		
Attitude	-.07	-.06
Alcohol use	.09	.06
Frequency of Marijuana Use:		
Parental effects		
Attitude	-.22*	-.09*
Alcohol use	.04	-.04
Best Friend's effects		
Attitude	-.28*	.06*
Alcohol use	.51*	.31*
Initiation into Marijuana Use:		
Parental effects		
Attitude	-.06	-.02
Alcohol use	.08	.11
Best Friend's effects		
Attitude	-.17*	-.15*
Alcohol use	.02	.07

[a]Other variables are included in the model.

*$p < .05$.

No significance tests are available for indirect effects that include effects through all endogenous variables assumed to be causally posterior.

Thus, adolescents' imitation of parents and peers occurs in a different manner at different phases of the use of a particular drug. Early in the process of initiation to alcohol, modeling of parental behaviors occurs when adolescents have an explicit awareness of parental drinking. Subsequently, once the drug behavior is established, parental modeling occurs in the absence of any explicit recognition of parental behaviors by their children. Modeling of peer behaviors in on-going situations is more likely to be based on the adolescents' explicit awareness of their friends' behaviors, as was observed for the use of alcohol and of marijuana. Similarly, on the basis of adolescents' perceived characteristics of their parents and peers in a small sample of adolescents (N = 149), Biddle, Bank and Marlin[56] concluded that with respect to adolescent drinking peers were influentials as role models and parents as definers of standards.

The role of the family as mediating between adolescents' drug use and involvement in drug-prone peer groups has been noted by Brook, Whiteman and Gordon.[2]

BOYS AND GIRLS

Adolescent friendships and peer influences have been discussed without any differentiation as to the adolescent's sex. There are similarities as well as differences in adolescent friendships between boys and girls. The trends observed are briefly summarized, although no supporting data are presented. General processes underlying the formation and dissolution of friendships and factors underlying interpersonal attraction are very similar for both sexes. Differences appear, however, in the relative influence of parents and peers. Girls appear to be more generally receptive than boys to interpersonal influences, whether those of parents or of friends, and within this general trend to be influenced more by their peers than by their parents. This was observed both as regards involvement in drug use[55,57] and the formation of educational aspirations.[36] The greater susceptibility of girls than boys to interpersonal influences is consonant with results reported by others and the observation that girls tend to form a greater number of friendships and more intimate ties than boys.[27,58-63]

CONCLUSION

The findings reviewed here provide only a modest beginning understanding of the role of friendships in adolescent drug use and adolescent development more generally. Longitudinal sociometric data provide insights into processes underlying the formation and dissolution of friendships and the nature of peer influences that are not available from cross-sectional data.

Adolescents coordinate their choice of friends and their behaviors and attitudes, in particular the use of marijuana, to maximize congruency within the friendship dyad. If there is a state of unbalance, such that the friend's attitude or behavior is incongruent with the adolescent's, the adolescent will either break off the friendship and seek another friend or will keep the friend and modify his or her own behavior and attitude.

Prior similarity (or homophily) on a variety of behaviors and attitudes is a determinant of interpersonal attraction as documented by the finding that friendships in process of formation are more similar than friendships that will dissolve. Similarity increases further as the result of sustained association. Thus, similarity between friends at one point in time results from two complementary processes, selection and socialization, whereby adolescents who share certain prior attributes tend to associate with each other and subsequently tend to influence each other as the result of continued association.

The finding that selection and socialization are approximately equal in importance has important implications for much of the published literature on the degree of influence on adolescent drug involvement attributed to peers. The present results lead to the conclusion that these estimates of peer influence are inflated, since they fail to take into account the role of prior similarity in friendship formation and the element of attribution contained in perceptual reports of friends' characteristics.

Clearly both parents and peers can have strong influences on adolescents, the degree of influence depending upon the arena of interest. Peer influences predominate on current lifestyles, while parental influences are especially strong with respect to basic values and future life goals and aspirations (see also [64-65]). To the extent that interpersonal influences of peers operate, they are more likely to be the result of modeling than of social reinforcement, while parental influences derive in part from the role of parents in setting standards and promulgating values for behaviors. Furthermore, parents and peers are not necessarily antagonistic to each other. As documented in an earlier study, there can be continuity of values across the generations, and parents and their adolescent children can maintain close relationships with one another.[15,43] A high proportion of adolescents in this sample report feeling extremely or very close to their mothers (62%) and their fathers (51%). Exclusive theories of interpersonal attachment in adolescence that stress attachment either to peers or to parents are too simplistic. Our task is to specify the domains of life and the conditions under which one type of influence predominates over the other.

The adolescent's susceptibility to various sources of interpersonal influence varies at different stages of drug involvement; and the processes through which the influence is exerted varies for different drugs and at different phases of involvement in a particular drug. To the extent that parents have an influence as definers and modelers, that influence is strongest at the early stage of drug involvement, preceding initiation. The most clear-cut instance of such a modeling effect is the impact of parental alcohol use and attitudes about alcohol on adolescent initiation into alcohol. Once drugs have been experimented with, however, parental influence exerts itself mostly indirectly through the choice of friends by the adolescent; direct effects on the children's behaviors are weak. Once the use of either alcohol or marijuana has begun, imitation of peers is the dominant mode of social influence. Neither for alcohol nor marijuana are parents successful in influencing their children's drug behavior through influencing the children's attitudes toward the harmfulness of these drugs. The effects of peer attitudes and behaviors, like parental ones, are mostly direct or mediated by other peer variables but not through their impact on the adolescent's attitude.

These differences in processes of socialization observed between peers and parents, especially as they characterize initiation into drugs versus ongoing drug use, may be accounted for in part by a fundamental difference in the nature of adolescent interpersonal ties with each group. Parental relationships are predetermined, although there are variations in the quality of the effective tie that unite parents and children. Friendships, on the other hand, result from deliberate choices. It seems plausible that peers come to exert a stronger influence once the adolescent is committed to a course of action and can select to associate with peers who will reinforce his norms and behaviors.

These insights provide a very modest understanding of the process of peer influences and of the role and nature of friendships in adolescence. The limitations of this understanding are many. No attention has been paid to individual factors, such as stage of cognitive or personality development, that may influence the type of developing interpersonal interactions.[23,27,60] Although balance[66] and social exchange[67,68] theories provide the most popular explanatory frameworks for conceptualizing interpersonal relations, our understanding of the rewards and costs that underlie adolescents' choice of friends is primitive. Yet, progress can only be made if more sophisticated accounting schemes, which specify the kinds of needs, interests and power that individuals have in and toward each other and how these elements affect dynamically the nature of interpersonal exchanges, are developed and tested.[30,69] Furthermore, dyadic involvements represent but a limited aspect of peer influences. The adolescents' relationships to their larger and more complex peer networks must also be examined.

Many additional issues relevant to our understanding of adolescent friendships and peer influences on adolescent drug involvement are unresolved. I would like to speculate about one issue in particular.

The question is why do peer groups come to have the prominence that they have in adolescence? The answer, I would suggest, is found in the conjunction of two conditions, structural societal factors and biological factors. One condition is the segregation of young people in schools, social structures that are completely age stratified and homogenous.[18] This setting provides a restricted age range of like-aged persons from whom young people can choose their friends, creates structural constraints on the types of interpersonal choices that young people can make, and leads to the absence of ties with other persons of different ages in society.[18,70-71] As stressed by Coleman,[18] these structural characteristics come to affect the way young people behave: their increasing reliance and psychic attachment to one another and their increasing drive for autonomy from adults.

The second condition that favors the emergence of reliance on peer groups is the experience of puberty, the same biological event within a relatively narrow age range.[72] Interpolating from Schachter's[73] work on affiliation and anxiety and Festinger's[74] theory of social comparison, Petersen[72] has suggested that the appearance of extensive physiological changes coupled with uncertainty about how to handle these changes intensify adolescents' need for affiliation. Schachter's experimental studies suggest that anxiety would intensify the need of adolescents to associate with other young people who experience the same biological changes. Furthermore, adolescents would also prefer to associate with other adolescents in order to determine appropriate standards and frames of reference against which to compare themselves.

Our understanding of the role of peers in adolescent drug involvement will be enhanced by models that incorporate structural, biological and personality factors within a developmental framework.

REFERENCES

1. Brook JS, Lukoff IF, Whiteman M. Initiation into adolescent marihuana use. J Genetic Psychol. 1980; 137:133-42.

2. Brook JS, Whiteman M, Gordon AS. Qualitative and Quantitative Aspects of Adolescent Drug Use: The Interplay of Personality, Family, and Peer Correlates. Psychol Reports 1982; 51:1151-63.

3. Brook JS, Whiteman M, Brook, DW, Gordon, AS. Paternal and Peer Characteristics: Interactions and Association with Male College Students' Marijuana Use. Psychol Reports 1982; 51:1319-30.

4. Glynn TJ. From family to peer: Transition of influence among drug using youth. J Youth Adolescence 1981; 10:363-83.

5. Huba G, Bentler PM. The role of peer and adult models for drug taking at different stages in adolescence. J Youth Adolescence 1980; 9:449-65.

6. Jessor R, Jessor SL. Problem Behavior and Psychosocial Development: A Longitudinal Study of Youth. New York: Academic Press, 1977.

7. Johnson BD. Marihuana Users and Drug Subcultures. New York: Wiley, 1973.

8. Kandel DB. Adolescent marihuana use: Role of parents and peers. Science 1973; 181:1067-70.

9. Kandel DB. Inter- and intra-generational influences on adolescent marihuana use. In V. Bengston and R. Laufer, eds., Special Issue on Generations and Social Change. J Social Issues 1974; 50:107-35.

10. Kandel D, Kessler R, Margulies R. Adolescent initiation into stages of drug use: A developmental analysis. In Kandel D, ed., Longitudinal Research on Drug Use: Empirical Findings and Methodological Issues. Washington, D.C.: Hemisphere-Wiley, 1978:73-100.

11. Kandel D, Kessler R, Margulies R. Antecedents of adolescent initiation into stages of drug use: A developmental analysis. J Youth Adolescence 1978; 7:13-40.

12. Kandel DB, Margulies RS, Davies M. Analytical strategies for studying transitions into developmental stages. Sociology of Education 1978; 51:162-76.

13. Bronfenbrenner U. Reaction to social pressure from adults versus peers among Soviet day school and boarding school pupils in the perspective of an American sample. J Personality Social Psychol. 1970; 15:179-189.

14. Hartup WW. The social worlds of childhood. Amer Psychol. 1979; 34:944-50.

15. Kandel DB, Lesser GS. Youth in Two Worlds. San Francisco: Jossey-Bass, 1972.

16. Mead M. Culture and Commitment. New York: Natural History Press-Doubleday, 1970.

17. Coleman JS. Interpretations of adolescent culture. In Zubin J, Freedman AM, eds. The Psychopathology of adolescence. New York: Grune and Stratton, 1970:20-29.

18. Coleman JS. Youth: Transition to Adulthood. A report of the panel on youth of the President's Science Advisory Committee. Washington, D.C.: U.S. Government Printing Office, 1973.

19. Blyth DA, Hill JP, Thiel KS. Early adolescents' significant others: grade and gender differences in perceived relationships with familial and non-familial adults and young people. J Youth Adol 1982; 11:425-50.

20. Huba GJ, Wingard JA, Bentler PM. Longitudinal analyses of the role of peer support, adult models, and peer subcultures in beginning adolescent substance use: an applica-

tion of setwise canonical correlation methods. Multivariate Behav Research 1974; 15:259-80.

21. Berndt TJ. Developmental changes in conformity to peers and parents. Developmental Psychol. 1979; 15:608-16.

22. Brittain CV. Adolescent choices and parent-peer cross-pressures. Amer Sociol Rev. 1963; 28:385-91.

23. Youniss J. Parents and Peers in Social Development. Chicago: University of Chicago Press, 1980.

24. Newcomb T. The Acquaintance Process. New York: Holt, Rinehart and Winston, 1961.

25. Hallinan MT. Structural effects on children's friendships and cliques. Social Psychol Qtrly. 1979; 42:43-54.

26. Hallinan MT, Tuma, NB. Classroom effects on change in children's friendships. Sociology of Education 1978; 51:270-82.

27. Epstein JL. Selection of friends in differently organized schools and classrooms. In Epstein JL, Karweit N, eds. Friends in Schools. New York: Academic Press, 1983a:73-92.

28. Epstein JL. The influence of friends on achievement and affective outcomes. In Epstein JL, Karweit N, eds. Friends in Schools. New York: Academic Press, 1983b: 177-200.

29. Coleman JS. The adolescent society. New York: Free Press, 1961.

30. Taylor DG, Coleman JS. Equilibrating processes in social networks: A model for conceptualization and analysis. In Holland PW, Leinhardt S, eds. Perspectives on Social Network Research. New York: Academic Press, 1979: Chapter 14.

31. Waldorf F, Coleman J. Analysis and simulation of reference group processes. In Dutton JM, Starbuck WH, eds. Computer simulation of human behavior. New York: Wiley, 1971.

32. Cohen JM. Sources of peer group homogeneity. Sociology of Education 1977; 50:227-41.

33. Duck SW, Craig G. Personality similarity and the development of friendship: a longitudinal study. British J Sociol Clinical Psychol. 1978; 17:237-42.

34. Duck S, Allison D. I liked you but I can't live with you: a study of lapsed friendships. Social Behavior and Personality 1978; 6:43-7.

35. Curry J, Kenny DA. The effects of perceived and actual attraction. Quantity and Quality 1974; 8:27-44.

36. Davies M, Kandel DB. Parental and peer influences on adolescents' educational plans: some further evidence. Am J Sociol 1981; 87:363-87.

37. Jessop DJ. Topic variation in levels of agreement between parents and adolescents. Pub Opin Qtrly 1982; 46:538-59.

38. Kandel DB, Single E, Kessler R. The epidemiology of drug use among New York State high school students: distribution, trends and change in rates of use. Am J Pub Health 1976; 66:43-53.

39. Kandel DB. Homophily, selection, and socialization in adolescent friendships. Am J Sociol 1978b; 84:427-436.

40. Otto LB, Haller AO. Evidence for a social psychological view of the status attainment process: four studies compared. Soc Forces 1979; 57:887-914.

41. Duncan OD, Haller AO, Portes A. Peer influences on aspirations: a reinterpretation. Am J Sociol 1968; 74:119-37.

42. Murstein B, ed. Theories of attraction and love. New York: Springer, 1971.

43. Kandel DB, Lesser GS, Roberts GC, Weiss R. Adolescents in two societies: peers, school, and family in the United States and Denmark. Final report submitted to the Office of Education, U.S. Dept. of Health, Education and Welfare, 1968.

44. Kandel DB. Similarity in real-life adolescent friendship pairs. J Person Social Psychol. 1978a; 36:306-12.

45. Verbrugge LM. The structure of adult friendships choices. Soc Forces 1977; 56:576-97.

46. Fischer CS. To dwell among friends: personal networks in town and city. Chicago: University of Chicago Press, 1982.

47. Kandel DB. Marijuana users in young adulthood. Archives Gen Psychiat 1984; 41:200-09.

48. Kandel DB, Lesser GS. Parental and peer influence on educational plans of adolescents. Am Sociol Rev 1969; 34:212-23.

49. Lucas WL, Grupp SE, Schmitt RL. Predicting who will turn on: a four-year follow-up. Int J Addict 1975; 10:305-26.

50. Kandel DB. On variations in adolescent subcultures. Youth and Society 1978; 9:373-384.

51. Akers RL, Krohn MD, Lanza-Kaduce L, Radosevich M. Social learning and deviant behavior: a specific test of a general theory. Am Sociol Rev 1979; 44:635-55.

52. Maccoby EE. The development of moral values and behavior in childhood. In Clausen JS, ed. Socialization and society. Boston: Little, Brown, 1968.

53. Bandura A, Walters RH. Social learning and personality development. New York: Holt, 1963.

54. Woelfel J, Haller AO. Significant others, the self-reflexive act and the attitude formation process. Am Sociol Rev 1971; 36:74-87.

55. Kandel DB, Andrews K. Processes of adolescent socialization by parents and by peers. Int J Addict 1984 (in press).

56. Biddle BJ, Bank BJ, Marlin MM. Parental and peer influence on adolescents. Soc Forces 1980; 58:1057-79.

57. Margulies R, Kessler RC, Kandel D. A longitudinal study of onset of drinking among high school students. Qtrly J Studies Alc 1977; 38:897-912.

58. Blyth DA, Hill JP, Thiel KS. Early adolescents' significant others: grade and gender differences in perceived relationships with familial and non-familial adults and young people. J Youth Adol 1982; 11:425-50.

59. Eder D, Hallinan MT. Sex differences in children's friendships. Am Sociol Rev 1978; 43:237-50.

60. Hansell S. Ego development and peer friendship networks. Sociology of Education 1981; 54:51-63.

61. Hartup WW. The peer system. In Mussen PH, Hetherington EM, eds. Carmichael's manual of child psychology 4th edition (Vol.4). New York: Wiley, 1983:1-282.

62. Kon I. Adolescent friendship: some unanswered questions for future research. In Duck S, Gilmour R, eds. Personal relationships Vol. 2. Developing personal relationships. New York: Academic Press, 1981:187-204.

63. Maccoby E, Jacklin C. The psychology of sex differences. Stanford: Stanford University Press, 1974.

64. Jennings MK, Niemi RG. The political character of adolescence: the influence of families & schools. Princeton: Princeton University Press, 1974.

65. Troll L, Bengston V. Generations in the family. In Burr WR, Hill R, Nye FI, Reiss IL, eds. Contemporary theories about the family, Vol. 1. New York: The Free Press, 1979:127-61.

66. Heider F. The psychology of interpersonal relations. New York: Wiley, 1958.

67. Emerson RM. Social exchange theory. In Inkeles A, Coleman J, Smelser N, eds. Ann Rev Sociol, Vol.2. Palo Alto: Annual Reviews, Inc., 1976.

68. Homans G. Social behavior: its elementary forms. New York: Harcourt Brace & World, 1961.

69. Coleman JS. Purposive action embedded in social networks. Presented at Conference on Social Networks, San Diego, California, 1983.

70. Feld SL. The focused organization of social ties. Am J Sociol 1981; 86:1015-35.

71. Karweit NL, Hansell S. School organization and friendship selection. In Epstein JL, Karweit N, eds. Friends in School. New York: Academic Press, 1983:29-38.

72. Petersen AC, Spiga R. Adolescence and stress. In Goldberger L, Breznitz S, eds.

Handbook of stress: theoretical and clinical aspects. New York: Free Press, 1982: Chapter 31.

73. Schachter S. The psychology of affiliation. Stanford: Stanford University Press, 1959.

74. Festinger LA. A theory of social comparison processes. Human Relations 1954; 7:117-40.

Father's Influence on His Daughter's Marijuana Use Viewed in a Mother and Peer Context

Judith S. Brook, EdD
Martin Whiteman, PhD
Ann Scovell Gordon, MA
David W. Brook, MD

ABSTRACT. A study of the fathers' impact on their daughters' marijuana use is presented viewed in the context of the mother and the daughters' peer group. Four hundred and three female college student volunteers and their fathers were administered closed-ended questionnaires which included a number of scales assessing various parental and peer characteristics. The results indicated that the domain (set) of paternal variables had a direct impact on daughters' marijuana use independent of the effects of the maternal domain. However, in the case of the peer group, the fathers' effects on daughters' marijuana use were not direct but were mediated through the peer domain. In addition, individual protective (nondrug-conducive) paternal variables served to mitigate the effects of certain maternal and peer risk (drug conducive) factors on the daughters' marijuana use. The findings underscore the importance of identifying those paternal factors that exert an influence on the daughters' marijuana use alone or in combination with other interpersonal (maternal, peer) factors.

Judith S. Brook, Ann Scovell Gordon and David W. Brook are with the Department of Psychiatry, Mount Sinai School of Medicine. Martin Whiteman is with the School of Social Work, Columbia University.

This investigation was supported in part by research grant DA 02390 and Research Scientist Development Award DA 00094 from the National Institute on Drug Abuse. The authors thank Drs. Dan Lettieri and Tom Glynn for their invaluable assistance and suggestions throughout the project. They are also grateful to Carolyn Nomura for her help.

Requests for reprints should be addressed to Dr. Judith Brook, Mount Sinai School of Medicine, 1 Gustave L. Levy Place, Annenberg 22-74, New York, N.Y. 10029.

INTRODUCTION

In the past decade, there has been a growing interest in the role the father plays in his children's development.[1-5] However, an emphasis on studying the father should not preclude the simultaneous examination of other important aspects of the child's life since the child is subject to many influences both inside and outside the family. In this study the focus is on the father's influence on his adolescent daughter's use of marijuana in the context of two other interpersonal influences, one intrafamilial (her relationship with her mother) and one extrafamilial (the daughter's peer group influences). In addition, a brief examination will be made of the "main effects" on marijuana use of individual father, mother, and peer factors.

In the present study, two aspects of the father's influence will be examined: his personality, including his drug behavior, and his relationship with his daughter. As regards the former, with few exceptions,[6-10] consideration has not been given to the influence of the father's personality characteristics on his offspring's marijuana use. Therefore, measures of paternal personality determinants that are known to be related to the child's adaptive behavior have been included. Theory and research findings suggest that the paternal personality attributes which facilitate the good psychological functioning and adaptive behavior of adolescents include conventionality, a healthy psychological adjustment, and the extent to which the father has control over his impulses.[11,12] In addition, in recent years Ainsworth and her colleagues,[13-15] in their elaboration of ethological attachment theory, have indicated the importance of examining the personality dimension of sensitivity. Therefore aspects of paternal sensitivity and how this affects the child's behavior will be briefly examined. Finally, the father's drug behavior affects the youngster, presumably through imitation. Imitation refers to the specific modeling of the father's drug behavior by the child, in accordance with social learning theory.[16]

Two processes involved in father-child relations will be explored: identification and positive and negative reinforcement (i.e., the father's socialization techniques). Our concept and measure of identification derive from cognitive developmental theory as stated by Hoffman,[17] and refer to the extent to which the youngster consciously emulates, admires, and perceives that he/she is similar to the father. As regards positive and negative reinforcement, our emphasis is on the affective and control dimensions of such techniques as delineated in research by Schaefer,[18] who has shown that these two dimensions comprehensively describe parental behavior towards adolescents. It is widely held that a nurturant parent-child relationship is basic to the development of adaptive behavior.[11] In our own past research, the findings indicated that fathers of marijuana nonusers were more likely to have established affectionate and child-centered relationships with their children.[10] Evidence that closeness to fathers is inversely related to marijuana use is provided by Kandel, Kessler, and Margulies.[9] Our interest in the control dimension has been fostered by studies of family interaction patterns which accompany adolescent psychopathology.[12] Adolescents who demonstrate behavior problems such as school failure, delinquency, disruption of ties with parents, and self-destructive behavior are often found to have parents with aberrant control styles. In sum, the various paternal dimensions outlined above will be examined in relation to the daughters' marijuana use both as "main effects" and in the context of maternal and peer influences.

As regards the maternal context, theories and research have long focused on the myriad ways in which maternal behavior affects children.[4,12] In this study the role of the father in relationship to two aspects of the mother-child relationship, the mother's socialization practices and the extent to which she serves as a role model (identification), will be studied. In recent years the ways in which mother-child relationships affect the drug use of children have been increasingly investigated. Less maternal warmth, less child centeredness, and lack of the child's identification with the mother have all been found to be related to greater drug use by the youngster.[19-21] All these maternal dimensions will be included in the present study both as "main effects" and as the contextual setting for further study of the father's role.

In studying the role of the father in the context of the mother's influences, one of our methodological approaches will be to examine the relative impact of sets (i.e., domains) of father and mother variables on the daughter's marijuana use. Based on previous research,[7] three models are hypothesized for explaining the interrelationship of paternal and maternal factors. In the case of an *interdependent* model each domain would be statistically significant without control of the other but each would lose significance with control indicating that certain paternal and maternal factors from both domains coexist in their impact on marijuana use. If a *mediational* model were operative, one of the domains would be prepotent to the other and mediate the relation of the other domain to the daughter's drug use. For example, if the mother domain were the mediator, it would be associated with adolescent marijuana use despite control on the father domain. However, the father domain would not be associated with the daughter's drug use when mother factors were controlled for. Thus father factors would be associated with mother factors which in turn would be associated with the youngsters' use of drugs. If an *independent* model were operative, both father and mother domains would have a direct impact on marijuana use, with and without control. Based on work done with fathers, mothers, and sons, it is expected that the father will have a direct impact on the daughter's drug use, independent of the mother-daughter relationship.[7]

In addition to studying the interrelationship of domains, examination will also be made of the *combined influences* of specific individual father and mother attributes. Two combinational types are of interest, both of which would reduce the likelihood of the daughter's marijuana use. In the first, attention will be focused on those positive aspects of the father that serve to ameliorate maternal risk factors in the adolescent (e.g., a distant mother-daughter bond). The second type of combination involves the degree to which positive father factors enhance protective maternal factors (e.g., an affectionate mother-daughter relationship). It should be noted that risk factors are defined as those variables that have been found in past research (our own, as well as others') to be related to adolescent drug use or maladjustment, and protective factors are those that have been found to be correlated with no (or little) drug use or good adjustment.[2,20]

The father's role in his daughter's marijuana use will also be viewed in the context of peer group influences. Numerous studies have been done on the crucial role that peer group processes play in the development of adolescent drug use.[20,22,23] Among the most significant peer influences are the peers' own use of illicit drugs, their engagement in deviant behavior, and their lack of achievement motivation. While it is important to include and evaluate these peer dimensions in their direct impact on the daughter's drug use, the present research is primarily concerned with studying fathers in the context of such peer influences.

Students of adolescence have noted that during this stage of the life cycle youngsters become less attached to their parents and more attached to peers. This change in orientation may occur during adolescence as a result of the dramatic changes during that time in the biological, psychological, and social spheres of the youngster (see, e.g., Jersild, Brook, and Brook,[12] Adelson[24] Coleman[25]). As Jersild, Brook, and Brook[12] indicated, it is during adolescence that youngsters seek independence for themselves emotionally, behaviorally, and in terms of their value system. While there is some disagreement as to whether parental influence decreases during adolescence,[26,27] there is widespread acceptance that peer influence increases.[26-28] There is also disagreement as regards the relative influence of parents versus peers during adolescence. An aim of the present research is to clarify this issue to some extent, since the influence of one of the parents (the father) relative to the influence of the peer group in its impact on the daughter's marijuana use will be studied.

It is also of interest to examine whether the father's personality and the father-child relationship help to shape the adolescent's integration into the peer group. According to a recent article by Hartup,[29] researchers have neglected to ask whether a developmental continuity exists between the social styles shown by adolescents in interaction with their parents and those used at a later point in time in interaction with peers. As noted by Lamb,[1] some investigators have assumed that because the father-child and peer-child systems are separate and distinct, and include diverse styles of interaction with very different effects on development, they should be considered as totally insulated from each other. However, Brook, Whiteman, Brook, and Gordon[6] found that the father's personality and the father-son relationship did have an impact on the youngster's relations with peers. This finding is significant since it demonstrates that father-son relations have an impact on the youngster's behavior not only within the context of the family, but also in extrafamilial situations.

Using the models approach described above, the interrelation of father and peer domains with respect to the daughter's marijuana use will be examined. In a previous study,[6] this approach was used to explore the relative influence of fathers and peers on marijuana use in sons. The findings indicated that the domains of father personality and father-son relationship variables were associated with a domain of peer factors which in turn was associated with the sons' use of marijuana (the mediational model). More specifically, the results suggested that boys whose fathers used drugs tended to select peers who also used drugs. In addition, the findings indicated that lack of a general emotional identification with the father was associated with a peer rather than a parent orientation. The present study is an attempt to extend the generality of these findings by examining fathers and daughters.

As with father/mother influences, the combined effects of specific individual father and peer factors on the daughter's marijuana use will also be studied. Again, it is expected that positive paternal factors will either ameliorate peer risk factors (e.g., peer drug use) or further strengthen the protective effects of positive peer dimensions (e.g., nondeviant friends).

The objectives of this study are therefore: (a) to examine the "main effects" on female adolescent marijuana use of three types of interpersonal influences—paternal, maternal, and peer factors; (b) to assess the relative impact of father influences in the context of the mother and the peer by using the "models" approach; and (c) to investigate how specific father factors combine with specific maternal and peer dimensions to lessen the risk of the daughter's marijuana use. Comparisons will also be made between the present study of fathers and daughters and our earlier studies of fathers and sons.[6,7,10]

METHODOLOGY

Sample

The sample consisted of 403 female college student volunteers and their fathers who also volunteered to participate in the study. The students were white, mainly middle class, and were recruited from all classes at a large state college in New Jersey. The students came from intact homes. The mean age of the student sample was 21.

Procedure

Student volunteers were obtained through posters distributed about the campus describing the nature of the study. In addition, a sign-up desk was placed near the student cafeteria where the students could find out more about the study and volunteer if they wished to do so. Each student and her father who volunteered to participate were given separate questionnaires to fill out in the privacy of their home. They were instructed to fill out the questionnaires alone and return them to us in sealed envelopes. Each father-daughter pair received

$10.00 for participating. The questionnaires were filled out anonymously. Identification numbers were used to match father and daughter questionnaires.

Measures

The questionnaires each contained approximately 200 closed-ended items assessing various personality and relationship dimensions, as well as drug use (self, peer, and family members). These items (except for drug use) were grouped into scales on the basis of item intercorrelations and reliabilities. For the most part, the scales were adaptations of existing scales with adequate psychometric properties. Delineated below is each scale and its source, grouped into the three domains of relevance for this study: paternal, maternal, and peer. Reliabilities (Cronbach alphas) for each scale appear in Table 1.

Domain of paternal personality and paternal relationship variables. The scales within the personality sphere were Attitude to Deviance,[30] Attitude to Marijuana Use,[31] Attitude to Tobacco Use,[31] Extraversion,[32,33] Object Relations,[34] Obsessiveness,[35*] Femininity,[36*] and Religion (one item assessing frequency of attendance at religious services). The scales used to measure the father-daughter relationship include: Child Centeredness, Possessiveness, and Communications,[18] Support,[37] Time Spent with Daughter (Original), Daughter's Resistance to Paternal Control,[38] Parental Authority,[39] three measures of Paternal Identification (Original), i.e., Admiration, Emulation, and Perceived Similarity, and three separate items, educational expectations for the daughter, attitude toward the daughter's cigarette smoking, and attitude toward the daughter's use of marijuana. With the exception of the three identification measures, all scales were based on the father's actual report.

Domain of maternal variables. Included in this domain were Child-Centeredness, Affection, and Extreme Autonomy,[18] Use of Power-Assertive Discipline,[37] Time Spent with the Daughter (Original), Admiration of, Emulation of, and Perceived Similarity to the Mother (Original). All the maternal scales were based on the daughter's perception.

---

*Obsessiveness and Femininity are being used, in part, as indicators of paternal sensitivity in that nonobsessiveness and an orientation toward femininity (expressiveness) appear to tap (or are related to) the parents' tendency to respond appropriately and promptly to the needs of their youngsters.

172   *ALCOHOL AND SUBSTANCE ABUSE IN ADOLESCENCE*

Table 1

Father, Mother, and Peer Measures: Their
Cronbach Alphas and Correlation
with Daughters' Marijuana Use

Variable	Alpha	$\underline{r}$ with Daughters' Marijuana Use	N[a]
I. Father Set			
A. Personality			
Tolerance of deviance (more)	.67(7)[b]	.19***	389
Object relations (poor)	.53(7)	.02	390
Extraversion (more)	.60(9)	.09*	390
Obsessiveness (more)	.71(4)	.02	389
Tolerance of tobacco use (more)	.65(3)	.11*	381
Tolerance of marijuana use (more)	.60(3)	.09*	365
Femininity (less)	.76(10)	.08	386
Religiosity (less)	--	.18***	388
Marijuana use (more)	--	.11*	387
Prescribed amphetamine/barbiturate use (more)	--	.04	386
Nonprescribed tranquilizer use	--	.00	387
Prescribed tranquilizer use (more)	--	.05	387
B. Father-Daughter Relations			
Child centeredness (less)	.74(5)	.10*	386
Communications (less)	.70(5)	.09*	387
Possessiveness	.44(4)	.01	388
Support (less)	.53(3)	.03	383
Parental authority (more)	.69(4)	.03	387
Resistance to paternal control (more)	.89(5)	.24***	386
Time spent with daughter (less)	.80(3)	.10*	381
Admiration of father (less)	.81(5)	.17***	388
Emulation of father (less)	.80(5)	.21***	388
Similarity to father (less)	.77(4)	.19***	389
Educational expectations for daughter (lower)	--	.10*	387
Tolerance of daughter's cigarette use (more)	--	.22***	388
Tolerance of daughter's marijuana use (more)	--	.14**	387

(Table continues on next page)

(Table 1 continued)

Variable	Alpha	r with Daughters' Marijuana Use	N
II. Mother Set			
Child centeredness (less)	.83(5)	.09*	386
Affection (less)	.79(4)	.04	389
Extreme autonomy (less)	.72(4)	.04	389
Power-assertive discipline (more)	.73(5)	.18***	388
Time spent with daughter (less)	.67(3)	.17***	378
Admiration of mother (less)	.79(5)	.22***	388
Emulation of mother (less)	.78(5)	.20***	388
Similarity to mother (less)	.75(4)	.20***	389
III. Peer Set			
Parent vs peer orientation (peer oriented)	.51(2)	.26***	385
Susceptibility to peers	.40(4)	.00	390
Number of deviant friends (more)	.71(5)	.34***	386
Number of achieving friends (fewer)	.39(3)	.20***	385
Number of drinking friends (more)	--	.38***	390
Number of smoking friends (more)	--	.30***	389
Number of marijuana using friends (more)	--	.59***	389
Number of other illicit drug using friends (more)	--	.65***	387

a N varies because of missing data.
b Number in parentheses refers to items in the scale.
*p <.05
**p <.01
***p <.001

Domain of peer variables. Included here were Peer Deviance,[40] Orientation to Parents as Opposed to Peers, Susceptibility to Peer Influences, and Number of Achievement-Oriented Friends (latter three original). All peer scales were based on the daughter's assessment.

With respect to drug use, fathers and daughters reported on their own self use of legal and illegal drugs. Peer drug use was based on the daughter's perception of friend use.* The distributions for father, perceived peer, and daughter's drug use can be found in Table 2. Frequency of daughter's marijuana use was the dependent variable.

RESULTS

Main Effects

Pearson correlations were obtained for the paternal, maternal, and peer variables with the daughter's marijuana use. (See Table 1) As shown in Table 1, fathers of marijuana users were less conventional, had poor father-daughter relations, and were less likely to have daughters who identified with them. Female marijuana users were less likely to identify with their mothers, spent less time with them, and had mothers who used power-assertive techniques of discipline. With regard to peer factors, the highest correlations with the daughter's marijuana use were for perceived peer deviance and perceived peer drug use.

Relative Impact of Father and Mother Domains (the "Models" Analysis)

Two regressions were run to examine the father and mother domains and their relative impact on the daughter's marijuana use. First, the set of father factors was examined with control on the set of mother factors and then the set of mother factors was examined with control on the set of father factors. As shown in Table 3, the father (as well as the mother) domain was significant without and with control (the independent model). Thus, father factors were not mediated by mother factors but had an impact on the daughter's drug use independent of the mother's influence.

Combination of Father/Mother Factors (the Interactive Analysis)

In order to examine the combined effects on marijuana use of individual paternal and maternal variables, two-way analyses of variance were performed. In each ANOVA, the two factors were one

---

*Please note that while data were obtained on maternal drug use (as perceived by the father), this study includes only mother-daughter relationships. Therefore the mothers' drug use was not included.

Table 2

Distributions for Paternal, Peer,
and Daughters' Drug Use

Drug Use Variable	N^a	%
Paternal Drug Use (Self-Report)		
Prescribed amphetamine/barbiturate use		
Never used	326	81
A few times a year or less	64	16
About once a month	3	1
Several times a month	3	1
Once a week or more	3	1
Prescribed tranquilizer use		
Never used	305	76
A few times a year or less	69	17
About once a month	9	2
Several times a month	8	2
Once a week or more	9	2
Nonprescribed tranquilizer use		
Never used	389	97
A few times a year or less	5	1
About once a month	4	1
Several times a month	1	-
Once a week or more	1	-
Marijuana use		
Never used	361	91
A few times a year or less	35	9
About once a month	0	-
Several times a month	0	-
Once a week or more	4	1
Peer Drug Use (Perceived by Daughter)		
Smoking (on a daily basis)		
No friends	48	12
Only a few friends	144	36
Some friends	133	33
Most friends	77	19

(Table continued on next page)

(Table 2 continued)

Drug Use Variable	N	%
Drinking alcoholic beverages (at least once a week)		
No friends	15	4
Only a few friends	48	12
Some friends	62	15
Most friends	278	69
Marijuana use (at least once a month)		
No friends	106	26
Only a few friends	124	31
Some friends	79	20
Most friends	94	23
Other illicit drug use[b] (ever used)		
No friends	132	33
Only a few friends	139	35
Some friends	69	17
Most friends	60	15
Daughter's Marijuana Use (Self-Report)		
Never used	117	30
A few times a year or less	159	40
Once a month	26	6
Several times a month	43	11
Once a week	15	4
Several times a week or more	36	9

Note. There is additional drug information for fathers and daughters (e.g., their legal drug use). This table presents only those father drug variables that were directly or indirectly related to the daughter's marijuana use. As regards the daughter, only her marijuana use is examined in this paper.
[a]Ns vary because of missing data.
[b]This included the following drugs for nonmedical purposes: amphetamines, barbiturates, cocaine, heroin, LSD or other psychedelics, quaaludes, tranquilizers, and the like.

father and one mother variable, each dichotomized into a high and low group. The dependent variable was the continuous measure of the daughter's frequency of marijuana use. Each father variable was examined in combination with each mother variable. Simple effects analyses were done for the significant interactions. (In order to make certain that the number of significant interactions was not simply a chance phenomenon, first the total number of potential father-mother interactions was calculated [25 father variables x 8 mother variables = 200]. Assuming that four types of interactions are possible [father protective x adolescent protective; father protective x adolescent risk; father risk x adolescent protective; father risk x adolescent risk], one would expect 50 [200/4] interactions of each type to occur. At the .05 level of significance, one would expect 5% [2.5 out of 50] of each type of interaction to be significant.)

As discussed in the introduction, positive father variables were expected to either mitigate maternal risk factors of drug use or serve as protective factors which further enhance maternal protective fac-

Table 3

Multiple Correlations (Rs) Between Paternal and Maternal
Domains and Between Paternal and Peer Domains
and Daughters' Marijuana Use

Domain	R for Domain; No Control on Other Domain			R for Domain; Control on Other Domain		
	R	F	df	R	F	df
Paternal and Maternal Domains						
A. Paternal	.47	3.22**	25,286	.44	2.67**	25,278
B. Maternal	.31	4.09**	8,303	.26	2.83**	8,278
A + B	.54	3.40**	33,278	--	--	
Paternal and Peer Domains						
C. Paternal	.47	3.22**	25,286	.20	1.00	25,278
D. Peer	.68	32.29**	8,303	.53	17.63**	8,278
C + D	.71	8.48**	33,278	--	--	

Note. Variables within the domains are presented in Table 1.

**p < .01

tors. The results are presented in Table 4. As shown in the table, there were several interactions in which positive father factors mitigated maternal risk factors. As a whole, mother risk factors (lack of child centeredness, use of power-assertive discipline, and not serving as a model for the daughter's emulation and admiration) were mitigated by paternal conventionality and a close father-daughter relationship. Findings regarding the second type of interaction (positive father factors which enhance positive maternal factors) are also presented in Table 4. As can be seen, positive maternal factors were enhanced by the father's nonuse of drugs, his psychological well-being, and time spent with his daughter. Results showed that 16% (8 out of 50) of the father protective x mother risk interactions were significant, this being greater than the expected figure of 5%. However, for father protective x mother protective interactions, 6% (3 out of 50) were significant, about the same as the expected 5%.

Relative Impact of Father and Peer Domains (the "Models" Analysis)

In order to determine the interrelation of father and peer domains and the daughter's marijuana use, two hierarchical multiple regression analyses were run. In one regression, the domain of paternal factors was entered last with control on the domain of peer factors. In the second regression, the peer domain was entered last, in order to partial out the effect of the father domain on the daughter's use of marijuana. The results are shown in Table 3. As can be seen, the father and peer domains were each significant without control on the other. However, while the peer set remained significant with control on the father set, the father set lost significance with control on the peer set. The findings regarding the father and peer domains therefore supported a mediational model: father attributes were associated with peer attributes which in turn were related to the daughter's marijuana use.

Having established the peer domain as the mediator between the father domain and the daughter's marijuana use, the next task was to determine how the variables in the father domain were related to the variables in the peer domain by using canonical correlation analysis. Two canonical correlations were significant. The first canonical correlation was .52 and explained 27% of the variance. Pearson correlations were obtained between the individual father domain variables and the first father canonical variate and the individual

Table 4

Significant Two-Way Interactions (Father Variables X Mother Variables X Daughter's Marijuana Use)

Mother Effect	Father Interactive Effect		F for Two-Way Interaction	df
	Less marijuana use Protective Condition	More marijuana use Augmented Risk Condition		
I. Risk Condition[a]				
Less child centeredness	Intolerance of tobacco use	Tolerance of tobacco use	5.19*	1,373
Less child centeredness	Less marijuana use	More marijuana use	8.15**	1,379
Less child centeredness	Intolerance of daughter's marijuana use	Tolerance of daughter's marijuana use	4.29**	1,379
Less child centeredness	Less parental authority	More parental authority	8.07**	1,379
More power-assertive discipline	More similarity to the father	Less similarity to the father	5.32*	1,383
More power-assertive discipline	Less nonprescribed tranquilizer use	More nonprescribed tranquilizer use	7.28**	1,381
Less admiration of mother	Nonresistance to paternal control	Resistance to paternal control	3.89*	1,380
Less emulation of mother	Intolerance of tobacco use	Tolerance of tobacco use	4.98*	1,375
	Protective Condition	Counter Protective Condition		
II. Protective Condition[b]				
More affection	More time spent with daughter	Less time spent with daughter	3.70*	1,376
Less power-assertive discipline	Less obsessiveness	More obsessiveness	4.87*	1,383
More time spent with daughter	Good object relations	Poor object relations	7.07**	1,374

Note. The mother and father variables were all significant ($p \leq .05$) as main effects in the ANOVAs with the exception of Paternal Authority, Paternal Tranquilizer Use, Paternal Object Relations, and Paternal Obsessiveness.

[a]For the interactions in Part I, daughters with mothers in the risk condition were less likely to use marijuana when their fathers were "protective" than when they were not. For example, in row one, simple effects test revealed that in the less mother child centeredness condition, the father's intolerance of tobacco use was associated with less daughter marijuana use whereas the father's tolerance of tobacco use was associated with more marijuana use by the daughter.

[b]For the interactions in Part II, daughters with "protective mothers were less likely to use marijuana when their fathers were protective than when they were counter protective.

*$p < .05$ **$p < .01$

179

peer domain variables and the first peer canonical variate using a procedure recommended by Levine.[41] The highest significant correlations between the father variables and the first father variate were father's control accepted by daughter (.69), father as model of emulation (.53), father-daughter similarity (.55), father as model of admiration (.47), paternal child centeredness (.47), father nonuse of marijuana (.35), father's intolerance of daughter's cigarette use (.33), and time spent with the daughter (.32). Peer variables associated with the first peer canonical variate were less friend other illicit drug and marijuana use, less friend smoking, and less friend drinking (.73, .71, .60, and .29 respectively); parental as opposed to peer orientation (.65), peer non-deviance (.28), more achievement-oriented friends (.27), and less susceptibility to peer influence (.24). Overall, these findings indicated that girls who identified with child-centered and non-marijuana using fathers and who accepted their fathers' control were less peer-oriented (relative to parent-oriented) and were less likely to have friends who used marijuana or were non-achievement oriented and deviant.

The second canonical variate (.41) explained 17% of the variance ($p < .01$). The father variables most highly associated with the second father canonical variate were father as model of emulation (.48), paternal support (.43), father as model of admiration (.39), similarity to the father (.38), intolerance of tobacco use (.27), prescribed use of amphetamines and barbiturates by the father (.26), and paternal tolerance of deviance (.26). The peer variables associated with the second peer canonical variate were parent relative to peer orientation (.50), more achievement-oriented friends (.37), more deviant friends (.36), more friends who use marijuana, tobacco, and other illicit drugs (.36, .35, and .21 respectively), and greater peer susceptibility (.24). Results of the second canonical analysis suggested that girls who identified with warm fathers, but whose fathers (in contrast to the first variate) were tolerant of deviance and used prescribed drugs, had friends who used drugs and were deviant.

Combination of Father/Peer Factors (the Interactive Analysis)

The combined effects on marijuana use of individual paternal and peer variables were examined in two-way analyses of variance and subsequent simple effects tests. In each ANOVA the two factors were one father and one peer variable each dichotomized into a high and low group. The dependent variable was the continuous measure of the daughter's frequency of marijuana use. Each father variable was examined in combination with each peer variable. All but two of the significant father-peer interactions were of the mitigating type in which positive father factors lessened the impact of peer risk factors. The results are presented in Table 5. Overall, the findings regarding the mitigating interactions indicated that adolescent peer risk factors (peer deviance, non-achievement orientation, and drug use) were offset by paternal conventionality, paternal identification, and paternal warmth. Thirty-eight percent (19 out of 50) of the father protective x peer risk interactions were significant, much greater than the expected 5%. For the two synergistic interactions, peer protective factors were enhanced by paternal support and his nonextraversion; however, only 2 out of 50 (4%) of the father protective x peer protective interactions were significant. Thus, it would appear that the number of protective synergistic interactions for both father-mother (reported earlier) and father-peer was no greater than what one would expect to obtain by chance.

DISCUSSION

Overall, the results of this study suggested that parental and peer influences were associated with the daughter's use of marijuana and that the father's role was of importance in both the maternal and peer contexts.

Paternal and Maternal Correlates of Daughters' Marijuana Use

Within the family area, parental personality attributes such as parental psychological well-being and conventionality and parental drug use have all been found in past research to be associated with the adolescent's drug use.[3,10,20,42-44] A second aspect of parental influence deals with parent-adolescent relations. Identification and social reinforcement, both rooted in psychoanalytic and social learning theory, have been shown to be of great importance.[1] In line with these findings, our results showed that fathers of marijuana users tended to be unconventional and to serve as models of drug use for their daughters' own drug use. There was also evidence that a close father-daughter relationship served as an influence on the daughter's nonuse of drugs. Further, in line with cognitive developmental theory,[17] the daughter's conscious identification with her father served to insulate her from drug use. The fact that positive reinforcement was associated with less drug use and excessive control was associated with more drug use is in keeping with social learning theories.[16,45] Results from earlier studies of the fathers' influence on sons' drug behavior[10,46] are also consistent with the present findings. As regards maternal correlates, female marijuana users were less likely to identify with their mothers and their mothers were more likely to use power-assertive techniques of discipline.

Paternal-Maternal Interrelationships and Interactions

The data relevant to the interrelationship of father and mother domains supported an independent model, with father factors remaining relatively independent of maternal factors in their effect on the daughter's marijuana use. In an earlier study of fathers and sons, Brook, Whiteman, Gordon, and Brook[7] reported similar findings, i.e., the father domain was not mediated through the domain of maternal variables but had a direct impact on the son's use of marijuana.

As regards the interaction of individual father and mother variables, certain protective father factors served to mitigate certain maternal risk factors. In general, it appeared that a weak mother-daughter attachment was offset by conventionality in the father and by a close father-daughter bond. At the same time father protective factors interacted synergistically with protective factors in the mother-daughter relationship resulting in less daughter marijuana use. For example, a close mother-daughter attachment was enhanced by the father's psychological well-being. Our findings relating to positive father-mother synergistic interactions need to be treated with far more caution than those dealing with the father as an ameliorator (mitigating) as there were more significant mitigating than synergistic interactions.

At the present time we need to ascertain whether these associations represent truly causal effects. In short, have the fathers and mothers through their influences actually affected the daughter's marijuana use or is it possible that youngsters who use drugs cause certain reactions or behaviors in their parents? This latter possibility demands serious consideration in that a number of studies have shown a bidirectional relationship between youngsters and their par-

Table 5

Significant Two-Way Interactions (Father Variables X
Peer Variables X Daughter's Marijuana Use)

Peer Effect	Father Interactive Effect		F for Two-Way Interaction	df
	Less marijuana use Protective Condition	More marijuana use Augmented Risk Condition		
I. Risk Condition[a]				
More peer deviance	Intolerance of deviance	Tolerance of deviance	4.62*	1,381
More peer deviance	Intolerance of daughter's smoking	Tolerance of daughter's smoking	6.79***	1,380
Fewer achieving friends	Religiosity	Nonreligiosity	5.50*	1,379
Fewer achieving friends	More child centeredness	Less child centeredness	8.64***	1,378
Fewer achieving friends	Good communications	Poor communications	4.60*	1,378
Fewer achieving friends	More similarity to the father	Less similarity to the father	9.35**	1,380
Fewer achieving friends	More admiration of the father	Less admiration of the father	8.21**	1,379
Fewer achieving friends	More emulation of the father	Less emulation of the father	19.19****	1,379
Fewer achieving friends	More possessiveness	Less possessiveness	6.28**	1,379
More peer marijuana use	Less prescribed tranquilizer use	More prescribed tranquilizer use	13.76***	1,383
More peer marijuana use	More similarity to the father	Less similarity to the father	10.29***	1,385
More peer marijuana use	More admiration of the father	Less admiration of the father	5.72*	1,384
More peer marijuana use	More emulation of the father	Less emulation of the father	13.48***	1,384
More peer marijuana use	Religiosity	Nonreligiosity	5.23*	1,387
More peer other illicit drug use	More femininity (i.e., greater sensitivity)	Less femininity (i.e., lesser sensitivity)	3.86*	1,379
More peer other illicit drug use	Intolerance of daughter's smoking	Tolerance of daughter's smoking	4.42*	1,381
More peer other illicit drug use	More similarity to the father	Less similarity to the father	10.29****	1,385
More peer drinking	More similarity to the father	Less similarity to the father	6.69***	1,385
More peer smoking	Less prescribed tranquilizer use	More prescribed tranquilizer use	5.27*	1,382

(Table continues on next page)

183

(Table 5 continued)

II. Protective Condition[b]	Less marijuana use Protective Condition	More marijuana use Counter Protective Condition		
Parental as opposed to peer orientation	More support	Less support	5.04*	1,375
Less peer smoking	Less extraversion	More extraversion	3.74*	1,385

Note. The peer and father variables were all significant ($\underline{p} \leq .05$) as main effects in the ANOVAs with the exception of Father Communications, Father Support, Father Tranquilizer Use, Father Femininity.

[a]For the interactions in Part I, daughters with peer risk factors were less likely to use marijuana when their fathers were "protective" than when they were not. For example, in row one, simple effects tests revealed that in the risk condition (a deviant peer group), the father's intolerance of deviance was associated with less daughter marijuana use whereas the father's tolerance of deviance was associated with more marijuana use.

[b]For the interactions in Part II, daughters who were in the "protective" condition were less likely to use marijuana when their fathers were "protective" than when they were "counter protective."

*$\underline{p} < .05$ **$\underline{p} < .01$ ***$\underline{p} < .001$

ents.[1] However, in support of the causative effects of parent factors, it should be noted that in previous research[7,47-49] parents have been shown to have an influence on subsequent initiation into drug use by the adolescent.

Peer Correlates of Daughters' Marijuana Use

A second broad area of interpersonal influence involves the peer group. Interpersonal influences of peer drug use, peer deviance, and the youngster's closeness to the peer group have been found to have an impact on his/her use of drugs.[6,9,23] The great importance of the peer group has been summarized by Kandel.[47] With respect to peer factors in the present study, female marijuana users reported a greater peer relative to a parent orientation, and greater perceived drug use and deviance among their friends. These findings for the most part are in accord with social learning theory and the peer studies just cited.[6,9,19,22,23,50-52]

Paternal-Peer Interrelationships and Interactions

The results indicate that the domain of father factors interrelated with the peer domain in a different manner from its interrelation with the maternal domain as regards the daughter's marijuana use. With respect to father/peer domains, the findings supported a mediational model, whereas for father/mother domains there was an independent model. The different models obtained for the interrelation of father/peer and father/mother may be explained by the fact that the peer domain may be more proximal to the adolescent's drug use and therefore more potent than the maternal domain. As for the ways in which the peer domain serves as the mediator of the father domain, our findings indicated that certain father attributes were associated with the daughter's selection of a particular type of peer group, which in turn was associated with her use of marijuana. These findings are consistent with those from our father-son study[6] which also indicated that father factors are mediated through peer group factors.

The canonical correlations suggested two possible father-peer linkages. First, girls who had a strong bond with their fathers, who identified with paternal traits, and whose fathers did not use drugs and were child centered tended to be parent as opposed to peer oriented, less susceptible to peer influences, and to have friends who were more achievement oriented and less likely to use drugs. These data support the thesis that having secure attachments within the father-adolescent social system and having fathers who serve as models of non-drug use promote active relations with friends who are conventional and conform to middle-class values. As such, the findings are consistent with Winder and Rau,[53] who found that fathers of high-status sons (e.g., well liked by peers) were favorably oriented toward their sons' competencies, provided them with reinforcement of a positive nature, discouraged antisocial behavior, and avoided punishing their youngsters. Our results regarding father-daughter relations and susceptibility to peers are also in line with studies which suggest that youngsters who are alienated from their parents are more susceptible to pressure from peers.[54]

The second possible father-peer linkage suggested by our data is that girls who identified with supportive fathers, but who, in contrast to the above findings, had fathers who were tolerant of deviance and used drugs, tended to select friends who were deviant and used drugs. The implication of this finding is that whether a close father-daughter relationship limits drug use may need to be qualified by the father's general orientation toward deviance and his more specific use of drugs. Our results suggest that a strong father-daughter relationship in the context of greater father acceptance of deviance and greater use of drugs may lead to the selection of peer groups which are drug conducive for the daughter. It is clear from this study, therefore, that individual differences in paternal personality attributes and the patterning of father-daughter relations have implications for the way the adolescent selects friends. In general, these results are consistent with those of investigators who espouse single process theories in which social competence is thought to arise for the most part in relationships within the family with the contributions of peer relationships serving to elaborate and extend those of the family.[29]

While the correlational evidence obtained in the present study is consistent with traditional notions of the intersystem model (mediational) being formulated here, it is important to note that correlations merely establish statistical associations between the father-adolescent and peer-adolescent measures and therefore do not demonstrate cause-and-effect associations between them. Longitudinal studies are necessary if we are to learn the manner in which the father-daughter relation affects later peer relations. As noted by Lamb,[1] a direct or linear continuity over time probably does not exist. It may be that the child selects unconventional peers because of his early experiences. The peer group members then have an influence on the youngster which may then affect the father-daughter relation in continuing reciprocal fashion.

The individual father factors in combination with certain peer group factors also seemed to have a direct impact on the daughter's drug use. For example, the findings suggest that positive attributes of the father may ameliorate peer risk factors in the youngster. Such father ameliorators of peer risk factors (e.g., peer drug use) include his conventionality, a positive father-daughter relationship (e.g., the daughter's identification with him, and his warmth) and paternal sensitivity. Fathers appear to be more likely to serve as ameliorators of peer risk factors in the case of daughters than in the case of sons.[6] One interpretation of this finding is that the father may be better able to serve as an ameliorator in the case of girls than in the case of boys since peer risk factors are less potent for girls. For example, comparative data from our earlier father-son study[6] and the current father-daughter study indicate that boys were more likely to report having friends who used marijuana than were girls ($\overline{X}_{boy}$ = 2.83; $\overline{X}_{girl}$ = 2.40, t = −4.85, p < .001).

SUMMARY

This study suggests the father's interpersonal influences upon the daughter can take place in a variety of ways. First, the father can act independently of the mother. Second, the father can operate indirectly through the mediating peer group. Third, the father can operate in a mitigating fashion—as an ameliorator of mother and peer risk factors. Finally, but to a lesser extent, the father can be a positive synergistic force, enhancing mother and peer protective factors.

These findings emphasize the importance of studying the effect of the father as a conjoint influence. Psychological research tends to examine parent-child relationships in terms of single dyads, mother-child or father-child, rather than as a triad. Valuable as this may be, such studies negate the reality that adolescents are subject to the influence of each parent separately and both parents together. How the adolescent internally integrates experiences with each parent, siblings, and peers is a research question in its own right, and that is still to be explored. This study demonstrates the various interactions between combinations of parental and peer behaviors, all of which have been shown to be related to the adolescent's drug behavior. Our findings based on the construction of causal models suggest several directions for future research. First, emphasis should be placed on how the diversity among families determines individual differences in parental traits, attitudes, and behavior which in turn affect the adolescents' drug use. Second, the social network within the family needs further systematic empirical examination. The tangled web of direct and indirect effects indicates that investigations in this area will remain complex and that progress in this area is likely to be slow. Lastly, further study is needed of the ways in which intrafamilial relationships affect integration into the wider social world and the impact of the latter on the youngster's drug use.

REFERENCES

1. Lamb ME (ed). The role of the father in child development (2nd ed). New York: Wiley, 1981.
2. Brook JS, Brook D, Whiteman M, Gordon A. Depressive mood in male college students: father-son interactional patterns. Arch Gen Psychiatry. 1983; 40:665-669.
3. Cath SH, Gurwitt AR, Ross JM (eds). Father and child. New York: Little, Brown, 1982.
4. Hinde RA. Family influences. In: Rutter M, ed. Developmental psychiatry. London: University Park Press, 1982.
5. Lewis M, Rosenblum LA (eds). The child and its family. New York: Plenum Press, 1979.
6. Brook JS, Whiteman M, Brook DW, Gordon AS. Paternal and peer characteristics: interactions and association with male college students' marijuana use. Psychol Rep. 1982; 51:1151-1163.
7. Brook JS, Whiteman M, Gordon AS, Brook DW. Paternal correlates of adolescent marijuana use in the context of the mother-son and parental dyads. Genet Psychol Monogr. 1983; 108:197-213.
8. Prendergast TJ, Family characteristics associated with marijuana use among adolescents. Int J Addictions. 1974; 9:827-839.
9. Kandel DB, Kessler RC, Margulies RS. Antecedents of adolescent initiation into stages of drug use: a developmental analysis. J Youth Adolescence. 1978; 7:13-40.
10. Brook JS, Whiteman M, Brook DW, Gordon AS. Paternal determinants of male adolescent marijuana use. Dev Psychol. 1981; 17:841-847.
11. Block J. Lives through time. Berkeley CA: Bancroft Books, 1971.
12. Jersild AT, Brook JS, Brook DW. The psychology of adolescence (3rd ed). New York: Macmillan, 1978.
13. Ainsworth MDS. The development of infant-mother attachment. In: Caldwell BM, Ricciuti HN, eds. Review of child development research (Vol 3). Chicago: University of Chicago Press, 1973.
14. Ainsworth MDS, Bell SM, Stayton DJ. Individual differences in strange situation behavior of one-year-olds. In: Schaffer HR, ed. The origins of human social relations. London: Academic Press, 1971.
15. Ainsworth MDS, Blehar MC, Waters E, Wall SN. Patterns of attachment. Hillside NJ: Erlbaum, 1978.

16. Bandura A. Social-learning theory of identificatory processes. In: Goslin DA, ed. Handbook of socialization theory and research. Chicago: McNally, 1969:213-262.

17. Hoffman ML. Identification and conscience development. Dev Psychol. 1971; 42:1071-1082.

18. Schaefer ES. Children's report of parental behavior: an inventory. Child Dev. 1965; 36:413-424.

19. Brook JS, Whiteman M, Gordon AS. Qualitative and quantitative aspects of adolescent drug use: interplay of personality, family and peer correlates. Psychol Rep. 1982; 51:1151-1163.

20. Brook JS, Whiteman M, Gordon AS. Stages of drug use in adolescence: personality, peer, and family correlates. Dev Psychol. 1983; 19:269-277.

21. Brook JS, Whiteman M, Gordon AS. Maternal and personality determinants of adolescent smoking behavior. J Genet Psychol. 1981; 139:185-193.

22. Lettieri DJ, Sayers M, Pearson HW. Theories of drug abuse: selected contemporary perspectives. NIDA Research Monograph 30 (DHHS No. ADM 80-967). Washington DC: US Government Printing Office, 1980.

23. Huba GJ, Bentler PM. The role of peer and adult models for drug taking at different stages in adolescence. J Youth Adolescence. 1980; 9:449-465.

24. Adelson J (ed). Handbook of adolescent psychology. New York: Wiley, 1980.

25. Coleman JC. Friendship and peer group in adolescence. In: Adelson J, ed. Handbook of adolescent psychology. New York: Wiley, 1980.

26. Berndt TJ. Developmental changes in conformity to peers and parents. Dev Psychol. 1979; 15:608-616.

27. Krosnick JA, Judd CM. Transitions in social influence at adolescence: who induces cigarette smoking? Dev Psychol. 1982; 18:359-368.

28. Bixenstein VE, DeCorte MS, Bixenstein BA. Conformity to peer-sponsored misconduct at four age levels. Dev Psychol. 1976; 12:226-236.

29. Hartup WW. Two social worlds: family relations and peer relations. In: Rutter M, ed. Scientific foundations of developmental psychiatry. London: Heinemann, 1980.

30. Jessor R, Graves TD, Hanson RC, Jessor SL. Society, personality, and deviant behavior: a study of a tri-ethnic community. New York: Holt, Rinehart, & Winston, 1968.

31. Kandel D. Study of high school students—student questionnaire, wave 1, fall, 1971. In: Nehemkis A, Macari MA, Lettieri DJ, eds. Drug abuse instrument handbook (Research Issues 12). Rockville MD: National Institute on Drug Abuse, 1976:259-260.

32. Cattell RB, Eber HW. The sixteen personality factor questionnaire. Champaign IL: Institute for Personality and Ability Testing, 1957.

33. Rehfisch JM. A scale for personality rigidity. J Consult Psychol. 1958; 22:10-15.

34. Jackson DN. Personality research form. Goshen NY: Research Psychologists Press, 1974.

35. Derogatis LR, Lipman RS, Rickels K, Uhlenhuth EH, Covi L. The Hopkins Symptom Checklist (HSCL): a self-report symptom inventory. Behav Sci. 1974; 19:1-15.

36. Bem SL. The measurement of psychological androgyny. J Consult Clin Psychol. 1974; 42:155-162.

37. Avgar A, Bronfenbrenner U, Henderson CR Jr. Socialization practices of parents, teachers, and peers in Israel: kibbutz, moshav, and city. Child Dev. 1977; 48:1219-1227.

38. Schaefer ES, Finkelstein NW. Child behavior toward parent: an inventory and factor analysis. Paper presented at the American Psychological Association Annual Meeting, Chicago, August 1975.

39. Schaefer ES, Edgerton M, Comstock MS. Parent interview. Unpub. 1976.

40. Gold M. Undetected delinquent behavior. J Res Crime Delinquency. 1966; 3:27-46.

41. Levine M. Canonical analysis and factor comparison. Beverly Hills CA: Sage Publications, 1980.

42. Hendin H, Pollinger A, Ulman R, Carr AC (eds). Adolescent marijuana abusers and their families. NIDA Research Monograph 40 (DHHS No. ADM 81-1168). Washington DC: US Government Printing Office.

43. Brook JS, Whiteman M, Gordon AS, Brook DW. Fathers and sons: their relationship and personality characteristics associated with the son's smoking behavior. J Genet Psychol. 1983; 142:271-281.

44. Newcomb M, Huba G, Bentler P. Mothers' influence on the drug use of their children: confirmatory tests of direct modeling and mediational theories. Dev Psychol. 1983; 9:714-726.

45. Bandura A, Walters RH. Social learning and personality development. New York: Holt, Rinehart, & Winston, 1963.

46. Brook JS, Whiteman M, Gordon AS. The role of the father in his son's marijuana use. J Genet Psychol. 1981; 138:81-86.

47. Kandel DB. Drug and drinking behavior among youth. Ann Rev Sociol. 1980; 6:235-286.

48. Brook JS, Lukoff IF, Whiteman M. Initiation into adolescent marijuana use. J Genet Psychol. 1980; 137:133-142.

49. Jessor R, Jessor SL. Problem behavior and psychosocial development: a longitudinal study of youth. New York: Academic Press, 1977.

50. Kandel D. Adolescent marihuana use: role of parents and peers. Science. 1973; 181:1067-1070.

51. Brunswick AF, Boyle JM. Patterns of drug involvement: developmental and secular influences on age of initiation. Youth and Society. 1979; 11:139-162.

52. Kandel D. Inter- and intragenerational influences on adolescent marijuana use. J Soc Iss. 1974; 30:107-135.

53. Winder CL, Rau L. Parental attitudes associated with social deviance in preadolescent boys. J Abnorm Soc Psychol. 1962; 64:418-424.

54. Condry J, Siman ML. Characteristics of peer- and adult-oriented children. J Marriage and the Family. 1974; 36:543-554.

SELECTIVE GUIDE TO CURRENT REFERENCE SOURCES ON TOPICS DISCUSSED IN THIS ISSUE

Alcoholism and Substance Abuse in Adolescents

Theodora Andrews

Each issue of *Advances in Alcohol and Substance Abuse* will feature a section offering suggestions on where to look for further information on that issue's theme. Our intent is to guide readers to sources which will provide substantial information on the specific theme presented, rather than on the entire field of alcohol and substance abuse. We aim to be selective, not comprehensive, and in most cases we shall emphasize current rather than retrospective material.

Some reference sources utilize designated terminology (controlled vocabularies) which must be used to find material on topics of interest. For these we shall indicate a sample of available search terms to that the reader can assess the suitability of sources for his/her purposes. Other reference tools use key words or free text terms (generally from the title of the document, agency or meeting listed). In searching the latter the user should look under all synonyms for the concept in question.

Theodora Andrews is Professor of Library Science; Pharmacy, Nursing, and Health Sciences Librarian, Purdue University, W. Lafayette, IN 47907.

191

Readers are encouraged to consult with their librarians for further assistance before undertaking research on a topic.

Suggestions regarding the content and organization of this section will be welcomed.

1a. INDEXING AND ABSTRACTING TOOLS

Biological Abstracts. Philadelphia, BioSciences Information Service, 1926- , semimonthly.

Index by keywords from specific words appearing in titles plus added terms.

Chemical Abstracts. Columbus, OH, American Chemical Society, 1907- , weekly.

These are complicated searches. The Chemical Abstracts Service suggests that users when using cumulative indexes should first use the Index Guide volumes and their supplements, using the most recent supplement first. The Index Guide does not provide direct access to references in *Chemical Abstracts,* but it guides the user to appropriate headings in the Chemical Substance and General Subject Indexes. The best approach is probably to check under the name of the substance of interest to get registry number and suggestions for additional headings. Weekly issues contain keyword subject indexes.

Dissertation Abstracts International. A., Humanities and Social Sciences. Ann Arbor, MI, University Microfilms International, 1938- , monthly.

Since 1970 (vol. 30) keyword title indexing has been provided as well as author.

Dissertation Abstracts International. B., The Sciences and Engineering. Ann Arbor, MI, University Microfilms Internation, 1938- , monthly.

Since 1970 (vol. 30) keyword title indexing has been provided as well as author.

Excerpta Medica: Drug Dependence. Section 40. Amsterdam, The Netherlands, Excerpta Medica, 1972- , monthly.

Search terms: Alcohol; Alcoholism (and listing beneath); Behavior; and also names of drugs.

Excerpta Medica: Internal Medicine. Section 6. Amsterdam, The Netherlands, Excerpta Medica, 1947- , 20 times per year.

Search terms: Alcohol; Alcoholism (and listing beneath); and also names of drugs.

Excerpta Medica: Pharmacology and Toxicology. Section 30. Amsterdam, The Netherlands, Excerpta Medica, 1948- , 30 times per year.

Search terms: Alcohol; Alcoholism (and listing beneath); Behavior; Drug Abuse; and also names of drugs.

Excerpta Medica: Public Health, Social Medicine and Hygiene. Section 17. Amsterdam, The Netherlands, Excerpta Medica, 1955- , 20 times per year.

Search terms: Alcohol; Alcoholism; Addiction; Behavior; Drug Abuse; Drug Dependence.

Index Medicus (including *Bibliography of Medical Reviews*). Bethesda, MD, National Library of Medicine, 1960- , monthly.

Indexing terms are called *MeSH* terms. See: Substance Abuse; Substance Dependence; Alcoholism; Substance Use Disorders. See also names of drugs.

NOTE: Indexing terms for the *Bibliography of Medical Reviews* are similar, except broader terms are used to enable grouping of similar material.

International Pharmaceutical Abstracts. Washington, DC, American Society of Hospital Pharmacists, 1964- , semimonthly.

Covers information on the pharmaceutical profession and the development and use of drugs. Search terms: Alcoholism; Dependence; Cannabis. See also names of drugs.

Psychological Abstracts. Washington, DC, American Psychological Association, 1927- , monthly.

Search terms: Alcoholism; Marihuana; Addiction; Drug Addiction; Drug Abuse; Behavior Disorders.

Psychopharmacology Abstracts. Rockville, MD, National Institute of Mental Health, 1961- , quarterly.

Indexed by keywords from specific words appearing in titles. See: Alcohol; Alcoholism; etc.

Public Affairs Information Service. Bulletin. New York, Public Affairs Information Service, 1915- , semi-monthly.

Search terms: Alcoholism; Marihuana; Drug Abuse; Drugs and Youth; Drug Addicts.

Science Citation Index. Philadelphia, Institute for Scientific Information, 1961- , bimonthly.

Usually searched through citations, but has a "Permuterm Subject Index" generated from title words of source items indexed in the publication. To use the citation index look up name of author known to have published material relevant to the subject area of interest. Cited authors will be listed. Then use source index for complete description of articles found through the citation index.

Social Sciences Citation Index. Philadelphia, Institute for Scientific Information, 1973- , 3 times per year.

Similar to *Science Citation Index.*

Social Sciences Index. New York, H. W. Wilson Co., 1974- , quarterly.

Search terms: Drug Abuse; Drug Addicts.

Social Work Research and Abstracts. New York, National Association of Social Workers, 1965- , quarterly.

Search terms: Alcoholism; Addicts; Drug Abuse; Drug Addicts.

Sociological Abstracts. San Diego, CA, International Sociological Association. 1953- , 5 times per year.

Search terms: Alcoholic; Addict/Addicts/Addicted/Addictive/Addiction; Drug Addict/Drug Addiction.

1b. ON-LINE BIBLIOGRAPHIC DATA BASES (Consult a librarian for search formulation).

BIOSIS PREVIEWS (Biological Abstracts and *Biological Abstracts Reports, Reviews, and Meetings)*

A search guide is available. Keywords from titles and concept codes similar to those used in the printed index are used.

BOOKS IN PRINT (data base)

Contains bibliographic information on virtually the entire U.S. book publishing output. Includes: *A Subject Guide to Books in Print; Forthcoming Books; Scientific and Technical Books in Print;* and *Medical Books in Print.*

BOOKSINFO (BOOK)

Contains citations to more than 600,000 English language monographs currently in print from approximately 10,000 U.S. publishers (including academic and small presses) and 200 foreign publishers.

CA SEARCH (Chemical Abstracts)

The "Index Guide" which is used for searching the printed index should be utilized.

CHEMDEX/CHEMDEX2, CHEMDEX3

These files are dictionaries of all compounds cited in *Chemical*

Abstracts since 1972. Each record describes a chemical substance by molecular formula, CAS Registry Number, CA Index Name, CAS Recognized Synonyms, and Full Ring Structure Information.

CHEMLINE *(The Chemical Dictionary On-Line)*
An interactive chemical dictionary file created by the Specialized Information Services of the National Library of Medicine in collaboration with Chemical Abstracts Service. Provides a mechanism whereby over 1,000,000 chemical substance names and corresponding CAS Registry Numbers representing over 500,000 unique substances can be searched online.

CONFERENCE PAPERS INDEX
Provides access to records of more than 100,000 scientific and technical papers presented at over 1,000 major regional, national, and international meetings each year. A guide, *Conference Papers User Index Guide,* is available.

DISSERTATION ABSTRACTS ON-LINE
Former name of this data base was *Comprehensive Dissertation Index.* It is a subject, title, and author guide to American dissertations accepted at accredited institutions. Contents correspond to *Dissertation Abstracts International, American Doctoral Dissertations, Comprehensive Dissertation Index,* and *Master Abstracts.* Beginning January 1984 abstracts were added to the file for the years 1980-present. These abstracts are about 350 words in length and describe the original research project upon which the dissertation is based.

DRUGINFO-ALCOHOL USE/ABUSE
Contains citations from two different agencies: Druginfo Service Center of the College of Pharmacy of the University of Minnesota, and the Hazelden Foundation.

EMBASE (formerly *EXCERPTA MEDICA)*
Search terms are those used in the printed index sections, but everything is combined rather than treated in sections. There are over two million records in the base. See: Excerpta Medica'a *Guide to the Excerpta Medica Classification and Indexing System.*

FOUNDATION DIRECTORY (Copyright Foundation Center)
Is indexed by fields of interest. Provides descriptions of more than 3,500 foundations which have assets of $1 million or more or which make grants of $100,000 or more annually.

FOUNDATION GRANTS INDEX (Copyright Foundation Center)
Subject access available. Contains information on grants
awarded by more than 400 major American philanthropic foundations representing all records from the "Foundation Grants
Index" section of the bimonthly *Foundation News.*

GPO (Government Printing Office) MONTHLY CATALOG
This is the machine-readable equivalent of the printed *Monthly
Catalog of United States Government Publications.*

GRANTS DATABASE
Provides subject access to information on currently available
grants. Produced by Oryx Press. Includes information on 2,200
grants offered by federal, state, and local governments com-
mercial organizations, associations, and private foundations.

International Pharmaceutical Abstracts (IPAB)
Search terms are basically those used in the printed index. A
thesaurus is available.

ISI/BIOMED
Biomedical disciplines worldwide are covered. Has a unique
search capability not available in any other database—direct access to the literature by research-front specialties.

MEDLINE (Medical Literature Analysis Retrieval System On-Line)
Search terms are those used in the printed *Index Medicus*
(MeSH).

MENTAL HEALTH ABSTRACTS
All areas of mental health are covered from 1969-present.
There is no equivalent printed publication.

NATIONAL FOUNDATIONS (Copyright Foundation Center)
Indexed by activity code. Covers the current year. Provides records of all 21,800 U.S. foundations which award grants
regardless of the assets of the foundation or the total amount of
grants it awards annually.

NTIS (National Technical Information Service)
This data base consists of government-sponsored research, development, and engineering reports as well as other analyses
prepared by government agencies, their contractors, or gran-
tees. An increasing proportion of the data base consists of unpublished material originating from outside the U.S. Several
thesauri are used since material comes from a number of
government agencies.

PAIS INTERNATIONAL
Corresponds to *Public Affairs Information Service Bulletin.*

Contains references to information in all fields of social sciences.

PRE-MED (PREM)
Contains citations indexed previous to their appearance in MEDLINE. Search terms are those used in *Index Medicus* (Mesh).

PRE-PSYCH
Begins with journals published in the fall of 1981. Citations appear within 4-8 weeks of their publication. Covers clinical psychology from 98 core psychological journals, and also psychological literature as it relates to criminal justice, the family, and education.

PSYCHINFO
Corresponds to the printed publication, *Psychological Abstracts.*

RTECS (Registry of Toxic Effects of Chemical Substances)
Search terms are the same as those used in the printed version, the names of substances.

SCISEARCH
Indexed like the printed sources (*Science Citation Index* and *Current Contents)* that is, keywords from titles.

SOCIALSCISEARCH
Indexed like the printed source (*Social Sciences Citation Index*) that is, keywords from titles.

SOCIOLOGICAL ABSTRACTS
Corresponds to the printed index.

SUPERINDEX
Available June, 1983, this data base allows one to identify the precise location (book title and page number) of specific reference information in all areas of science, engineering, and medicine. Twenty-one major publishers participate.

TDB (Toxicology Data Base)
A file of chemical, toxicological, and pharmacological facts extracted from standard reference sources. File may be searched by keywords in titles, names of chemical substances, and by MeSH terms.

TOXLINE (Toxicology Information On-Line)
An extensive collection of bibliographic citations on human and animal toxicity, effects of environmental pollutants, adverse drug effects, and analytical methodology. The file can be searched by keywords in titles and by words which the indexer has added.

1c. BIBLIOGRAPHY OF BIBLIOGRAPHIES

Bibliographic Index. Bronx, NY, H. W. Wilson Co., 1937- , 3 times per year.
    Search terms: Alcohol; Alcoholics; Alcoholism (with various subheadings); Drug Abuse; Drugs and Youth.

1d. CURRENT AWARENESS PUBLICATIONS

Current Contents: Clinical Practice. Philadelphia, Institute for Scientific information, 1973- , weekly.
    Indexed by keywords from titles, examples: Alcohol; Alcoholism; Alcoholics; Drug Abuse; Addiction, Addicts; Behavioral Problems.
Current Contents: Life Sciences. Philadelphia, Institute for Scientific Information, 1958- , weekly.
    Indexed by keywords from titles, examples: Alcohol; Alcoholism; Alcoholics; Drug Abuse; Drug Abusers; Behaviors; Addiction.
Current Contents: Social and Behavioral Sciences. Philadelphia, Institute for Scientific Information, 1968- , weekly.
    Indexed by keywords from titles, examples: Alcohol, Alcohol Abuse; Alcoholics; Alcoholism; Addicts; Behavioral Problems; Drug Use.

2. SOURCES OF NOTICES OF BOOKS, PERIODICALS, AND OTHER PUBLICATIONS

Andrews, Theodora. *A Bibliography of Drug Abuse, including Alcohol and Tobacco.* Littleton, CO, Libraries Unlimited, Inc., 1977.
Andrews, Theodora. *A Bibliography of Drug Abuse, Supplement 1977-1980.* Littleton, CO, Libraries Unlimited, Inc., 1981.
Bemko, Jane. *Substance Abuse Book Review Index.* Toronto, Addiction Research Foundation, 1980- , Annual.
    Begins with 1978 material. Does not contain actual reviews, but guides the user to journals that have reviewed publications in the substance abuse field.
Critiques. Madison, WI, Wisconsin Clearinghouse of Alcohol and Other Drug Information, 1979- , bimonthly.
    A review periodical that publishes evaluations of new films, books and pamphlets in the substance abuse field.

Health Science Books, 1876-1982. New York, R. R. Bowker Co., 1982. 4 vols.
  Includes indexes by subject, author, and title. Search term: Drug Abuse.
Irregular Serials and Annuals, 1984: An International Directory. 9th ed. New York, R. R. Bowker Co., 1983.
  Arranged by broad subjects, e.g., Drug Abuse and Alcoholism.
Medical Books and Serials in Print: An Index to Literature in the Health Sciences. New York, R. R. Bowker Co. Annual.
  Arranged by author, subject, and title.
National Library of Medicine Current Catalog. Bethesda, MD, U.S. National Library of Medicine, 1966- , quarterly.
  Search terms the same as those used in *Index Medicus* (MeSH).
Ulrich's International Periodicals Directory. 22nd ed. vol. 1-2. New York, R. R. Bowker Co., 1983.
  Arranged by broad subjects, e.g., Drug Abuse and Alcoholism.

See also in Section 1b, on-line bibliographic data bases BOOKS IN PRINT and BOOKSINFO.

3. U.S. GOVERNMENT PUBLICATIONS

Government Reports Announcements and Index. Springfield, VA, National Technical Information Service. Biweekly.
  Contains a biological and medical sciences section, further sub-divided. Has a keyword index of words selected from a controlled vocabulary of terms. Examples: Alcoholic Beverages; Alcoholism.
Monthly Catalog of United States Government Publications. Washington, DC, U.S. Government Printing Office. Monthly.
  Has a subject index and also can be approached through keywords in titles. Search terms: Alcoholism (and also subdivisions); Drug Abuse; Marihuana.

4. SOURCES OF INFORMATION ON GRANTS

Annual Register of Grant Support. Chicago, Marquis Academic Media. Annual.
  Has a section on life sciences and indexes by subject, organization and program, geographic area, and personnel.
Foundation Grants Index. Edited by Lee Noe, et al. New York, Foundation Center. Annual.
  Has a subject index.

Fund Sources in Health and Allied Fields. Compiled by William K. Wilson and Betty L. Wilson. Phoenix, Oryx Press. Monthly.
A newsletter of interest to professionals who need to know what fund sources are available. Government and foundation grants both are included.

NIH Guide for Grants and Contracts. Washington, DC, U.S. Department of Health and Human Services.
Published at irregular intervals to announce scientific initiatives and to provide policy and administrative information to individuals and organizations who need to be kept informed of opportunities, requirements, and changes in grants and contracts activities administered by the National Institutes of Health.

See also in Section 1b, on-line bibliographic data bases FOUNDATION DIRECTORY, FOUNDATION GRANTS INDEX, GRANTS DATABASE AND NATIONAL FOUNDATIONS. In addition, see Raper, James E., Jr., et al., "Grantsmanship, Granting Agencies and Future Prospects for Grant Support" in *Advances in Alcohol and Substance Abuse,* Vol. 2, No. 3, Spring, 1983, p. 71-79.

5. GUIDES TO UPCOMING MEETINGS

World Meetings: Medicine. New York, Macmillan Publishing Co. Quarterly.
See: Keyword subject index, sponsor directory and index.

6. PROCEEDINGS OF MEETINGS

Conference Papers Index. Louisville, KY, Data Courier, Inc., 1973- , monthly.
  Directory of Published Proceedings, Series SEMT—Science, Engineering, Medicine and Technology. Harrison, NY, InterDok Corp., 1965- , 10 times per year.
  Principal indexing is by keyword in the name of the conference and the titles. Also has a sponsor index.
Directory of Published Proceedings, Series SSH—Social Sciences/ Humanities. Harrison, NY, InterDok Corp., 1968- , quarterly.
Index of Conference Proceedings Received. The British Library, Lending Division, 1964- , monthly with annual, 5 and 10 year cumulations.

Search terms: Addiction; Drug Abuse; Addictive Drugs; Drug Dependence; Alcohol; Alcohol Abuse; Alcohol Studies; Alcoholism.

Proceedings in Print. Arlington, MA, Proceedings in Print, Inc., 1964- , bimonthly.

Covers all subject areas and all languages.

7. MISCELLANEOUS RELEVANT PUBLICATIONS
NOTE: Some of the publications in this section are guides to sources of information on the topic under review; other provide relevant information directly.

Barnes, Grace M. *Alcohol and Youth: A Comprehensive Bibliography.* With special assistance from Robert J. Brown. Westport, CT, Greenwood Press, 1982.

Contains 4,600 citations including books, journal articles, theses, government reports, and popular literature.

Blane, Howard T., and Linda E. Hewitt. *Alcohol and Youth: An Analysis of the Literature, 1960-75.* Pittsburgh, PA, University of Pittsburgh, 1977. Prepared for the National Institute on Alcohol Abuse and Alcoholism.

An extensive bibliography of more than 1,000 references has been provided with the report.

Blane, Howard T., and Morris E. Chafetz, eds. *Youth, Alcohol, and Social Policy.* New York, Plenum Press, 1979.

Papers from a conference organized by the Health Education Foundation and held October 18-20, 1978 in Arlington, VA. Provides recent information on the epidemiology of drinking behavior and drinking problems among the young, theories that may explain drinking behavior, social policy implications of youthful drinking, and a review of programs designed to reduce problems associated with alcohol.

Beschner, George M., and Alfred S. Friedman, eds. *Youth Drug Abuse: Problems, Issues, and Treatment.* Lexington, MA, Lexington Books, 1979.

A comprehensive work that examines major issues in the field. Deals with epidemiology, methodology, issues and aspects, special problems, special youth populations, and treatment. Most of the statistical data included was obtained from the national drug data bases.

Brake, Mike. *The Sociology of Youth Culture and Youth Sub-*

cultures: Sex and Drugs and Rock'n'roll? London and Boston, Routledge & Kegan Paul, 1980.

    The author examines research done on youth culture, subcultures, and delinquency covering the early thirties period until recently in both Great Britain and the U.S.

Cohen, Sidney. The Alcoholism Problems: Selected Issues. New York, Haworth Press, 1983.

    Topics covered relating to young people include: teenage drinking, problem drinking in adolescents, blackouts, the now people, alcohol-drug combinations, and how social drinkers become alcoholics.

Cohen, Sidney, ed. Drug Abuse and Alcoholism: Current Critical Issues. New York, Haworth Press, 1980. (Collected Essay Series.)

    An analysis of the current scene in substance abuse.

Cohen, Sidney, ed. The Substance Abuse Problems. New York, Haworth Press, 1981.

    A remarkable overview of the subject. The coverage is diverse, and includes problem drinking adolescents.

Hawker, Ann. Adolescents and Alcohol: Report of an Enquiry into Adolescent Drinking Patterns Carried out from October 1975 to June 1976. London, B. Edsall and Co., Ltd., 1978.

    Makes a limited contribution to the understanding of the problem of youthful drinking. Reports on the outcome of a self-administered questionnaire survey of young people, ages 13-16, in schools in England. Data provided relate mainly to the epidemiology of adolescent alcohol use. A little discussion, interpretation, and analysis of the finds has been provided.

Institute of Medicine. Division of Health Sciences Policy. Marihuana and Health. Report of a study by a Committee of the Institute of Medicine. Washington, DC, National Academy Press, 1982.

    The major conclusion reached is that what little is known for certain about the effect of marijuana on human health justifies serious national concern.

Mayer, John E., and William J. Filstead, eds. Adolescence and Alcohol. Cambridge, MA, Ballinger Publishing Co., 1980.

    Contains 17 papers by experts who examine the research done on the alcohol abuse problem and suggest future policy directions that may improve the currently used treatment and prevention programs.

Menditto, Joseph. *Drugs of Addiction and Non-Addiction, their Use and Abuse: A Comprehensive Bibliography, 1960-1969.* Troy, NY, Whitson Publishing Co., 1970. (Supplementary volumes are published approximately annually under the title *Drug Abuse Bibliography for (date).*
These volumes make up a near complete bibliography of the world literature on the subject for the period covered. Include citations to books and essays, dissertations, and periodical literature.

Smart, Reginald G. *The New Drinkers: Teenage Use and Abuse of Alcohol.* Toronto, Canada, Addiction Research Foundation, 1980.
A current edition of an earlier work, this publication answers questions raised by parents, educators, and others regarding youthful drinkers. In addition, it pulls together information from research studies.

U.S. National Institute on Drug Abuse. *Young Men and Drugs in Manhattan: A Causal Analysis.* By Richard B. Clayton and Harwin L. Voss. Washington, DC, GPO, 1981. (DHHS Publication No. (ADM) 81-1167; NIDA Research Monograph Series No. 29.)
Points out the factors that account for the use of illicit drugs.

U.S. National Institute on Drug Abuse. *Drug Abuse and the American Adolescent.* Editors: Dan J. Lettieri and Jacqueline P. Ludford. Washington, DC, GPO, 1981. (DHHS Publication No. (ADM) 81-1166; NIDA Research Monograph 38; a RAUS Review Report.)
A review by the Research Analysis and Utilization System treating the epidemiology of drug abuse, emphasizing marijuana. Six papers emphasizing research findings and an overall summary are presented.

U.S. National Institute on Drug Abuse. *Marijuana and Youth: Clinical Observations on Motivation and Learning.* Washington, DC, GPO, 1982. (DHHS Publication No. (ADM) 82-1186.)
Included are ten papers by noted clinicians who have observed the effects of drugs, particularly marijuana, on teenagers.

U.S. National Institute on Drug Abuse. *Student Drug Use in America 1975-1981.* By Lloyd D. Johnston, Jerald G. Bachman, and Patrick M. O'Malley. Washington, DC, GPO, 1982. (DHHS Publication No. (ADM) 82-122.)
A publication in a series from the University of Michigan's In-

stitute for Social Research. Presents detailed statistics on the prevalence of drug use among American high school seniors in 1981, and on trends since 1975.

8. SPECIAL LIBRARIES WITH COLLECTIONS OF NOTE

Alcoholism and Drug Addiction Research Foundation Library, 33 Russell St., Toronto, Ontario M5S 2S1, Canada.

Rutgers University Center of Alcohol Studies Library, Smithers Hall, Busch Campus, New Brunswick, NJ 08903.

Information for Authors

Advances in Alcohol & Substance Abuse publishes original articles and topical review articles related to all areas of substance abuse. Each publication will be issue-oriented and may contain both basic science and clinical papers.

All submitted manuscripts are read by the editors. Many manuscripts may be further reviewed by consultants. Comments from reviewers will be returned with the rejected manuscripts when it is believed that this may be helpful to the author(s).

The content of *Advances in Alcohol & Substance Abuse* is protected by copyright. Manuscripts are accepted for consideration with the understanding that their contents, all or in part, have not been published elsewhere and will not be published elsewhere except in abstract form or with the express consent of the editor. Author(s) of accepted manuscripts will receive a form to sign for transfer of author's(s') copyright.

The editor reserves the right to make those revisions necessary to achieve maximum clarity and conciseness as well as uniformity to style. *Advances in Alcohol & Substance Abuse* accepts no responsibility for statements made by contributing author(s).

MANUSCRIPT PREPARATION

A double-spaced original and two copies (including references, legends, and footnotes) should be submitted. The manuscript should have margins of at least 4 cm, with subheadings used at appropriate intervals to aid in presentation. There is no definite limitation on length, although a range of fifteen to twenty typed pages is desired.

A cover letter should accompany the manuscript containing the name, address, and phone number of the individual who will be specifically responsible for correspondence.

Title Page

The first page should include title, subtitle (if any), first name, and last name of each author, with the highest academic degree obtained. Each author's academic and program affiliation(s) should be noted, including the name of the department(s) and institution(s) to which the work should be attributed; disclaimers (if any); and the name and address of the author to whom reprint requests should be addressed. Any acknowledgements of financial support should also be listed.

Abstracts

The second page should contain an abstract of not more than 150 words.

References

References should be typed double space on separate pages and arranged according to their order in the text. In the text the references should be in superscript arabic numerals. The form of references should conform to the Index Medicus (National Library of Medicine) style. Sample references are illustrated below:

1. Brown MJ, Salmon D, Rendell M. Clonidine hallucinations. Ann Intern Med. 1980; 93:456-7.
2. Friedman HJ, Lestèr D. A critical review of progress towards an animal model of alcoholism. In: Blum K, ed. Alcohol and opiates: neurochemical and behavioral mechanisms. New York: Academic Press, 1977:1-19.
3. Berne E. Principles of group treatment. New York: Oxford University Press, 1966.

Reference to articles in press must state name of journal and, if possible, volume and year. References to unpublished material should be so indicated in parentheses in the text.

It is the responsibility of the author(s) to check references against the original source for accuracy both in manuscript and in galley proofs.

Tables and Figures

Tables and figures should be unquestionably clear so that their meaning is understandable without the text. Tables should be typed double space on separate sheets with number and title. Symbols for units should be confined to column headings. Internal, horizontal, and vertical lines may be omitted. The following footnote symbols should be used:* † ‡ § ¶

Figures should be submitted as glossy print photos, untrimmed and unmounted. The label pasted on the back of each illustration should contain the name(s) of author(s) and figure number, with top of figure being so indicated. Photomicrographs should have internal scale markers, with the original magnification as well as stain being used noted. If figures are of patients, the identities should be masked or a copy of permission for publication included. If the figure has been previously published, permission must be obtained from the previous author(s) and copyright holder(s). Color illustrations cannot be published.

Manuscripts and other communications should be addressed to:

Barry Stimmel, MD
Mount Sinai School of Medicine
One Gustave L. Levy Place
Annenberg 5-12
New York, New York 10029